The Mask of Normalcy

Social Conformity and Its Ambiguities

The Mask of Normalcy

Social Conformity and Its Ambiguities

George Serban

Transaction Publishers
New Brunswick (U.S.A.) and London (U.K.)

Copyright © 2014 by Transaction Publishers, New Brunswick, New Jersey.

All rights reserved under International and Pan-American Copyright Conventions. No part of this book may be reproduced or transmitted in any form or by any means, electronic or mechanical, including photocopy, recording, or any information storage and retrieval system, without prior permission in writing from the publisher. All inquiries should be addressed to Transaction Publishers, 10 Corporate Place South, Piscataway, New Jersey 08854. www.transactionpub.com

This book is printed on acid-free paper that meets the American National Standard for Permanence of Paper for Printed Library Materials.

Library of Congress Catalog Number: 2013012616
ISBN: 978-1-4128-5269-2
Printed in the United States of America

    Library of Congress Cataloging-in-Publication Data

Serban, George, 1926-
  The mask of normalcy : social conformity and its ambiguities / George Serban.
    pages cm
  Includes bibliographical references and index.
  ISBN 978-1-4128-5269-2
  1. Conformity. 2. Compliance. 3. Adjustment (Psychology) I. Title.
  HM1246.S47 2013
  303.3'2—dc23

                                        2013012616

Contents

Acknowledgments		vii
Introduction		ix
1	Unstable Social Conformity within "Normal" Behavior	1
2	Theories of Personality and the Equivocation of "Normalcy"	37
3	Stress, Coping, and Social Conformity	75
4	Conformists versus Nonconformists	111
5	The "Normal" Psychopath	139
6	Social Conformity in a Polarized Society	165
Index		189

Acknowledgments

I want to thank and show my appreciation to Andrew McIntosh, who tactfully and expertly directed the process of producing a book from my manuscript. I also wish to extend my thanks to all the members of the production department and editorial staff of Transaction who contributed to the publication of this book.

Introduction

The individual's conformity to the social norms of organization and behavior has become a topic of much debate in view of the complex and somewhat divisive changes experienced lately by our society. Social conformity has been considered by psychosocial scientists as the backbone of proper social adjustment and of community integration, and also as an indicator of a healthy and stable society. As Émile Durkheim, the father of sociology, concluded a long time ago, social facts require social constraints which are "unfortunate restrictions on the individual's freedom." He surmised that it represents a small price paid to avoid societal disorganization and ultimately anarchy. It works as a "supra-individual social force" regulating the interaction between people. People are inclined to act in agreement with the social constraints. Society as a rule tends to constrain people to behave in a manner which they would not follow if uncompelled. There are constraints related to the material structures of society like urbanization, technologies, communications, and external structural constraints induced by kinship, family ties, or outer social framework. There are also constraints of moral nature and cultural ones.[1] All these social agents and social structures play their role in the formulation of social conformity.

From a sociological point of view, a smoother functioning of society could be achieved when people have incorporated as self-constraints the most significant social constraints directing their regular interactions with others. In this case, people harmonize their behavior with that of others facilitating an easier and more satisfying social conduct. According to Norbert Elias, a sociologist theorist, a higher regulated and differentiated pattern of self-restraint occurs in societies where there is a relatively stable monopolization of physical force and of the central organs of society.[2] Ironically, this situation is achieved in totalitarian states where the militant groups that orchestrate the capture of political power change the structure of society to conform to their ideological beliefs. They suppress individual freedoms in a methodical and ruthless manner and grossly violate people's civil liberties, compelling them to conform automatically to the authorities' demands. Otherwise, they are subject to harsh punishments.

This brings into focus the role of social conformity in a free society where it is part of the social interactive processes. Here social conformity acts as a mediator between the norms and regulatory acts of the state that protect the social rights of all citizens by reinforcing their freedom and enforcing respect for their civil rights. In reality, as we will see, the loose and twisted interpretation of social conformity has led to the ongoing debate regarding its fairness and validity. It is seen as inadequate in dealing with the social conditions brought about by the policies imposed by the government. Some of these decreed policies have affected specific segments of the population with regard to what they perceive to be a serious encroachment on their civil rights and free expression.

This issue of social conformity had been part of a larger, classical study dealing with the interaction between the society and the individual's social character. In their book *The Lonely Crowd*, David Riesman et al. forwarded the hypothesis that for society to function properly it has to ensure a degree of conformity from its population that has to be willing to act in a manner acceptable to all members of the community. They found that this condition does occur based on an assumed link between the existing social system and the social character of the people defined as a "product of the experience of that group."[3] They concluded that there are three types of social characters: the tradition directed, the inner directed, and the other directed. According to them, each of these social characters evolved to a great extent in a specific type of social organization and order. The tradition-directed type belongs to societies with high-growth potential which fostered the tendencies to follow the traditions of the family, kin and clan, together with the cultural rituals in its members. The individual's conformity seems to be commanded largely by the social power of his family and relatives in that social organization. In case of misbehavior, the tradition-directed individual feels guilt and/or shame.

The inner-directed type is the product of a "transitional growth," in a society in which there is constant expansion of the production of goods, and of exploration, where people show high personal mobility. There are a few subtypes of inner-directed character depending on the region and the religion practiced. The inner-directed type who is considered very stable is expected to maintain the fragile balance between his wants and the coping with community pressures. A sense of guilt acts as the emotional constraint for behaving inappropriately in response to inner impulses.

The other-directed type emerged in a society showing signs of a population decline, but otherwise with material abundance and interest in leisure-time activities. They are the people who want the approval of others and look to receive direction from contemporary others. They draw their "signals," or cues from a wider circle of resources than the tradition- or inner-directed types. The authors consider the other-directed as cosmopolitan since the line separating the familiar from the strange is loose and blurry. Whenever they trespass the social rules, they tend to experience "diffuse anxiety."[4]

The researchers viewed these social character types as abstractions that were arrived at from studying the actual character traits of individual personalities, from which the common elements forming the social character were extracted. They also remarked that a society may change faster than the social character or vice versa. This incompatibility between the required behavior by society and the inadequate social characters could act as a factor for change in the social order. Social characters that were well adapted to their tasks could find themselves under pressure from newer, better adjusted persons. The latter would replace them while the former would be relegated to subordinate positions, creating resentment or rebellion.

These findings might be relevant for explaining today's problems of poor adherence to social conformity as potentially related to a disparity between our information-centric, pluralistic and multicultural society and the competing needs of its diversified population.

This brings us to the social character who fails to adjust to the social demands. If they fail to conform they might be classified according to the researchers as either anomics or autonomous. Anomic means maladjusted, but the authors felt the word had too strong a negative connotation. Anyway, the meaning is the same, namely, they are "ungoverned" and noncompliant with the social rules. They might range from outright outlaws to "catatonic" types who are apathetic. In modern psychiatric nosology they seem to be people with severe personality disorders, antisocial personalities, and psychotics in relative remission.

On the contrary, the autonomous, though able to conform, is highly selective. He transcends his culture and risks acting against the social norms of proper behavior, going instead with his personal drives and needs. For him, the acceptance of the social and political system is always conditional by reserving the judgment for the protection of his personal agenda.

On the other hand, there is the category of adjusted people who have the right social character to adjust to society even when they deviate either by error or misjudgment. These three types of approach to social conformity are viewed by the researchers as universal. It is also understood that no one can be slotted rigidly in one type; it can only be said that one mode of adaptation predominates.

However, there are particular types of autonomous who consistently disregard the norms of social conduct in varying degrees. One group is represented by Bohemians, people who tend to accuse society of being hypocritical and manipulative, while they would like to think of themselves as free of "kowtowing to custom" when in reality, they pursue their own code of unrestrained marginal behavior. They are mildly nonconformist and would represent what it is known today as hobos and hippies. The other group described by them was the eccentrics who behave in an exhibitionist manner by dressing unusually in order to attract attention. Others project themselves as sexually emancipated people. A final category is that of the allegedly emancipated African American of that time, who by the sixties evolved to become those street demonstrators and protestors demanding equality and implementation of their civil rights.

The authors emphasized the heightened self-conscious of the autonomous individual who recognizing his feelings for self-respect tries to pursue his own potentialities and limitations, concepts borrowed from the humanist psychologists that will be amply discussed in the book.

It is interesting that the researchers speculated that in "a permissive and easy going" social environment people striving for autonomy have difficulty in identifying the "enemy."[5] However, one decade later, the civil rights movement identified its enemy as the biased policies of the government. They became the new autonomous nonconformists. The study doesn't mention the extreme nonconformists, such as the religious fanatics and the political rebels who have a different perspective on society which from their point of view have been oppressed by it. As will see, later studies on terrorists have shown that most of them are normal nonconformists.

This stimulating study raised in passing an important issue as discussed by Martin Hoffman, a psychologist, who emphasized the conflict between the autonomous behavior mostly cultivated by the other-directed character to show initiative, reliance on his own judgment and abilities to achieve his goals, and the pressure of society to conform to what was called "American character structure."[6] The problem is even more evident when applied to the social conformity of today, considering that the degree of autonomous nonconformity is related to the prevailing mode of individuals' pseudo-conformity. Then, one may wonder about the kind of conformity to be expected from a multicultural, polarized, contentious society where many norms of conduct are viewed as arbitrary and unfair.

In the other area of interaction between the social sciences and psychology, sociologists have made significant contributions to the interpretation of the complex functioning of the society with its social processes and specialized institutions and of their role in the life of the individuals. Nevertheless, they showed a tendency to dwell only briefly on the deviant, dissonant societies which have twisted, distorted social interactions with its members. In this respect, the political work of the Frankfurt School with theorists like Max Horkheimer, Theodor Adorno, and others is better known. The school attempted to study fascism from a Marxist-psychoanalytic point of view.

Coming back to the contributions of sociologists to the exploration of psychological issues such as the social context of the interaction between the mentally ill and their families, the pioneering work of Erving Goffman is important. In the chapter "The Insanity of Place" from his book *Relations in Public* he analyzed the multifaceted psychological interactions between psychotics and their families. It is an insightful and sensitive discussion of the plight of the families having to deal with the deviant behavior of their unaware relative patients.[7] The study is also historically important because it raises the awareness of mental health workers about the dramatic emotional effects of mental illness. One mentally ill member can disrupt the routine functioning of the whole family. At that time this issue was of less concern to clinical psychiatrists who treated the mental illness of the patient outside the context of his family.

It should be mentioned that at that time the causes of mental illness were still being debated by some dissident psychiatrists and psychologists, who, relying on their empirical observations and assumptive knowledge, argued that the medical model was paying insufficient attention to the social and cultural roots of the alleged psychotic diseases. Ronald Laing has been the best-known exponent of the theory that the psychopathology of schizophrenia should be understood within the context of person's psychotic behavior and of his speech with its alleged symbolic communication as an expression of his suffering.[8]

Independently, Thomas Szasz talked of mental illness as an "ambiguous label" used for the purpose of "avoiding the conflict of interests between patient and his social environment." He tried to make his case against mental illness using hysteria as an example, a condition which he viewed as "unconscious malingering," a part of the play in his version of a social game.[9] All these intriguing theoretical assumptions attracted other followers in the seventies like Theodore Sarbin and so forth.[10]

In this context, I conducted a clinical study of 950 schizophrenics, the results of which were published in *Adjustment of schizophrenics in the community*. In this study, I documented the role of the environmental factors acting as stressors on individuals who appeared to be hereditary predisposed, and which could have triggered the manifestation of the disease.[11] Gradually, during the nineties, it became accepted the role of genetics in psychiatric disorders; namely that of biogenetic vulnerability which was translated into an imbalance in the neurotransmitters that would interact with social stressors. All these factors were recognized to play a role in causing schizophrenia and bipolar disorders. These new findings put to rest any further debate about the factors contributing to the etio-pathogeny of the disease.

Another meaningful contribution to the field are the psychosocial studies of self, by George Mead[12] and Herbert Blumer[13] who explored the self as "an object to itself" that "distinguishes it from the body." Blumer described it in dynamic terms as "a process and a social structure." He concluded that self is a "mechanism of self-interaction with which we meet the world."

Mead has also tackled the psychological problem of self-hood and of self-consciousness relating them to the process of social conduct or activity that in finality involves the "apparatus of reason." Thinking on similar lines, he conceptualized the self as an object to itself which makes it distinct from consciousness that "indicates an experience with, an experience of, one's self." He further commented that consciousness can't be applied to behavioristic acts since "no physical organism can become an object in itself." Moreover, he raised an intriguing issue about the unity of the mind as not being the same as the unity of the self. According to him, the self represents the unity of the entire relational pattern of social behavior and experience in which the individual is involved. Based on these assumptions, he attempted to explain the dissociation of personality and multiple personalities, a controversial diagnostic issue in psychiatry, as the breaking down of the unity of self. The validity of this intriguing view has been discussed by others and myself, and we have reached different conclusions.[14] Anyway, Mead's hypotheses added a new dimension to the examination of the processes of social interaction for psychology and social psychology.

Furthermore, an approach from this perspective could incline one to assume that among its other functions, self is at the center of people's "gut reaction" to the exigencies and demands of social conformity. It is vaguely implied as being intrinsically fused with the genetic traits of the individual to which are added the gained social developmental experiences, giving it its specific individual outlook on societal interaction.

Other aspects of the core of self, expressed in self-consciousness were examined by Goffman, a sociologist who analyzed the claimed territories of one's self in relating to others and individual use of markers as identifiers of a rightful personal possession. In "The Territories of the Self," a chapter from the book, *Relations in Public*, he explored these issues systematically showing that any violation of these personal claims by intrusion, obtrusion, transgression, encroachment, defilement, and so forth are viewed as social offenses that could lead to an interpersonal conflict.[15] The discussion of these areas of potential conflict among regular people signaled some aspects of nonlegislated social conformity that are part of the community norms of interaction.

To appreciate the importance of this unwritten code of social conduct, one has to consider situations where the ignoring of these rules has disastrous effects. Take the recent case of D. Pagan reported by the press. Pagan, a thirty-eight-year-old married man was in a bar with his wife. He became furious after the leash of his little dog became entangled with another miniature dog. His wife tried together with the other owner to untangle them. When he came out of the bar, Pagan suddenly accused the owner of the other dog of inappropriately touching his wife. An argument ensued and Pagan took a knife out of his pocket and stabbed the man twice in the stomach. The victim died. Another man who tried to intervene was slashed in the neck. Pagan was sentenced to thirty years of imprisonment.[16]

Continuing with the discussion on presenting one's self to others with an appearance of normalcy in routine interactions, Goffman described the multiple modalities of conveying this image in another chapter of the same book, entitled "Normal Appearances." It is used for reassuring and appeasing other people in a regular interaction by not giving a cause for alarm or concealing fraudulent intentions under a cloak of normalcy. In the first case, the person exercises his competency acquired from his trade, social status, and the expected conduct of people in his community, while in the latter he enacts an image of normalcy by pretending to be that social identity which he tries to imitate and simulate. In both situations the individual, in one case legitimately and in the other fraudulently, tries to display in his "umwelt," (the social sphere surrounding him) that he is a safe person by doing what he considers as acting normally in order to be viewed by others as one of them. A special category of dissimulation is that of secret intelligence, covert spying activities, or the secret monitoring by government agencies, which are concealed for obvious reasons. Goffman concluded that while "normal appearance" becomes, as it is, a broad cover under which persons and agencies may try to monitor someone, approach him for attack, conceal things vital to him, attempt to make secret contacts with him, and the like, "it makes that individual's 'umvelt' hot for him." However, this doesn't affect their normal appearance for the enemy.[17] He viewed normal appearance as a mode of alerting an individual to a possible danger that would induce a sense of security after he reached the conclusion that the surrounding is "safe and sound," to be able to continue his activity. This might not be always true in the present unsafe environment of big cities.

In this context, let's examine a dramatic New York event as reported by the press: E. Menandez a thirty-one-year-old woman who was pacing the platform muttering to herself, suddenly pushed a forty-six-year-old man into the path of an oncoming train. The man, who was unknown to her was killed instantly. The woman later confessed to the crime, calling it an act of vengeance against Muslims and Hindus for 9/11. The man was an Indian. According to the court, she was found mentally fit to stand trial, though later on it was disclosed that she attacked and bit the hand of a police officer at the precinct station. These senseless crimes are not isolated cases. So much for our alarm system of protection![18]

The awareness about the social dynamics of appearance of normalcy in social interaction is extremely important since it is encountered routinely in our life and could create emotional and legal problems if we are not attuned to it for our own protection. As a sociologist, Goffman gave an account of the social process of interaction among people, ranging from acceptable behaviors to illegal ones without

Introduction

any underlying psychological assumption. Using different terms, he described the reinforcement of a conformist behavior by normal people who attempt to reassure others of their normalcy, and conversely, by the fraudulent people who by pretending to do the same thing, act as nonconformists.

From this point onwards, the role of torchbearers has fallen on psychologists and psychiatrists. They have to explain, analyze, and find corrective solutions for those people who intend to act in an illegal or deviant manner.

From Goffman's presentation it can be concluded that either the group of people with legitimate normal appearance or the illegitimate ones are striving for achieving the impression of normalcy in order to be able to reach their social goals. Without clearly defining normalcy, he used this notion as the basis for his presentation. He theorized that it was a way of concealing various underlying types of illegitimate social behaviors. Indirectly, he separated the normal from the illegitimate behavior.

The psychological model of normalcy tends to be more precise, defining for better or for worse, its complex psychosocial meaning. Nonetheless, it took the cue from the work of sociologists by basing normalcy on social conformity which presupposes obeisance to the norms and regulations of the society. It also added, in line with the medical model, the notion of the individual's relative freedom from emotional distress while coping with various stressors of daily life. From this point of view, a normal individual conforms to the framework of rules and regulation of the state without experiencing any serious emotional distress in dealing with adverse situations. However, this model of normalcy has proven to be incomplete and inadequate in defining normal behavior in a modern multicultural and polarized society. There are many reasons for the need to reevaluate and change the unworkable concept of normalcy; among them, is the exacerbation of the conflict between individual and society with its changed rules for competition at work and with biased governmental policies, to mention just two. On another level, the conflict is aggravated by "the individual's desire to actualize himself, live authentically and autonomously" and society's desire to treat him as a statistic performing specific tasks, as emphasized by the sociologist Georg Simmel.[19]

At the same time, society has gradually enlarged the notion of normalcy to include nonconformist behaviors of those people who refuse to follow various societal rules perceived by them as either absurd or detrimental to their well-being, but who otherwise act relatively as adjusted normals. In this respect a big issue has been the conflict between the individuals who have felt that some government policies are discriminatory and that those enforcing them are infringing on their civil rights. Ironically, the subjective interpretations of various social conducts by political correctness or the abusive actions of Transportation Security Administration agents at airports are ultimately nonconformist acts. This further questions the legitimacy and validity of social conformity when viewed as being imposed by biased and arbitrary rules of authorities.

Not to be ignored is the fact that normalcy tends to include those people who are socially marginal like hippies, and has tacitly accepted the religious or political fanatics who might have seriously disturbed personality. Intriguing are the findings that most terrorists could be considered normal, regardless how puzzling it might appear to be. A body of research documentation has dispelled any doubt about this fact, though it sounds inconceivable by Western standards, particularly when applied to suicide bombers.

Another interesting issue about normalcy is the special category of psychopathically bent people who act most of the time as well-adjusted citizens until they commit frauds believing that they would never be caught. They are basically opportunists miscalculating their chances in taking illegal advantage of a situation viewed by them as profitable and safe.

Not necessarily presenting psychopathic bents are the imposters, assuming a different personality as part of spying, activity in the service of the country or others just operating fraudulently for personal gains. The former are normal well-adjusted people performing a dangerous task for the national purpose while the latter are basically crooks, though until caught appearing well adjusted. Both groups are acting as nonconformists for diametrically opposite reasons. The symbolic use of "mirrors, masks, lies and secrets" as suggested by Karl Scheibe in his book, *Mirrors, Masks, Lies, and Secrets: The Limits of Human Predictability*, is employed not only by imposters to make their concealment harder to be discovered by others but also by politicians, inside traders, lawyers, and so forth. Nonetheless it is not a foolproof method of concealment making any prediction by the others of their activity a sheer speculation.[20]

Since time immemorial, as a part of the human condition, people have lied, misrepresented the truth, and cheated either to protect

Introduction

themselves or for personal gains. In a psychosocial study, *Lying: Man's Second Nature*, I discussed the role of lying in the daily interaction among people.[21] The issue of lying is a moral, social, and political reality affecting all aspects of our life. Society has always been unable to maintain a balance between acceptable protective lies and the harmful ones. This is even more evident today in our multicultural society beset by contrary social convictions which most often represent personal and self-serving interpretations of truth. Factual truth itself becomes subject to interpretation depending on the individual's perception which is colored by his social background and past experiences integrated in his view of society. From this perspective, truth becomes relative, subjective truth, which tends to impact society.

Under the umbrella of relative truth which has blurred the distinction between right and wrong, social conformity itself is dealing with multiple truths resulting from the interpretation of factual reality by the individual's self-serving needs or biased social posture. Either way, everything could be justifiable to him under the egis of moral relativism.

Notes

1. E. Durkheim, in *Classical and Modern Social Theories*, ed. H. Andersen and L. B. Kaspersen, chap. 5 by W. Guneriussen (Blackwell Publishers, UK, 2000), 59–6.
2. N. Elias, in *Classical and Modern Social Theories*, ed. H. Andersen and L. B. Kaspersen, chap. 22 by G. Olofsson (Blackwell Publishers, UK, 2000), 364–68.
3. D. Riesman, N. Glazer, and R. Denney, *The Lonely Crowd*, chaps. I and II (New York: Doubleday Anchor Books, 1953).
4. D. Riesman, N. Glazer, and R. Denney, *The Lonely Crowd*, chaps. V, VI, VII, VIII, XII, and XIII (New York: Doubleday Anchor Books, 1953).
5. D. Riesman, N. Glazer, and R. Denney, *The Lonely Crowd*, chap. XIV (New York: Doubleday Anchor Books, 1953).
6. M. Hoffman, "Conformity, Conviction and Mental Health," *Merrill-Palmer Quarterly* 4, no. 3 (Spring 1958): 145–50, published by Wayne State University Press.
7. E. Goffman, "The Insanity of Place," in *Relations in Public, Microstudies of the Public Order* (New York: Basic Books, Inc., 1971), 335–90.
8. R. D. Laing, *Sanity, Madness and the Family* (London: Penguin, 1964).
9. T. Szasz, *The Myth of Mental Illness* (New York: Delta Book-Dell Publishing, 1961).
10. T. Sarbin, *Schizophrenia, Medical Diagnosis and Moral Verdict* (New York: Pergamon Press, 1980).
11. G. Serban, *The Adjustment of Schizophrenics in the Community* (New York: Spectrum Press, 1980).

12. G. H. Mead, *On Social Psychology, Part V, VI, VII* (Chicago, IL: Phoenix Books—The University of Chicago Press, 1964).
13. H. Blumer, in *Classical and Modern Social Theories*, chap. 12 by N. Mortenson.
14. G. Serban, "Dissociative Identity Disorder and Crime: A Forensic Issue: In Explorations," in *Criminal Psychopathology*, ed. L. Schlesinger and C. Charles (Springfield, IL: Thomas Publishers, 2006), 276–96
15. E. Goffman, *The Territories of the Self in Relations in Public* (New York: Basic Books, Inc., 1971), 28–62.
16. J. Saul, "Rabid Slayer Gets 30 Years," *New York Post*, January 12, 2013, 14.
17. E. Goffman, *Normal Appearances in Relations in Public* (New York: Basic Books, Inc., 1971), 238–333.
18. J. Saul, "Subway 'Pusher' is Sane," *New York Post*, January 15, 2013, 17.
19. G. Simmel, in *Classical and Modern Social Theories*, chap. 7 by H. Ornstrup, 7–106.
20. K. E. Scheibe, *Mirrors, Masks, Lies, and Secrets: The Limits of Human Predictability* (New York: Praeger, 1979).
21. G. Serban, *Lying: Man's Second Nature* (New York: Praeger, 2001).

1

Unstable Social Conformity within "Normal" Behavior

Didi is a professional woman in her late forties. Single and somewhat attractive, she is moderately successful in her career. However, Didi is worried that she is going nowhere. She works too hard at a job that is no longer very challenging. Her emotional life is unsatisfying. The happiness she earlier obtained from making good money has diminished. Now the over-riding feeling is that she is making no further progress, either in her career or in her relationships with men. She wonders whether her career has become stagnant and her private life reached an impasse.

Some knowledge of her life history might help us to understand her predicament. As a young, financially poor, but ambitious woman, she labored hard, surviving on various scholarships in college and during her post graduate education to get a master's degree in economics from a prestigious university. Armed with the degree, she decided to become a successful career woman and to prove herself by working in an elite financial investment house. In order to climb the corporate ladder faster and be appreciated by her bosses, she would spend long hours at work, almost completely sacrificing a regular social life.

For a long while, the financial rewards combined with regular promotions gave her a sense of achievement, and confidence in her ability to eventually become a well-placed executive, if not a chief executive officer. She was proud of her feminism and of her determination to take men head-on. However, her private life was less successful, punctuated by occasional short-lived affairs with men who were also career-driven and who viewed the relationship as flings with no strings attached. She was unable to develop a steady relationship with a man because she traveled abroad frequently and was often held back in office attending late-hour meetings. This led to dates being postponed or cancelled much to the irritation of her lovers.

After years of casual dating, she met a charming, older Wall Street account executive, John, at a social gathering. He was not only well off but also courted her with persistence. He fitted perfectly into her hectic life style since he was already married and led a life independent of her. John convinced her that his was a marriage of convenience and that he was free to live as he pleased. He said that he wasn't ready for a divorce because he had a teenager son who his wife wasn't able to handle alone.

These "true confessions" didn't bother Didi too much at the time because it allowed her to pursue her busy schedule. In fact, she found that it was nice to have "her man" available when she returned home from a long trip. It worked for a while to her satisfaction until she started to get irritated by his unavailability on holidays or for regular vacations with her because of his family obligations. Upset, she started to protest, forcing him to make small concessions by taking her with him on short business trips when she was available.

However, over the years, Didi gradually became dissatisfied with the limited time they spent together. She began to insist that he officially separate from his wife since their son was now in college. Furthermore, she had a new job which required much less traveling and she was looking forward to spending more time with him. To her disappointment, she was spending most of her free time alone or with female friends because he was never there. As if this wasn't bad enough, she was fast reaching the age of forty. She was worried that she would lose her chance to have a child if John did not get a divorce or at least a legal separation from his wife.

When Didi pressurized him, John promised to consult a lawyer, but the expected separation papers never materialized.

At this time she met a man about her age who fell in love with her and wanted to marry her. After some deliberation she decided that she didn't love him, because of he had some annoying personality traits. She made up with John with whom she had a strong sexual bond. Their short separations following arguments about his dilly dallying succeeded, ironically, in reinforcing their attachment. He could calm her down with solemn assertions that he was working hard to change his marital status. The reality was, that despite so many years of being together with Didi, he was still not ready to leave his wife.

Then, unexpectedly, Didi's career took a downturn. Her company was bought out by a conglomerate and she was fired. This was a devastating blow, particularly since she believed that her contribution was essential to the profitability of the company. Looking for a job again at her age, was a rude jolt. It was worse, since there was a recession and jobs were hard to come by.

Regardless of how much energy and time she devoted to find a job, it took her over one year to nab another position. It was with a less prestigious firm, with less pay and bonuses. Meanwhile, she decided to terminate her relationship with John. He continued to stay solidly married while giving her superficial support. He claimed that he had his own problems with his clients. She became aware of how lonely she was, coming home every evening and having nobody to talk to.

The feminist position advocating commitment-free live-in relationships with men was not working for her. She found it disheartening to spend most of the evenings without John because either he claimed he was seeing clients or he just could not be reached.

At the same time, the new job was not only not giving her too much professional satisfaction but also revealed to Didi her distressing lack of marketability that excluded her from competing for the top post in the company. The recognition and success she desired seemed a shimmering mirage dancing in front of her eyes, but always out of reach. She was beginning to have doubts about her future, wondering whether her high expectations of her career and personal life were out of sync with reality Did she actually possess those professional abilities that the professors in her master's program and previous bosses had praised so lavishly? Was there something wrong with her attitude? Was she missing the traits of personality that were required to move up the corporate hierarchy and break the proverbial glass ceiling? She had been aware for a long time that she wasn't good at handling office politics, though she thought that it was compensated for by her professional efficiency, dedication, and skills.

Had her feminist stance of independence, self-sufficiency, and confidence rubbed her bosses and her lovers the wrong way? In retrospect, she was sure that some of the men with whom she had short-lived affairs had felt rather uncomfortable with her directness, forwardness and easy camaraderie, which also possibly cooled their passion.

John's rejection combined with mishandling of her intimate relationships with men and the regret of not having a child were haunting her from time to time.

Didi also questioned the wisdom of her tolerant attitude during her relationship with John. It had led her nowhere, but messed up her life. Looking at her other relationships in the light of this new wisdom, she felt that her less accommodating attitude toward some past lovers had led to the premature termination of the relationships. She concluded that she didn't understand men and her feminist approach didn't help her handle her interaction with them better. Now, thinking back, she believes that she tried to dazzle them with her professional success and affluence. Love and sex were treated casually as a psychobiological function within the framework of a relaxed interaction of equal partners. Now she was pushing fifty and it seemed harder than ever for her to find the right man. Also she no longer had faith in her ability to hold him if she did find one.

To alleviate her endless frustrations, she started to drink alone in the evening at home. From time to time, John called her trying to renew the relationship, professing eternal love while making the same empty promises.

Didi, by our conventional standards, may be viewed as a well-adjusted normal person, a conformist trying to succeed in her chosen career. In fact, humanistic psychologists would say that she was pursuing self-actualization. However, looking at her situation objectively, her ambitious drive for self-actualization turned out to be the cause of her distress. She ended up unable to deal with her unrealistic expectations. While her feelings of frustration over the stagnation of her career were natural, gradually they eroded her self-esteem and made her emotionally insecure.

The relevant question is whether her emotional behavior fits the definition of a well-adjusted person. Any qualified answer assumes a value judgment. However, by our social standards, she lives a relatively unfulfilled emotional and social life that affects her self-esteem and induces bouts of depression alleviated by drinking; yet on the surface she appears to function normally. Nevertheless, from a social perspective she seems to have an adaptive problem induced by her difficulty in making the right decisions about the men in her life. To some extent, Didi resembles Sophie, the protagonist of *Sophie's Choice*, the novel by William Styron.[1] Didi might be considered, in retrospect, a woman who often made the wrong decisions about men. But, unlike Sophie whose crucial decisions were out of her control, a matter of fate, Didi reached her judgments of her own free will. Her distress is the result of a deliberate effort to act in keeping with her vision of herself as a feminist . Her failure to live up to her standards of a fulfilled career questions her objective appraisal of her aim, particularly because of her inability to cope emotionally with setbacks. In this sense she tends

Unstable Social Conformity within "Normal" Behavior

to be a self-deceiver. But even though her social adjustment is filled with anxieties and passing states of depression, she still acts within the realm of conformist-normalcy.

According to prevailing social views, people are "well adjusted" as long as they conform and adapt to the customs, rules, and regulations of the society. The ideal societal concept of proper adjustment has been freely equated with being normal which is only partially true as will be shown later. It is, in general, represented by people who are able to achieve the life tasks of working, raising a family and playing by the social rules. As long as they function within the norms of society and are able to deal with changing social conditions without social or emotional disruptions, they are judged to be well adjusted, a state that has become synonymous with being normal. For convenience, for the time being, the two terms are used interchangeably. In this context, society would consider equally normal a conformist who works sixty hours a week to earn a meager living for his family and one pretending to be a conformist. An example of the latter would be a Wall Street investment banker who makes a pot of money by deliberately misleading and cheating customers, selling them fancy investment schemes of dubious quality that are profitable to him and to his investment house. Furthermore, the assumed notion of being well-adjusted normal ignores the emotional drama of unfulfilled ambitions, or inner conflicts that may consume, exasperate, and frustrate people unless they decide to disobey social rules and regulations.

I should mention here that the concept of "proper adjustment-synonymous-with-normalcy" is viewed differently when it relates to a religious code of behavior. The latter assesses a person in terms of the moral values that guide his conduct. People who are self-centered, greedy, and ruthless are viewed as morally corrupt and sinners, though society does not reject or convict them. The disconnect between the religious and secular view of proper behavior can create serious emotional conflict in some people. The inability of the faithful to follow precepts viewed by their religious denomination as sins, makes them sinners fallen from God's grace. However, this may be irrelevant for the social mores that accept their alleged sinful behavior. A good example of such a conflict is the new liberal sexual standards which approve abortion and homosexuality but which go against the tenets of many religions.

Take the case of David, a professional man in his thirties who was brought up in a religiously oriented family in which the parents expected him to perform well in school, get a good job, and raise a family. David tried hard to follow the family religious and social norms by working hard in school in order to become an accountant and secure a good job.

But, socially he was withdrawn, had few friends, and rarely dated a girl; the few dates were the result of family and peer pressure. He was not interested in women.

In fact, he felt different in this respect from other boys since his high school years. He avoided the company of girls in contrast to his mates. Instead, David had fantasies of sexual intimacy with boys, though the idea of actually experiencing it horrified him. In college, he was seduced by a friend into the practice of mutual masturbation which he enjoyed very much but which left him guilty and depressed. After a while, he avoided having similar encounters, though he continued to fantasize about them while masturbating. He was upset that he was a homosexual, although by then homosexuality was socially acceptable. In fact, he went into therapy to treat his alleged sexual deviation. After one year of therapy, he was advised to have sex with a surrogate sex partner, but he had difficulty performing with the woman and didn't enjoy it all. This made him even more depressed, particularly since he had a hard time explaining to his family why he didn't have a girlfriend. After exhausting a variety of excuses including an inability to find the right girl, he said he was depressed and that interfered with any desire to date. The depression was real because he was unable to accept his sexual orientation and at the same time realized that he was unable to change it. To accept it, meant that he was committing a sin by having "unnatural" sexual needs, though society did not think so. The HIV/AIDS epidemic relieved him of any thought of having any sexual contact with men. Staying sexually neutral was a compromising solution that did not change his negative feelings about himself. Was he socially maladjusted because his needs were running counter to his strong religious beliefs? In a sense, yes! By not accepting the new social norms while feeling caught in a clash of values, he was being pulled apart. He opted for following a set of religious values, but at a high price.

The unfulfilled expectations of Didi or the religious-social conflict of David have not only created significant psychological problems for them but also brought out the arbitrariness of the concept of social conformism. Their plight viewed from a psychological standpoint questions their alleged psychological normalcy while acting as conformists, Didi, socially and David, religiously. Psychologically, the concept of a well-adjusted person is a little different. Psychologists view people torn by inner conflicts, who doubt or deceive themselves as emotionally impaired, hence not quite socially adjusted.

All of us are familiar with Willy Loman, the character in Arthur Miller's play *Death of a Salesman*.[2] He is an average fellow who fought hard to succeed and failed while attempting to work within the customary social framework. Eventually, he committed suicide. By our social standards, Willy might have been considered adjusted. Yet psychologically, he was torn inside by unfulfilled dreams and unrealistic ambitions that magnified his feelings of social failure making his life less bearable. It slowly led to his sense of defeat and his wish to die as expressed in the suicidal act. The play is popular not only because of its intrinsic literary value but also because it epitomizes the tragedy of so many common people who labor hard within the system but are unable to meet their social expectations. Nonetheless, even if one seems to function normally from the legal, religious, or psychological points of view, he still may perceive himself as an outsider, performing his social duties mechanically because he feels alienated from society. He appears to be doing alright by the social standards, but from his perspective, his style of life has lost its meaning because he feels that he lives an absurd, illogical life. These feelings were well expressed by Meursault, the character in Albert Camus', *The Stranger*.[3] He felt bewildered by the irrational social rules that did not make any sense to him. He just could not understand or relate to them. Somewhat similar feelings of alienation of a dysfunctional suburban American family were expressed more prosaically by the protagonist of the movie—*American Beauty*—by the main character Lester Burnham.[4] Interestingly, the ultimate fate of both heroes was dramatic: one was sentenced to death by an insensitive judicial system and the other was discarded by his dear ones like unwanted baggage.

The individual's feelings of alienation and estrangement are intensified by the conflicting norms of conduct imposed by society that appear to him as meaningless and absurd. Society is ambivalent toward these people and treats them as odd characters or labels them as strange or weird.

A case in point is that of Fred, a fifty-year-old entrepreneur who built a successful business worth about fifty million dollars from scratch. It had seventy-five employees and a high growth potential. He was married, had two grown-up children and lived a very comfortable life. He had every reason to be content with his life, surrounded by all the trappings of wealth, but he became dissatisfied. Instead of looking forward to new business challenges and higher financial rewards, he felt detached and saw his business activities as purposeless. In the past, he had enjoyed playing by the rules of social success, honing them almost to perfection in order to achieve his goals of wealth, recognition and social status, but now he questioned the meaning of his previous relentless efforts and of his socially self-imposed style of life.

This change in his philosophy of life occurred after he had a close encounter with death. He escaped with relatively minor injuries when his car collided head-on with another car coming from the opposite direction and which jumped over the highway divider. His closest friend died in the accident. This tragic experience gave him time for reflection on the unpredictability of life and the relativity of his social condition.

Fred started to wonder whether his daily scramble to outdo others, outsmart competitors, monitor production, negotiate favorable contracts and manipulate business regulations were all there was to life. All of it had been achieved at the expense of his family life and by neglecting the pursuit of his intellectual and personal needs. Even on weekends, he felt obliged to entertain his clients on the golf course. He asked himself whether he had not sacrificed too much for success and a good life, all of which could become irrelevant in case of an unexpected terminal illness or catastrophic death. After months of agonizing and soul-searching, he decided to sell his business and to change his style of life by getting far away from it all. He tried to become a nonconformist.

However, after Fred became free from all the commotion and trepidation which had previously surrounded him, he found himself confronted with a new set of social conditions hampering the expression of his previously suppressed intellectual needs.

His dilemma seems intractable: on the one hand, he questions any commitment to any activity or style of life that might turn out to be another shimmering mirage and on the other, he still feels trapped in a web of social obligations viewed by him as meaningless and suffocating. Is anything emotionally wrong with him?

By our social standards, he behaved until recently as a "normal-well-adjusted" individual who cleverly applied the accepted social script for success for his own benefit. Now, he wonders about the power of social inculcation that led him to forfeit the joys of being true to his own self and which forced him to live an inauthentic life.

However, an outside observer may question Fred's decision as possibly related to an emotional state induced by being overstressed. Is he an emotionally burnt out businessman? Are all these signs part of a masked depression that resulted in a loss of the meaning and zest of living or does he experience a spiritual conversion? On the other hand, is anything wrong for one to try to do his own thing? Does he need psychiatric counseling to bring him back in line with the social and family expectations of him? For some people he may be a callous egotist avoiding his social responsibilities in favor of a self-indulged style of life. It all depends on someone's concept of normalcy and its set of ethical values.

All the disparate lifestyles presented above show the variety of individual approaches to life under the umbrella of conformity or, a relative deviation from conformity as part of acting normally. The notion of normalcy becomes even more debatable when viewed in the context of the diversity of cultural factors that identifies behavioral norms in different societies.

Cultural Variations in the Concept of Well-Adjustment

It is known that the concept of what may constitute a well-adjusted person has changed from time to time within the same society depending on the set of prevailing social values. One of the most noticeable variations recorded throughout social history has been in the domain of the male-female relationship and sexual morality. Some societies have been monogamous while others have been polygamous; certain societies have appreciated virginity in girls before marriage, whereas others didn't care. Initially, in our puritanical society, most marriages were not a result of love but of a social-economic arrangement with a negotiated dowry and sometime spurred by the need for a political or social alliance. Today, on the contrary, passionate love is the most powerful reason for marriage. Furthermore, the marital relationship has undergone drastic changes with regard to the economic dynamics, sharing of household responsibilities, and bringing up of the children. Moreover, the role of the parents in the care and upbringing of children has been reduced by the transfer to the community of many of their functions to nurseries and day care centers or after school-hours programs. Most of the child's socialization is taking place outside of the home, supervised by social agencies and people hired for this purpose. As a result, the role of the parents in their children's upbringing has been restricted to that of financial and emotional support. At the same time, the family bond has been weakened by the newly cultivated self-assertion of spouses. In many cases, it has led to the dissolution of the marriage.

Divorce, previously an ignoble and socially decried act, has become a casual event with 40 to 50 percent of marriages ending in divorce. Adultery, which was considered a reprehensible marital offense in the past, is now socially ignored and in most states doesn't have any legal consequences.

The sexual misadventures of Bill Clinton, while in the Oval Office or of John Edwards,[5] former senator and presidential candidate or Jesse Jackson,[6] a high-profile political leader and minister chairman of the Rainbow Coalition or the most recent case of Arnold Schwarzenegger,[7] who while governor of California had a long-term affair with a housemaid with whom he had a child; all of them were married men, which amply proves the point made above.

If we expand our inquiry by looking at other cultures, a kaleidoscopic picture emerges of those societies' norms of proper behavior. For example, a cursory look at some Muslim societies shows us that men can have up to four wives, women have minimal participation in the decisions regarding the family business or social affairs, and in case of adultery they are harshly punished, sometimes stoned to death. It has been reported by Al Arabyia, news channel that 943 Pakistani women and girls were murdered last year for defaming their family honor. About 595 of the killed women were accused of having "illicit relations" and 219 of marrying without parental permission. Some of them were raped and gang raped before being killed.[8]

In the same vein, certain child-rearing practices in some societies may raise eyebrows in our country. For example, Eskimo and Vietnamese mothers allow their children to breastfeed till the age of four or five. It was also reported that in certain New Guinea communities, homosexuality is routinely practiced by boys between puberty and the age of marriage. It was suggested that some of these social customs reinforced passive-dependent attitudes. Yet, in the context of their culture one can't assume that the mothers or others adults are maladjusted because they follow these practices or that these customs induce maladjustment in adult life.

The self-evident conclusion is that there are no universal standards of normalcy, and the notion of normal-well adjusted has currency only within the context of a particular society with its peculiar customs and beliefs. As previously mentioned, even within the same society the customs may undergo changes after social, political or religious revolutions, conquests by another culture, and so forth that introduce new ways and norms for social relationships.

It is interesting to note how our social customs and values have evolved and changed dramatically under the influence or pressure of new political and social multicultural beliefs. There is a significant impact of these changes on people depending on their ability to adapt to them. It has separated those who have learnt how to cope with the changes and are viewed as well adjusted from those who are struggling or have failed to adjust. Those who succeeded seemed to have relied on a well-balanced evaluation of reality and a control of their emotional drives, all parts of their adaptive personality make-up. Translated into personality traits, their capacity to adapt indicates an overall flexibility and amenability while those with difficulty or inability show inflexibility and intransigence. It simply indicates that some people who are considered well-adjusted-"normals" are unwilling or incapable of adapting even when the stakes are high, affecting their social achievements or their status in the community. However, this is not always so.

The American Premise about the Nature of Man

From its inception, the notion of adaptation has been widely prevalent in our society, since it is optimistically assumed that man has the intellectual capacity of reasoning and learning which can help him overcome his emotional shortcomings and improve his social condition. This concept about the nature of man was embraced by Thomas Jefferson and became the basic tenet of our Constitution. In contrast to the widespread traditional belief held by Alexander Hamilton, James Madison and other founding fathers about the common man's inability to always act rationally and hence his inability to self-govern, Jefferson championed the progressive idea of the common's man ultimate ability to use reason instead of passion in deciding the course of his actions. This concept emphasized the ordinary man's capability to expand his intellectual resources, to learn from his environment and to self-govern. Bluntly said, it was thought that all men are products of their circumstances and environment. By relying on the very limited knowledge of his time, Jefferson inadvertently attempted to answer the controversial question: Is it whether the inherited or the acquired traits of behavior that play a predominant role in the formation of human nature?

Jefferson, an enlightened man, embraced the social concept that promoted unlimited possibilities of achievement for the nascent state that relied on the pioneering, entrepreneurial spirit of the thousands of immigrants fighting to build a better life. The losers were replaced with fresh waves of new immigrants. In reality, society unknowingly applied the most brutal criteria for competition—what would later be known as natural selection.

As a matter of fact, these egalitarian principles justifying the governing of the nation by its people fitted well with the ideals for which they fought in the revolution. These social ideals, enshrined in the Declaration of Independence have reverberated for centuries in the American society shaping to a large extent the thinking of its social institutions. This concept of the plasticity of man's mind that can overcome almost any natural or artificial hindrance has been enthusiastically embraced by modern culturalists. It has been the buzz word of social researchers who have attempted to document that man can change not only his environment but also himself.

Despite all the knowledge accumulated by science showing the significant role played by man's genetic make-up or biological factors in the design and organization of human behavior, the supporters of the environmental theory still tend to give priority to social factors. In fact, it is assumed that the social–ethical changes undergone by our country in the last part of the twentieth century are proofs of man's adaptability to new conditions. However, the reinterpretation of the existent social system of values was justified by the parallel expansion of the meaning of the factual truth to incorporate the relative truth with its novel use in the rules of work competition and social conduct. The result has been the blurring of the distinction between factual and relative truth. Under these circumstances, our multicultural society has liberalized the meaning of social adjustment to incorporate a wide range of beliefs and customs of the significant ethnic groups. Within the larger framework of moral relativism, society has redefined many concepts about what constitutes normal behavior, compelling people to alter their ways of dealing and adapting to the new social conditions.

In view of all these social reinterpretations of the concept of normal behavior it is important to know what is the definition of a "normal"-well-adjusted personality provided by the researchers of human behavior.

Society's View of "Well-Adjusted Behavior"

The concept of social adjustment that identifies an individual's ability to act within the framework of acceptable social behavior and avoiding the unacceptable varies according to the field of social science which evaluates it and of the society under discussion. By the same token, this approach infers that if the individual acts outside the arbitrary norms of the acceptable behavior he is maladjusted-abnormal. This controversial idea has been espoused by many social agencies and communities which simplistically assume that the failure to adapt to the societal standards is indicative of personality disorder. In reality, it is amply documented that it can well be a part of successful normal functioning, and that it all depends on the social circumstances.

In passing, it should be mentioned that some societies don't make a clear distinction between the behavior attributed to so-called normal conduct and the one associated with abnormality. While all societies have developed their own social conventions and rules of behavior, some differ from others by considering behavioral transgressions as not necessarily abnormal unless they appear to be in the domain of irrational behavior. Even so, psychotic behavior has been attributed in many societies to being caused by demons that need to be exorcized.

Lately, this view has started to change due to the expanded knowledge about abnormal behavior relying on the hard data furnished by biological-neurophysiological research. In this context, mental illness is generally viewed as a result of brain's neurological impairment linked either to chemical dysfunctions of specific neurotransmitters triggered by distinct defective genes or related in other circumstances to certain physiological changes induced by specific medical illnesses. This is the view currently put forward to explain mental illness but it remains vague in setting out the parameters of what is socially acceptable normal behavior.

Our society has distinctly divided human behavior into "normal" and "abnormal." Using these distinctions, it has formulated the concept of well-adjustment normalcy. The domain of recognized psychotic disorders is treated separately. Plainly, in this context, well-adjustment means the absence of symptoms associated with distressful abnormal responses or with psychoses. This notion of proper adjustment has been functionally related to the ability to fulfill one's major life-work and obligations, while psychologically possessing a sense of identity and a capacity for intimate and meaningful social relationships. Seen clinically, it is supposed to convey feelings of emotional control, freedom from discomfort, distress, or mood liability. But when it is clinically compared to the emotions elicited by disorders of personality like anxiety or depression, the lines between "normal" and "abnormal" become blurred because these very emotional states can also be exhibited in clinically defined "normal" personalities. Though it could vary in intensity and duration, the fact remains that the alleged normals under condition of stress could experience the whole gamut of negative emotions.

In this context, therefore, the clear-cut distinction between a so-called normal and maladjusted personality becomes blurry, presenting problems of interpretation of the duration and intensity of emotional responses or the objective evaluation of the distressful psychological symptoms. In fact, Sigmund Freud considered "normalcy" an ideal condition not met by the average individual. In his opinion, normal behavior (identified by him as the genital personality) addresses the same underlying conflicts that abnormal behavior attempts to resolve, except that the alleged normal person has developed better ways of dealing with such events. However, "well-adjusted-normals" when faced with personal crises beyond their level of tolerance, may show various degrees of behavioral dysfunction. Since the psychoanalytic model is mainly oriented toward explaining the dynamics of emotional pathology as induced by inner drives, it has not directed its inquiry into the analysis of the psychological dynamics that might identify what can be called "normalcy-well-adjustment."

Later, the humanistic-oriented clinicians who were ignorant or unaware of the role of the innate drives,[9] didn't consider them in their attempt to create a psychosocial model to identify the attributes of their view of well-adjusted behavior. They related psychological well-being to a set of alleged psychosocial indicators, such as self-control, social responsibility, and integrative adjustment determining the expression of one's social potentials. These attributes could be interpreted as belonging to a continuum of arbitrary qualities of social functioning ranging from highly present in well-adjusted normalcy to that of lacking in abnormality. This approach describes personality disorders that fall between well-adjusted behavior and psychoses. Although personality disorders are outside of the state of well-being, they are only qualitatively but not categorically distinctive from well-adjusted-normal behavior. These disorders that may be graphically presented on a continuum from "normalcy" to "psychoses" do not address the issue of whether they represent various types and degrees of genetic impairment, not yet fully understood.

Yet the assumption remains that each person, considered well adjusted or not, has his own adaptive strengths and weaknesses that decide his responses to events and crises and shape the organization of his life. It is assumed that one's degree of "proper adjustment" would evolve from the interplay between the undefined "inner factors" and learned adaptive abilities responding to the crises perceived by the individual as threatening and harmful. A prevalent belief is that this process starts in childhood, and in case of repeated failure to properly solve situational conflicts, it would tilt the balance toward maladjustment. The explanations for it were related to the unfavorable factors in the environment. To evaluate these complex factors, we have to evaluate their role in the making of personality. However, the past formulation of the concept of personality met with serious problems because of the lack of biogenetic knowledge on the part of the researcher or of his biased indoctrination.

Clinical Issues in Identifying the Assumed Components of Personality

Basically, personality is an abstract theoretical concept that attempts to identify an enduring set of traits and drives that regulate one's behavior during one's life, while expecting that an individual may show temporary changes in his behavior in response to new situations never experienced before. It is also anticipated that he will return to his old patterns of behavior after the crisis like loss of a loved one, undesirable job assignment, moving to an unwanted new location, military call to duty, and so forth have been solved.

The lasting traits of personality should be the markers of one's behavior, determining to a great extent the individual's style of coping with life events. However, there are other responses to social encounters that vary with the situations and are not necessarily part of one's characteristic pattern of coping. These changeable behaviors depend on immediate factors influencing the outcome of the event as it may happen when someone decides to unusually increase the expenses for a vacation trip, occasionally eating exotic and unfamiliar types of food, dressing in different style of clothes than usual, and so forth.

Another characteristic of personality is the uniqueness of one's consistent traits of behavior that differentiates him from others. In fact, from this point of view no two people are alike.

The pattern of behavioral responses to events is unique for a person and in a sense identifies him. This uniqueness of personality is a result of one's specific way of using, analyzing, and interpreting reality based on the totality of his psychological traits that, however, are not specific to that person. The variation in behavioral responses is accounted for by the breadth and strength of inter-relationships among the psychological components responsible for the formation of one's personality. And here starts the problem of defining the components of personality responsible for his adjusted social functioning.

For example, is it the degree of one's intelligence, his cognitive processes, his encoded inborn dispositions or his learned mode of emotional responses as reflected in the acquired experiential world that shape his social adjustment and contribute to the differences between him and another person? Would these elements be sufficient to explain the preferences and behavioral differences among people, beyond the knowledge that most of us have similar motives and drives? How could we explain that the individual's behavior which might sometimes appear fragmented or haphazard in reality is well structured and organized in distinctive patterns that give coherence and meaning to his acts and identify his personality? If so, how can someone prove that these patterns are at the core of his coping with various crises and events that occur in his life?

What we currently know is that these patterns of coping have been developed as a result of the continuous interaction between the innate mental capacity of the individual and the learned experiences from his family and social environment which have become incorporated in his perception and evaluation of reality according to his innate make-up. But the processes involved in these complex activities have been partly assumed and only partly understood.

The innate mental dimension represents an individual's genetic-biological make-up in which his temperament and his distinctive cognitive capacity are subsumed. Temperament is viewed as a sum of inborn dispositions and sensitivities that have left their deep mark on the developmental style guiding an individual's functioning. The latest research indicates that these temperamental dispositions indeed, dictate a preference in the child for certain environmental surroundings that are more or less maintained in later adulthood.[10] As we will see, this specific interaction between temperament and environment defines one's personality. It is well known that children vary in the uniformity of their biological functioning, in their responses to new situations, mood qualities, alertness to stimuli, attention, intensity of response, degree of adaptability, and so forth. This has been fully documented by researchers[11] who found that children display three broad temperament styles from infancy onward, clinically described by them as easy child (40 percent), slow-to-warm-up (15 percent) and difficult

(10 percent), the remaining 35 percent represent a mixture of the three types. Furthermore, children of a particular disposition, let us say energetic or robust (easy child), will be treated differently by his parents or caretakers than a child that is slow or cranky (difficult child). For example, it has been documented that highly alert and active children gain faster knowledge about their immediate environment. They are more exploratory than the ones who are slow or passive. These temperamental dispositions can elicit reactions from others that sanction and reinforce those traits. It is also important to note that parental reactions differ to some extent from child to child according to their perception of children's dispositions and sensitivities. A lively, easygoing child will tend to receive positive responses from the mother or caregiver, while a difficult child may bring out negative responses of uneasiness and frustration. When the frustrations of parents or caregivers are repeated through attempts to control the exploratory activities of active children or conversely attempts to stimulate the passive ones beyond their threshold of temperamental acceptance, the adults might create conditions for the development of maladaptive patterns of behavior in the children. This is a clinical proof of the complex interaction between the genetic-biological make-up (nature) and the outside cultural milieu (nurture) in the formation of personality. It also suggests, as we will see in the next chapter, that these primary biological dispositions shape a child's behavioral responses to his cultural environment, defining those learning experiences that lead to the development of what it is loosely called normal or abnormal personality. At the same time, the cultural forces acting upon the biological substrate reinforce, modify, or even suppress the experiences. It can be described as a circular interaction that aims to preserve his existence and to allow him to adjust to the environment under optimal available conditions.

Maternal and Environmental Influences upon Child's Development of Personality

The role of the social environment in the socialization of the child and believed to contribute to the shaping of his personality has been better known and researched, though not in the context of the child's genetic traits. The mother, an agent of the society, either deliberately or inadvertently tries to manipulate certain basic drives of the child. It is based on the hypothesis that some primary drives can be affected by the child's socialization during the developmental years. For example, hunger and thirst are primary drives which are present at birth. They are universal human drives but the way in which they are satisfied greatly depends on the mother or mother-surrogate. It has been claimed, without rigorous longitudinal scientific documentation, that this interaction has implications for the formation of the child's personality. Some mothers prefer to feed the baby "on demand," or whenever he cries. It is believed that babies brought up in this way will cry less, will be inclined to take action whenever they feel a compelling need to act, and will not develop long-term habits. By contrast, babies fed "on schedule," let us say every four hours, regardless of how much they may cry, if hungry, may develop a different social learning set. Gradually, they realize that regardless of how demanding they are, it is useless. It was noticed that these children may learn to endure frustration, to be more passive and inclined to give up easier than the ones fed on demands. But this is only one variable of interaction between an innate drive and the social milieu. There are other factors, such as breast or bottle feeding, early or delayed weaning, stable or labile mood of the mother, and presence or lack of affection in the stimulation of the baby that could not only reinforce or minimize these behaviors but also add new dimensions to the personality formation of the baby as developmental psychologists suggest. The open question is whether the acquired characteristics of personality are maintained throughout life and applied to situations and events that may require more flexible approaches.

For example, a great deal has been made out of the toilet training that represents a socialization of a basic physiological necessity that of elimination of body waste. It has been thought, particularly by psychoanalysts, that it plays an important role in the formation of certain traits of personality. Parental practices related to toilet training have been linked to the individual's responses to authority figures and social control. It has been assumed that the nature of interaction between the parents and child is generalized to other coercive social situations where the child uses the same patterns of response. Psychoanalysts have also hypothesized that the same strict or liberal approach used by the parents in relation to toilet training, is used in other social situations that require discipline and strict rules of behavior. Claims have been made that there is a correlation between the parental approach to toilet training and their method of socialization of the child in the domain of cleanliness, modesty, expression of aggression, obedience, and sex. It creates the basis for shaping the social conformity of the child. However, it has been speculated that toilet training accompanied by severe punishment allegedly induces certain responses in the child that lead to the formation of a definite personality type, the anal retentive personality.[12] Except for an assumptive analogy between anal retention and retention (hoarding) of goods in adult life, no systematic research has proven this point. This concept was further elaborated by Erich Fromm, a psychologist,[13] in his formulation of the "hoarding" orientated personality, quite similar to the anal personality. Intriguingly, the compulsive-obsessive traits of personality observed in the anal personality and also described by Fromm in his hoarding personality have been recently related to faulty genes.

Furthermore, the assumption that the acquired-learned behavioral set persists throughout one's life and may be only slightly modified by ulterior experiences is still debatable. One argument brought forth in favor of the persistence of the acquired learned responses to controlling inner drives is the supposition that the learned responses during infancy are potent since they are strongly reinforced by the reduction of the need for satisfaction of the drives. An alleged supporting argument is the assumed strength of the individual's conditioning to this modality of response that strengthens their endurance. Many of these conditioned behaviors associated with parental reward and avoidance of pain have been considered as excessively resistant to extinction. However, it is also acknowledged that in adulthood they may become extinct under the repeated exposure to different sets of social conditions acting as stimuli. Furthermore, it may also provoke paradoxical reactions in case of repeated absence of the conditioning reward or punishment. In this case it may lead to a behavioral acting out that is out of character with that individual's basic personality. This has tried to explain why a person considered as passive, may suddenly act assertively and defiantly in a new situation in which the old inhibitory factors are meaningless.

If all the above hypotheses interpreting clinical observations offer a very incomplete understanding of the personality's role in determining an individual's behavioral functioning, at least the interplay between an inner drive and social learning is more evident in the manipulation of the sex drive, which is relatively controlled by society. It was taken for granted in the past that children should be taught to suppress any sexual stimulation, at least until adolescence. The sex drive could be easily inhibited or hidden because of fear of social disapproval or punishment. In addition, it was assumed that the suppression does not harm the body in any significant way. The sexual activity of teenagers and particularly pregnancy of teenage girls were supposed to be prohibited until marriage or at least until reaching financial or social independence. Masturbation was frowned upon as undesirable behavior. Today, in our society, most of these inhibitions have been discarded because of the change in social mores that has resulted in a permissive attitude toward sex. The reversal of the attitudes toward juvenile sexual activity shows the extent to which society manipulates sex for pleasure or reproduction.

By the same token, it is well known that sex inhibitions developed in early childhood may interfere with satisfactory sexual functioning in adulthood by inducing anxiety that affects performance and/or pleasure. Since sexual stimulation leading to satisfaction of the sex drive is a private affair, it was acceptable to secure it using a variety of means, from self-stimulation to heterosexual or homosexual intercourse. A new liberal attitude toward sex was born.

Only intercourse with animals is viewed as a sexual deviation punishable by law. All forms of gratification of the sex drive, except for rape and pedophilia, fall within the range of acceptable-normal behavior. At the same time, the biological premise of sex for reproduction has been recast to include gender surgical reassignment or display of the ambiguous he-she sex (shemale) status. A new concept of man-made sex-gender emerged that has been equated with normalcy.

Nevertheless, society has been less successful in manipulating the natural sexual orientation of the child by relying on parental guidance and reinforcements of socially acceptable behavior for boys (masculine) and girls (feminine conduct.) This role training attempts to reinforce the gender of the child at birth according to the socially acceptable gender roles. Over the years, children tend to identify with the parent of the same sex by internalizing his (her) mode of behaving and attitudes by a process known as learning by imitation. In this way children get to learn not only patterns of responses of the same-sex parent but also a self-concept based on the parental praise and criticism of him or her. However, many things could go wrong with the child sex identification, some brought on by the improper or deviant behavior of the parents or by the absence of the role model of the significant parent, most often of the father. A different contributing factor that may affect child's self-image has been assumed to be induced by marital disaccord in which both parents discredit each other or punish the child for showing affection for the other parent.

However, cultural psychologists have also speculated that the child's acquired sex role is the function of the parent with whom he or she identifies and tries to imitate regarding the same-sex-linked interests, attitudes, and behaviors. This has been a standard explanation for sissy behavior in boys and tomboyish behavior in girls. It does not take into account the genetic elements, albeit not clearly understood, but strong enough to sabotage an identification of the child with the opposite sex instead of his or her own gender

The power of gender in the sex orientation of the child cannot be denied as supported by the cases of genetic sex dysphoria in which boys with ambiguous genitalia have been brought up as girls only to find out at puberty that they wanted to be boys. A famous case is that studied at the Johns Hopkins gender clinic,[14] where an identical twin boy who accidentally lost his penis at circumcision, was brought up as a girl until he was fifteen years old. At that age, he refused to have full sex change surgery because he felt like a boy and wanted to be a boy. In fact, his previous behavior was of a tomboyish-maladjusted girl.

The study of the socialization of the acquired drives in contrast to those of inner drives presents intriguing problems for the formulation of the concept of what is considered normal personality. Besides that, there are speculative explanations of the role of mother-child interaction in the formation of adult personality. In this context, it has been theorized that the overly dependent adult who clings for help and support to others may trace his condition to maternal deprivation or paradoxically to the mother's overprotection and overindulgence. Maternal deprivation could be the result of the early death of the mother or separation from her and his confinement in an unloving foster home or orphanage. In fact, it is viewed as axiomatic by developmental psychologists that for the first six to nine months after birth, maternal care is essential for the child to develop healthy relationships with others throughout adult life.

However, the role of socialization becomes even more debatable in certain unsettled issues related to specific acquired drives such as a child's learning to handle frustration. Frustration is a child's response that stems from dealing with regulations and prohibitions imposed by the parents, school authorities and even playmates. Empirical observations about children in the Balinese society trained by parents to accept frustrations showed that they were passive and as adults they did not respond angrily to unusual delays, conflicting actions and discomforts. It is hard to generalize since the observations were not based on any longitudinal, double blind research testing. On the contrary, in general, people frustrated by the barriers between certain strong drives and the ability to satisfy them, perceived the situation as a threat to their well-being. In many cases this led to outright aggression. Aggression is a drive that has generated much controversy since opinions are divided over whether it is an innate drive as Freud and ethnologists believe, or an acquired one as humanists would like to assume. Either way, the fact remains that aggression plays an important role in the human interaction.[15] Aggressive behavior is more noticeable in children that are more often punished for misbehavior. It is hypothesized that less physically punitive mothers do not arouse aggression in children while more punitive mothers do and reinforce it by also physically punishing any display of aggressive behavior.[16] It is assumed that the same pattern is reinforced by school authority figures when they physically punish children. However, while punishment increases the aggression drive, at the same time it reduces its expression because of the fear of renewed punishment. The attempt for self-control exercised by the child leads to frustration and anger that are directed toward other weaker people that cannot retaliate like younger siblings. Furthermore, this theory assumes that a parent who hits his child in anger is teaching him to do the same thing when angry in addition to learning to resent that parent.

Another possibility for the child is to introject the anger by directing it toward himself, though there is no clear explanation for the psychological dynamics leading to the previous approach or this one. In the second scenario, it is assumed that he blames himself for the reasons leading to his punishment. This becomes part of a larger expiatory approach known as guilt that is gradually developed by the child and is triggered by the fear of punishment, loss of love, rejection or shame of being discovered. Guilt is interpreted in psychodynamic terms as redemption for committed punishable transgressions. It acts either as a deterrent to executing any prohibited activity or if it was executed, as a self-imposed way of undoing it by a symbolic restitution. Guilt is assumed to be in a way a self-retribution in order to avoid further repetition of a wrongful act. It is reinforced by parents when they repeatedly deliver stern warnings of severe punishment to the child if he was caught pursuing prohibited activities. This is further supported by the self-instilled feelings of shame and worthlessness if discovered.

According to these hypotheses, the child, more likely by trial and error, develops a pragmatic understanding of what is permissible and what is prohibited behavior by figuring out the consequences of his actions. When the child is old enough to grasp the distinction between right and wrong, he is able to accept that the prohibited punishable actions were wrong. Then he might feel guilty or afraid to pursue it. This explains why self-restraint is not necessarily practiced in the absence of the grown-up when the child realizes that his offenses cannot be discovered and he wouldn't be punished. Furthermore, when the need for satisfaction of a strong drive such as sex is pressing him or the desire to pursue another pleasurable activity is overwhelming, then the child will attempt without any guilt to circumvent the prohibitions by manipulating others through lying and deception.

A case in point is the story reported by newspapers about the sex-play of children at a kindergarten in New York City. Parents complained that a group of children of five-year-olds took their pants off and proceeded to expose their genitals and play sexually under the desks with the teacher present in the classroom. The sexual play allegedly continued for months despite the alleged complaints of the parents. The result is that one of the mothers sued the city for $5 million for show-and-touch sex activity, which was not stopped by the teacher or school.[17] It is obvious that the children demonstrated that they knew what they were doing was wrong by hiding under the desk. They realized that they were not seen and so potentially could not be punished. Only after children have been exposed to the right and wrong actions of others and put under society's pressure, does the sense of right and wrong in most cases become part of their self-regulatory internal mechanism. This sense is integrated into what is known as conscience and moral conduct. Going against this pat concept of the development of a social conscience and of morality, is the recent assumption that a genetic element might play a role, at least in the cases of antisocial personality formation.

Anyway, it has been assumed that the interplay of these psychological processes represents by and large, the main mechanism used later by the alleged normal adult or deviant one in dealing with his environment. It is also believed that over the years these psychological responses may undergo various degrees of modifications according to individual experiences and the quality of his cognition.

However, assuming that one agrees with the major role of family and environmental factors in the development of personality, one will still be unable to explain the differences in behavioral responses between the alleged well adjusted and maladjusted person. For instance, the role of acquired attributes of frustration, aggression, guilt, and conscience, assumed to be developed in response to the upbringing of the child and believed to influence the formation of the individual's personality, as against the role played by genetic factors, still remains controversial. Except for antisocial behavior where these assumed learned traits are recognizable as being out of balance, there has been no meaningful formulation of their role in the formation of other abnormal personalities.

The paucity of clinical research studying their interaction with basic biological drives doesn't help either. Nevertheless, the latest knowledge from genetics throws a ray of light on the early interaction between innate drives and some cultural-parental influences. These findings could permit unbiased researchers of personality to use the genetic results and integrate them with the environmental elements ranging from home and school to peers and community. They become even more crucial in understanding the psychological responses at puberty and adolescence, which are driven by the dramatic hormonal changes. These should be viewed as part of the continuum of influences shaping an individual's personality into adulthood.

Most of the social studies of personality either tend to speculate hypothetically about what might have gone wrong with the development of personality by assuming a faulty interaction with the parents during infancy or childhood or by simply describing flawed behavioral patterns of an individual in response to conflicting events within his social milieu. For example, the social theorists who underscore the role of environment in shaping the individual's behavior fail to tell us the specific reasons for the differences in the reactions of children in a family brought up in the same social conditions. Furthermore, they are unable to explain why identical twins adopted by different families, hence living in dissimilar environments, have similar personality patterns. To understand the complex interaction of factors contributing to the formation of personality, the hereditary-genetic component can't be ignored. To attempt to decipher the complexity of factors shaping what we call a well-adjusted normal personality, a more scientific approach is required.

Societal Factors Affecting an Individual's Adjustment

The general consensus is that people who tend to function within the range of society's norms of acceptable behavior are loosely equated as being "normal." This belief fails to consider the different options for social adjustment offered by different types of social organizations. For example, people living under a dictatorship conform to the imposed social rules regardless how adverse they might be in order to survive. They appear to be well adjusted hence "normal" by hiding their frustrations and true feelings of resentment. Shouldn't we assume that their responses dictated by fear are nothing more than signs of a pure struggle for survival? Is forfeiting any sense of independence of thought or action an act of true choice or one imposed by these coercive circumstances? No wonder that people in the former Soviet Union who dared to demand more freedom were considered mentally ill and placed in mental institutions. This would suggest that people who adjust either act as deft opportunists using better coping skills or they obey the state's rules because they are afraid to confront the system. Anyway, this is a telling comment on how the concept of normal-well-adjusted behavior is manipulated by the social system.

Nonetheless, regardless of the type of organization of society, the individual's social adjustment to daily living is highly personal depending upon the quality of his decision-making process in finding solutions to crisis situations. In this context, personality could be viewed as an information-processing system which has to weigh the constraints of the situation and skillfully either try to solve it favorably or to circumvent or negotiate a compromise that relatively meets his own set of values and needs. If he fails, he might try to minimize the impact of the situation while turning his interest to other areas of activity. In this case the individual is supposed to act within the constraints of conformity. However, he might fight the harmful social rules and regulations while he pretends to accept them for the moment, biding his time till more favorable circumstances occur. Thus he acts ambiguously, as a pseudoconformist. Otherwise, unable to solve the conflict satisfactorily, he might act rebelliously, in the nonconformist manner of a maladjusted person.

What is important to note is that the people previously defined as well adjusted may end up maladjusted due to irresolvable clashes between their held values and the social ones. To put it differently, whenever their sense of proper adjustment is confronted by situations that they cannot solve favorably within the framework of their self-image, status or strong beliefs, or because of the high stress experienced attempting to cope, they might act in a disruptive manner that affects their well-being. On the contrary, if they comply with the social dictates imposed on them, their self-image may suffer because of their inability to reconcile the social demands with their inner needs. This raises again the issue of the extent to which being "normal" can always be equated with being socially adjusted.

In a sweeping statement, social adjustment can be viewed as a set of changes occurring in people's behavior in response to the external demands and experienced stresses brought about by societal constraints. These responses are not necessarily the expression of a reflexive response triggered by a set of beliefs and perceptions that compel an individual to try to adjust or not, but are rather deliberate decisions determined by one's complex motives and restraints elicited by the event. This explains why people tend to adjust selectively to social situations and events. Since socially, adjustment is most often equated with conformity, a good adjustment is considered an ability to match social standards of acceptable behavior with personal needs. A person able to do so is seen as socially well adjusted, a condition that has become interchangeable with the state of being normal. And here is the basic flaw of equalizing social adjustment with normalcy instead of seeing them as partially overlapping. As we will see later, "normal" people could be socially adjusted or not depending on the encountered situation. After all, social adjustment is a qualitative assessment based on a value judgment about conforming to a particular social system.

Conversely, a maladjusted person is presupposed to display behaviors that do not meet the standards of the community either because of his inability to follow it or unwillingness and defiance. Certainly, this evaluation based on a value judgment is arguable since the system's values differ not only from society to society but also within the same one depending on a variety of racial and cultural factors, as will be thoroughly discussed in another chapter. At this time, we might say that adjustment is a very relative notion when it is automatically integrated within the concept of normalcy. The extent of one's conformity is also debated by an individual within his personal concept of the fairness of the social system viewed through the prism of his general philosophy of life. Then, any decision is highly personalized and varies from one situation to another.

A case in point is of Mary, a thirty-seven-year-old career woman who inadvertently became pregnant in the course of a love affair with a man who did not want either to get married at that time or to continue the relationship in case she decided to keep the baby. He felt that the pregnancy was her fault hence he had no reason to get involved. But, regardless of whose fault it was, she became extremely distressed at the prospect of either losing her boyfriend or having an abortion. Neither one of the alternatives available to her was satisfying. To get an abortion was out of the question because of her strong moral beliefs and to put the baby up for adoption was thought by her as equally bad. The idea of keeping the baby was enticing but would have meant losing her boyfriend and sidetracking her career. Since she did not have an extended family to help her, she was supposed to take care of the baby all by herself. The raising of the baby alone would not only interfere with her job but also not give her a chance to provide adequate attention to the baby even if she hired the help of a surrogate mother. The dilemma seemed hard to resolve.

After extensive and tormenting soul-searching and discussions with a variety of counselors, Mary decided to keep the baby, to get a less demanding job in a smaller city where she could go home to check on the baby if necessary, and to terminate the affair with her lover. She did so, but decided to name him officially as the father of the baby and to ask for child support. But this did not mean that she was happy with the solution. Mary thought that this was the best decision that she was able to reach by reconciling conflicting moral values with adverse social circumstances. It had required a total reorganization of her life with a downgrading of her career expectations. She made all these drastic readjustments to her life, but for a price, namely, strong feelings of rejection and defeat resulting in episodes of frustration and bouts of depression. Her self-esteem and confidence in herself were shaken, and the future direction of her life became unsettled because she thought that the cards had been stacked against her.

Then, what does it mean to be well adjusted, as well as a normal person? Does it mean that the assumed absence of the psychopathology associated with the abnormal personality is sufficient to identify proper adjustment-normalcy? Is it realistic to think so? Moreover, the symptoms of soft psychological pathology are subjective and depend to a large extent on the individual's perception of an allegedly unfavorable environment affecting his well-being and could be present either in the assumed normal or in the abnormal one. As we have seen, inappropriate emotional responses may be present in people who are otherwise thought to be normal. In view of this fuzzy distinction, clinicians have surmised that the intensity and long-term persistency of symptoms experienced by the subject may separate normalcy-conformity from abnormality. While this may be true, it does not tell us whether the alleged social adjustment was warranted or not.

Take for example the case of Sudik a middle-aged, mid-level manager at the United Nations (UN). He has worked for over twenty years for the UN and gradually, he was promoted to this responsible position.

In the regular course of his job, he came across certain financial manipulations of funds by his chief of service who illegally diverted tens of millions of dollars to his native country. Sudik brought this to the attention of the appropriate authorities and his boss was suspended with pay during the investigation. In the interim, he was temporarily appointed in charge of the service. Six months later his former boss, a political appointee, came back to reclaim his old position, while it was decided that Sudik stayed as his deputy. Unaware of the strong political connections of his boss to the governing body of the UN, he was shocked to see the culprit back at work with no further action proposed against him for the misuse of funds. Meanwhile, he was accused of exceeding his authority by reporting the alleged fraud to the executive branch. Realizing his predicament, he asked to be transferred to another section, but the request was denied.

From then on, his life in the office became hell: His boss constantly belittled and accused him of incompetency, in addition to giving him periodic bad job evaluations. Sudik reported the continuous harassment to the higher ups without any favorable result. He was enraged by the injustice done to him, particularly since he was a professional, while his boss was a political careerist. Getting no remedy from the UN grievance committee, he went to a lawyer who advised him that since UN is not under the US labor jurisdiction, it might refuse to honor a court decision even if he won. After months of complaining and fighting for his rights, he slowly became depressed. Now, he actually functioned poorly at work and was advised to take sick leave and get psychiatric help. He felt crushed and lost because he realized that he did not have a chance to win back his rights. He felt left at the mercy of his tormentor and a manipulative bureaucracy.

This sad situation may remind someone of the classic Milgrim's experiment on obedience by conditioning dogs to passivity in response to receiving a painful electric shock while restrained and unable to avoid the shock. The dogs became passive, apathetic, and nonresponsive.

Sudik, by all conventional standards, was a conformist behaving "normally" until faced with a threatening situation which was beyond his ability and social resources to control. He was unable to protect himself against this overpowering political force—the boss—who wanted to get rid of him. The alternative for him was either to retire on medical grounds or to resign and look for a job in the private sector. To find a job with a similar pay was out of question, but to settle for a minor job would not have helped his mental state either. In retrospect, one may assume that behind his facade of being well adjusted, was hidden an inadequate, limited coping ability which under stress triggered a fair amount of anxiety and depression affecting his efficiency at work. A simple assumption could be his inadequate judgment in handling the conflict and his poor understanding of the office dynamics of power with the result that the vulnerable shield of "conformity-normalcy" was shattered. But, according to him, the nature of his job created the conflict. Sudik claims that had he glossed over his negative accounting findings, they would have been discovered later by the regular team of outside auditors and he would have been fired outright. He emphasized that he did not have any choice in this matter. Not an enviable situation to be in. However, if his view of the situation was the correct one, on hindsight one may claim that he was supposed to protect himself before taking any official action by discreetly investigating the political power of the boss and informally discussing the matter with his higher-ups. But this is sheer speculation. In his case, to be well adjusted would have required a high ability to manipulate others in order to protect himself, while creating the illusion that he was asking only for their advice for handling his job properly. He did not pass the test of cleverness, sophistication and dishonesty required by his job. This means that one's social adjustment may be judged relative to the individual's capacity to function within his social status and condition. A threatening and crooked social situation could be overcome by smart operators or by skillful but disingenuous manipulations that only would pretend to be within a framework of conformity-normalcy.

Sham Social Adjustment and Deceptive "Mask of Normalcy"

Take the intriguing case of Gail, a widow, a charming, intelligent, well educated, financially well-off woman in her mid-fifties who recently had some legal problems. She had difficulty in recovering a series of loans of hundreds of thousands dollars made to a close business partner. According to her, she gave him, on various occasions, these substantial sums of money for business purposes without any contractual agreement because she liked and trusted him. But a closer look at her pattern of social interaction suggests more likely a miscalculation on her part. Apparently, Gail's expectation of obligating and emotionally binding him did not materialize. In fact, the charming guy turned out to be a smooth operator who used the money for personal purposes. Their game of trying to outwit each other ended in court when she sued to recoup her money.

At this point, some revealing information of her past life is in order. It shows a pattern of deceit ranging from improper manipulations during her career, to pursuing calculated, profitable marriages followed by well-timed divorces. Years ago she had married a young professional whom she divorced shortly afterwards but not without getting a generous settlement extracted by blackmailing him for alleged perverse sexual behavior while she was carrying on at the same time, an affair with her divorce lawyer. Later, Gail secured a professional degree with the help of a professor infatuated to the point of writing her master's degree thesis himself.

After all these successful manipulations, her career came to a standstill when she was investigated for professional insurance fraud that affected her reputation in the community. At a later date, she compensated for her losses by collecting a large insurance award by faking a physical disability and inability to work related to an alleged car accident.

Married again to another professional man who spent lavishly on her, she persuaded him to buy two adjacent houses and give one as a gift to her mother. She later sued her mother for the house repossession since she was not living in it and reached a settlement. When her husband unexpectedly developed an illness diagnosed as terminal she panicked and sought solace in the arms of his treating physician. Although her husband's health and prognosis improved, she decided to divorce him for alleged infidelity and mental abuse.

After an acrimonious court battle and threats of blackmailing him professionally, she got a big settlement and married the physician who left his family for her. To assure his total separation from his children, she insisted on relocating thousands of miles away. While still unsettled professionally in the city, the new husband suddenly died while undergoing treatment in a prestigious hospital and she became the sole heiress to his substantial assets, including a hefty insurance compensation for his accidental death, obtained after artful manipulations of facts with the help of a husband's friend in insurance business. Before trying to get the money, she decided to immediately cremate him in order to avoid any contact with his family. After all, at her insistence he had disinherited his children because of their alleged disapproval of the marriage.

In her new role of a wealthy socialite seeking advice for business ventures, she targeted a rich man in his eighties who she romanced for months while pushing him to finance a sham, million-dollar social project. But he died before signing the final papers.

Undaunted, she continued her phony pitch for other deals until she met the charming lawyer and would-be business partner. Gail gambled to win him over and she lost but she recouped her money only after court action. In court she played the role of a distressed, naive widow cheated by the defendant who she said had misrepresented himself as a business consultant. After winning she refused to pay her lawyers the balance of the fees.

Besides belonging to the category of ruthless, callous, and predatory persons, displaying behavior from habitual lying to deception, she is a normal-conformist by our social standards. She is viewed as well adjusted, socially coping well and with minimum distress during her financial and marital shenanigans. She has never been arrested for any crime, thereby creating the illusion of being an abiding citizen. In fact, she flaunted her social success expecting to be treated as a respectable citizen. Certainly, one may discern psychopathic patterns of behavior but since her actions were more or less within the boundary of the law and since she sought discreet legal counseling before embarking on any new dubious activity, she managed to stay a step ahead of the law.

In the same vein, baffling questions are raised about the sham conformity of politicians, investment bankers, or businessmen who may lie, deceive, or abuse their office and others and still pretend to be models of normalcy as long as they are not indicted or convicted by a court. The new ambiguous social values and moral relativism seem to be slowly incorporating within the structure of the society and drastically changing our view of what used to be called normal behavior. It seems that the ones who fail to function within the new rules of moral ambiguity could easily become losers, if not maladjusted. In this period of social transition the social moral standards appear fuzzy to many people affecting their shaky social adjustment. What would we say about a congressman convicted of appropriation of federal property and later pardoned by a departing president? Could he claim to have been an honest man ignorant of the law or was he a crook? What about a minister or rabbi who diverted his congregation's money and was treated leniently by the court on ground of ignorance of financial matters? Are they swindlers or part of the new definition of people displaying "normal behavior?" From the legal point of view these cheaters are rational but just corrupt, while being leniently treated by activist judges and opportunistic politicians. Psychologically, they might be at least regarded as maladjusted if not suffering from a serious personality disorder. Ethically, they are for sure immoral.

Legal versus Psychological Conflict in Defining Social Conformity

It is important to note that the legal presumption of socially adjusted behavior does not necessarily match the mental health concept of it. An individual who legally deviated from conformity is considered not normal only if he is incompetent to stand trial by inability to pass the test for it or to prove that he was insane at the time when the crime was committed. The defense has to prove the incapability of the accused to understand the nature and quality of the charges and to show his inability to follow the court procedures. Basically, the defendant acts at various degrees of legal nonconformism claiming nonresponsibility for the act.

However, even these rules can be interpreted according to the situation. A person who may act irrationally in a situation under the influence of a delusion or false belief may act rationally in a different situation that is not part of his delusional system. This means that one may be responsible for his behavior in some situations and invoke insanity in others. For example, someone suffering from delusional persecutions may physically attack and harm the object of his delusion, while at the same time he is able to handle his financial matters quite well. In the same vein, a person committed involuntarily to a mental institution may be able to refuse participating in a research project with a new drug because he understands the unwarranted consequences of its use.

It should be also noted that some states have broadened the purview of the insanity plea by permitting a defendant to assert an affirmative defense of extreme emotional disturbance at the time of the offense. His legally nonconformist behavior was the result of a temporary "aberration." This defense is closer to the psychiatric concept of impairment of judgment under severe emotional stress but without the concomitant presence of a mental disorder.

However, the mental health point of view of abnormality is more liberal, embracing all types of behaviors that fall outside the social standards of acceptability, from antisocial behavior to irrational acts, which are all believed to be induced by a personality disturbance or mental disorder. The basic premise of the mental health concept of abnormality is that the irrational behavior of the mentally disordered person is inevitable, in the sense that the mentally ill person is unable to act otherwise owing to his condition. This approach of "unavoidable irrationality" leads to clashes with the legal concept of abnormality. For instance, alcoholics or drug addicts may commit crimes under the influence of the used substances, but since their mental state induced by drugs could have been prevented by avoiding use, they are considered rational and subject to prosecution. This brings us to the issue of the role of will within the context of the law and mental health.

While mental health clinical practice distinguishes disorders of will-impulse as a special category that may affect the individual's judgment and impair his social functioning, the law does not consider it a reason for abnormality, unless it is part of an insanity plea. As a matter of fact, volitional problems affecting conformity are more subjective in scope and harder to identify legally than issues of rationality, hence their possible abuse by the defense.

Anyone faced with this variety of concepts of assumed conformity ranging from social and psychological to moral and legal ones may be confused and practically unable to accurately apply them in order to identify the well-adjusted-appearing-normal people in their daily interactions. Yet, all these diverse concepts only succeed in obfuscating the concept of what practically should constitute a normal-conformist person.

Psychologically versus Socially Well-Adjusted Person

As a matter of fact all these psychological and social constructs of identifying normal behavior have little value for defining conformity in routine social interaction.

Interestingly, the concept of well adjusted, proper behavior, initially it had only tribal connotations, meaning someone's obeisance to the community's moral customs and traditions. It implied compliance with the moral rules of behavior as propounded by religious beliefs, strictly monitored by the priests. Later, standards of social behavior were evolved and imposed by the leaders of community that became norms of conduct, required to be followed by all the members. The religious prescriptions and secular rules were intertwined while organizing the structure of society and together were guiding and regulating the behavior of the tribesmen. The punishment was either divine retribution or secular punishment, mainly by ostracism for offenses against religious precepts that would bring down Gods' wrath and revenge on the tribe. This tells us how greatly disposed were the tribesmen to conform to the rules of authority.

Now, most common people still rely on customary norms of acceptable behavior according to the standards of the community, except that traditional values have undergone significant alterations and have been replaced in our multicultural society by moral relativism. As a result, a new notion of well-adjusted social behavior has emerged which has altered drastically what had been understood in the past as well-adjusted normal behavior. Could these "pseudo-adjusted" people be considered as behaving normally? As long as they operate, more or less, within the ill-defined moral framework of our social organization they appear to be "normal," though they might be either dishonest, untrustworthy liars, or deviants practicing sexual perversions or spouse/child-abuse relatively tolerated in their community. Take, for example, the recent scandal of Brooklyn, New York District Attorney (DA) Charles Hynes who has refused to name the orthodox Jewish child molesters prosecuted by his office, an incident that has fueled a firestorm of community outrage.[18] He claims that by naming the perpetrators he would compromise victim confidentiality. However, the critics claim that by keeping the community in the dark, he panders to the all-powerful ultraorthodox leaders. The irony is that the same DA office recently released the name of an offender, a nonultraorthodox, who raped an eleven-year-old girl, the daughter of his girlfriend. Is this circumvention of law according to the DA's interpretation of what is good and bad for the community, justifiable? The fact is that in the last three years, eighty-five sex predators have been accused and arrested for molesting or raping children in this ultraorthodox community. There were 117 victims, eighty-nine under the age of seventeen, which resulted in fourteen being sentenced to jail and twenty-four being sentenced to probation. The problem for the DA is that the community doesn't cooperate with him because many victims are pressed by their families not to testify. Parents allegedly hesitate to report the sex crimes because they are afraid of retaliations from the community leaders, rabbinic schools, and local institutions.[19]

Judging by the norms of well-adjusted behavior are these citizens acting to protect their interests in the community or are they in contradiction to the generally acceptable conduct of obeying and supporting authorities? Most of them seem to believe that as long the interests of the community do not coincide with those of the society at large, they have to support their community. But this attitude makes them maladjusted nonconformists because they are going against the social norms of conduct while adjusting to those of the community.

This shows the degree of relativity of well-adjusted behavior when one is caught in a conflict of allegiance to different levels of social obligations which affect one's daily life in dissimilar ways.

The behavior of some of these people could be judged to be closer to what is assumed as well-adjusted normalcy while others' behavior can be judged as closer to abnormality. Ultimately, "conformity-well-adjustment" represents either an ideal state of functioning in the community or is used as an arbitrary working concept that would offer general guidelines for describing a person with a relatively integrated self-identity and who resolves most of the problems affecting his life within the prevailing cultural framework of shared beliefs of his community.

People loosely considered well-adjusted-normal present a variety of qualitative and quantitative facets and nuances in their behavioral traits in the process of relating and coping with their environment that vary according to the encountered social conditions and challenging events. This variation in the individual's attitudes and behaviors toward society throw wide open the concept of conformity, suggesting that an individual usually displays flexibility and creativity in handling new situations. They may act and respond in an unexpected manner to similar demands, but are still viewed as normal but nonconformist if they are able to organize their life in ways that appear to them as purposeful and meaningful.

Notes

1. William Styron, *Sophies's Choice* (New York: Knopf, Doubleday, 1993).
2. Arthur Miller, *Death of a Salesman* (New York: Penguin Books, 1976).
3. Albert Camus, *The Stranger* (New York: Vintage Books, 1954).
4. "American Beauty," Actor, Kevin Spacey, Directed by Hollywood Film Dir. Sam Mendes, 1999.
5. "John Edwards Indicted on Campaign Finances," *The Washington Post*, online, November 1, 2011.
6. "Jesse Jackson Admits Affair, Illegitimate Child," ABC news.go.com, January 18, 2001.
7. "Schwarzenegger: Affair with Housekeeper Hurt Shriver, Kids, Family," Los Angeles Times.com, October 1, 2012.
8. "943 Women 'Honor Killed' in Pakistan in 2011," Al Arabiya, News Channel, March 3, 2012.
9. Abraham Maslow, *Toward a Psychology of Being* (Princeton, NJ: Van Nostrand, 1968).
10. Christopher Badcock, *Evolutionary Psychology* (Malden, MA: Blackwell Publishers, 2000).
11. A. Thomas, S. Chess, H. Birch, and M. Hertzig, "A Longitudinal Study of Primary Reaction in Children," *Comprehensive Psychiatry* 1 (1960): 103–12.

12. Freud Sigmund, "Character and Anal Eroticism," in *Collected Papers*, vol. 11, chap. 14, 20 (London: Hogarth Press, 1938).
13. Erich Fromm, *Man for Himself, An Inquiry into the Psychology of Ethics* (New York: Henri Holt & Company, 1990), 65.
14. John Money, "Boy Raised as Girl/David Reimer Case," Wordpress.com, November 5, 2010.
15. Robert Baron, *Human Aggression* (New York: Plenum Press, 1977), 77–122.
16. Gordon E. Jesse, *Personality and Behavior* (New York: Macmillan, 1963), 282–88.
17. Giove, C. and S. Edelman, "School Fondle Shock," *New York Post*, February 2, 2012, 18.
18. Colin Moyniham, "Victim Suffered Rapes for Years, Prosecutors Say," *New York Times*, June 24, 2011.
19. Collin Moynihan, "One Defendant is Freed in Brooklyn Rape Case," *New York Times*, April 18, 2012.

2

Theories of Personality and the Equivocation of "Normalcy"

PART I
The Ambiguity of Defining Well-Adjusted Normal Behavior

The facade of well-adjusted "normalcy" could be quite deceptive. Someone while appearing well adjusted, normal at the time of an interview for hiring, let's say, as a security guard, suffers from recurring episodes of panic attacks and abuses alcohol frequently but was never treated and as such his true story is unbeknown to the interviewer. At best, the interviewer can ascertain the alleged well-adjusted-normal state of functioning at that time. Even if someone has official knowledge of that person's past social history, free of serious entanglements with the law, or of not significant medical history, such a person still might miss any correct evaluation because of hidden abuse of drugs, alcohol, or of an unknown sexual perversion not to mention of a partner's physical abuse.

Furthermore, the identifying of "normalcy" with its corollary social conformity depends to a large extent on the definition used by the interviewer or researchers of human behavior. For some, social conformity as part of acting "normally" is viewed as one's ability to reach excellence in his social activity, to be in good health, and to experience a sense of fulfillment. From these desiderata at least two of them are subjective relative value judgment items. It reflects the individual's view of himself and the arbitrary criteria used by the interviewer. One overall criterion is the ability to adjust to unfavorable events mostly outside of one's control by accepting their adverse results upon his life which is translated in well adjustment. If he is not content with the status that he has achieved and is burning inside, this fact is irrelevant for his adjustment. Even if his conformity is a pretense, just a temporary period for rethinking his choices of redressing the balance of his life, he is still considered well adjusted. This situation poses the question whether there are better methods for identifying well-adjusted people allegedly normals.

Many psychologists think that psychological tests could separate the normal conformists from the others emotionally or socially impaired or dysfunctional. This approach though considered more accurate, it has almost the same shortcomings as the interviews by capturing some arbitrary traits of behavior postulated to be characteristic of a social, well-adjusted functioning, but to which there is attached a value judgment. At best, one can say that on the surface they attest one's stated conformity to the social rules of social conduct. In fact, the questionnaires focus on specific types of social activities and behaviors assumed to identify traits of personality reflecting individual's degree of conformity to society. Even so, the responses might contain elements of distortion created by the possible unreliability of people interviewed who may answer the test questions in a careless or misleading manner.

In general, it is hypothesized that the traits identifying "normalcy-conformity" represent individual's ability to organize life in acceptable social patterns. This presupposes identifying the salient points about individual's organization of life which meets the standards of the community and also about his state of mind with its subjective view of himself and his style of life determined by and large by his cultural standards. As one may realize, the notion of normalcy and social adjustment could conflict in case of the individual's nonconformist behavior that might be acceptable or not depending on the possible discrepancies between the society's standards and his personal cultural beliefs. This arbitrary approach of defining "well-adjusted normalcy" has inadvertently opened Pandora's box.

Psychosocial Theories of Personality within the Context of Conformity

To understand the problems of defining conformity in the context of normal behavior one has to review the many prevailing cultural theories embraced by the theoreticians of personality who used them as circumstantial arguments in support of their view of social adjustment as indicator of normalcy. In fact, most of the theoretical underpinnings were drawn from the old psychosociological view about the overriding role of nurture in determining what has been commonly called human nature. As strange as it may sound, human nature had been conceived by humanists as represented by an inner core comprising its hereditary determinant and biological-instinctual factors, though repressed or controlled by cultural and environmental forces. The role of the inner nature in the formation of personality has been considered weak and imprecise, ego alien and mostly unconscious. It revealed itself in the case of "authentic selfhood" which according to Abraham Maslow is "able to hear these impulse voices within oneself." He went on to say: "they are instinct-remnants as impulses and drives, weak, subtle and delicate, easily drowned out by learning, by cultural expectations, by fear."[1]

Based on these naïve and speculative premises about human nature, the psychosocial theories of personality were formulated. Appealing to imagination and cultural trends, but undocumented by research because of lack of better knowledge the human nature has dominated our notions about normal and abnormal human personality for almost a century. Only recently, the advances in biology and genetics have started to bring a slow shift toward a new and more comprehensive formulation of personality. This happened when researchers from the field of biology and genetics questioned some of the previously untouchable but unproven premises held by the "culturalists." Basic premises of social-cultural tenets became vulnerable to the scientific fresh data provided by the biological-genetic findings about human behavior. The previous "irrefutable" arguments about the all-encompassing role of the psychosocial factors, hypothetically assumed to determine the formation of personality, fell short of adequately explaining the gamut of complex human behavior.

For a long time socially oriented psychoanalysts and humanist psychologists influenced by the sociological and anthropological theories "on vogue," developed hypothetical models of normal and abnormal social functioning exclusively relying on the social/nurture factors in explaining human nature. Taking their cue from Emile Durkheim, the founder of sociology,[2] they went along with his unproven idea of collective consciousness, developed in the process of human's socialization, and with Franz Boas, a cultural anthropologist, who advanced his own theoretical version of the mind as shaped by the individual's social environment to the point of accepting the ultimate speculation of Alfred Kroeber, anthropologist, who declared the human mind and behavior as not being subject to the laws of biological evolution but determined by society.[3,4] Their writings influenced a great deal the post-Freudian psychoanalysts theorists who were unhappy with Freud's reductionist biological premises about the human development of personality.

The Influence of the Post-Freudians on the Formulation of Personality

Alfred Adler, Karen Horney, Erich Fromm, and Harry Stack Sullivan are the most known psychoanalysts, exponents of the social dimensions of the development of personality while ignoring or implying a reduced role for a few biological factors in its shaping. Each one made his clinical suppositions about various social dynamics inducing abnormal behavior and by their resolution of the assumed normal personality.

For example, Adler introduced the hypothetical concept of man's striving for superiority as a compensatory need to conceal inferiority feelings related either to one's body or mind inadequacies. From childhood he continuously strived to reach a higher level of betterment and social recognition, driven by his "creative self," which is ultimately responsible for one's style of life and personality by making man unique in his configuration of interests and values. Another element in the formation of personality is the "will to power" an alleged universal goal of men, a concept borrowed from Frederick Nietzsche, an influential German philosopher. His assumption of a normal person has been that the individual is responsible for his own formation of personality since it is based on conscious processes which mold one's personality.[5]

Horney dispensing with what she considered Freud's mechanistic and biological orientation that has hindered the understanding of human condition, emphasized the interpersonal relationships. An inadequate interpersonal relationship leads to various "neurotic" strategies that are summed up by her three orientations: moving toward people, away from them, or against them. For her, the normal person either resolved or is able to control somehow any inner conflict, and is able to function and cope favorably when faced with aggravating social situations.[6]

Fromm's position is unequivocal about man's ability to transcend his biological drives because of his self-awareness, intellectual pursuits, and ability to satisfy his spiritual needs.

For Fromm, a well-adjusted normal individual is one who possesses a set of characteristics clustered under the umbrella of a productive personality that creates the ability to realize one's potentialities in accordance with the circumstances offered by society. His implication is that normal people learn the rules of society's conformity. However, this alleged normal individual may become upset and alienated if society frustrates him in the gratification of his social needs. In this general framework he described other types of personality created by our capitalistic system. He speculated that these personalities represent distorted style of life in response to strong neurotic traits.[7]

For Sullivan social interaction defines man's personality because the individual's psychic make-up is a result of one's interpersonal relationships. He also emphasizes the role of anxiety in the process of properly functioning socially and man's attempts to contain it by developing his own system of protection. Generally speaking, Sullivan had attempted to define normal personality in terms of proper interpersonal relationship introducing anxiety as a part of the normal structure of functioning.[8]

Later, Maslow, an exponent of humanistic psychology, developed eleven social-clinical criteria for "normalcy" required to be met by a well-adjusted individual. Their mix identifies more or less certain general traits of one's personality. These theoretical characteristics attempt to represent the foundation for the individual's style of coping and degree of adjusting to his social condition.[9] They haven't been validated.

A relatively recent pseudoscientific support for the assumed decisive role of the social factors in the development of personality has been offered by the speculative theory of the "cultural determinism" supported by Richard Dawkins, an ethologist. According to his far-fetched argument, people develop their personality under the influence of the cultural "meme." These assumed meme(s) are pieces (units) of culture that are passed on from generation to generation, exactly as the selected genes are genetically passed on to produce the body and its brain. The brain is the storage house. Dawkins speculated these cultural determinants, as units of the culture, to be inculcated in the brain and to be responsible for the human behavior. This conjectural theory does not add anything to the social development of personality.[10]

Behavioristic Theories Supporting Conformity as Part of Normal Social Conduct

A different avenue for the evaluation of the role the social factor in the formulation of personality has been provided by the conditioned reflexes theory, initially studied by Ivan Pavlov. Later, Burrhus F. Skinner, the best known authority in the field of behavioral conditioning, concluded his laboratory research with animals on the premise that human behavior is determined by social conditioning. The school of behaviorists believes that it is possible to mold the mind in order to respond in accordance with any social conditioning. They praise the power of nurture over nature in the formation of the human behavior, while they gloss over the simple fact that conditioning itself has a neurophysiological basis that determines its limitation in accordance to certain vital inner drives of each species.[11] For example, researchers found that rats could be conditioned to the size of the food after receiving electric shocks, but not to the taste of food. This indicates an innate control against conditioning of taste that is vital for their survival. Taste of the food protects them against potential illnesses while size does not. Similar examples could be found in other animals or birds when attempts were made to condition them to factors contributing to the suppression of their basic survival instincts. Pigeons easily connect sound with delivery of food but they cannot link sound to electroshocks. The shocks are associated with an imminent danger, attacks of hunters or predators.

An offshoot of the conditioning theory is the school of learning that formulates human behavior based on the stimulus-response theory supported by the assumption that the child's instinctual needs are regulated by gradual and repeated conditioning. John Dollard and Neal Miller have elaborated a comprehensive theory of child's personality development based on reinforcement-reward principles involving habits, cues, primary, and secondary drives that are conditioned on hierarchical responses. To note, all this learning occurs in a cultural framework, conditioning the child individual to conform to the norms of the culture. It could be negatively affected by the improper interaction between child-parents and child-society. In this context, social maladjustment presupposes a deficient learning of the social rules by the individual.[12] However, it does not tell us anything about the role of the child's temperament.

In fact, these social theoreticians in the field of personality have expounded on ideas popular during their times when the field of genetics was just emerging. The result has been the development of theories of personality with wrong interpretations of data by lack of knowledge about the role of constitutional-genetic factor. Poorly informed or uninformed, they dismissed or ignored the role of genetics, relying on explanations already offered by the speculations of culturalists, by now entrenched and their speculations treated as irrefutable facts.

Constitutional Factors Indicators of Personality Types

Other clinical researchers like William Sheldon, influenced by Ernest Kretchmer, an European researcher who emphasized the role of the constitutional elements in the formation of the individual personality, expanded this line of research by studying the link between the constitutional factor and types of personality. In fact, it has been known for a long time that asthenic people are more reserved and inhibited than the portly, heavy set ones who are more gregarious and jolly. Sheldon empirically distinguished three main body types, the endomorph (the digestive type), the mesomorph (the athletic type), and ectomorph (the asthenic-cerebral type). He linked these three body types statistically to particular sets of traits of temperament.[13] Sheldon's classification envisioned the constitutional-genetic factors as fixed, unalterable traits of an individual, hence less responsive to social-psychological manipulations. This immutability of traits may explain the reason for the reluctance of most social researchers of human behavior to pursue and emphasize the role of genetic factors in the formation of personality. Other reasons were into play as well, such as the education of the neopsychoanalytically or psychosocially oriented clinicians that fitted well with American social concept of the self-made man, a master of himself.

Another group of researchers known as organismic holists have tried to bridge the gap between biological and social components of the behavior by approaching human behavior from the perspective of body and mind unity. Relying heavily on Gestalt concepts, Kurt Goldstein, an exponent of organismic theory, underscored the integration of psychological processes with the physiological ones since together they determine any response to social stresses and demands. The holists are mainly interested in the general psychosocial dynamics processes that interact with a given biological structure and are together responsible for one's functioning in society.[14]

While attempting to explain this elusive balance in functioning is a highly desirable goal, none of them addressed the role of nonconformity in defining normalcy. Furthermore, normalcy defined only in terms of social adjustment, disregarded the potential conflict between self-realization and antagonistic social rules glossed over by the humanists-culturalists.

However, culturalists have continued to elaborate in an extensive but unconvincing manner about cultural forces as determining individuals' behavioral responses. In general, negative behavioral responses have been viewed as part of a poor or a nonsocial integration that is supposed to be associated to unfavorable cultural and social conditions created by dysfunctional parents or by a hostile surrounding environment. At the same time, it has been assumed that the choices for adjustment and self-actualization are by and large, within the reach of most people under the right social circumstances. This optimistic and naïve view has created an illusion of equal ability for all people by disregarding their unique and inalterable traits of their temperament.

Current Approaches to the Study of Personality

As one may notice, all these speculations and theories about the formation of personality are tidbits of clinical observations of limited theoretical or practical values, framed in sociopsychological generalizations that hardly could be integrated in a comprehensive formulation of personality. It has required a more comprehensive exploration of the traits of personality responsible for human behavior to draw some meaningful conclusions about what might constitute the matrix of a normal well-adjusted personality. Later, a relative progress was made when better trained clinicians attempted to separate people who behave "normally" from those who don't do it successfully based on their ability to function in their environment.

The theoretical assumption was that there were specific positive behavioral responses enhancing person's functioning in his environment and implicitly favoring his or her genetic reproduction. By contrast, inadequate responses that induce serious distress and/or impair individual's social functioning with the potential of negatively affecting the offspring characterized maladjusted or abnormal personality. One of the flaws in this approach is that not all people with a personality disorder experience distress and not all people feeling distressed show noticeable impairment of functioning. For example, antisocial people do not experience distress or remorse caused by their harmful behavior while obsessive-compulsives can function socially quite well, albeit upset about their rigid behavior. Ignoring for the moment the nosological shortcomings of this arbitrary separation of "normal" from abnormal personality, the important fact is that the difference between them is more than what appears to be a simple qualitative one. Their diagrammatical representation on a behavioral continuum of a linear vector with normalcy at one end and abnormality at the other indicates only one dimension of the relation between them. Another dimension to be considered along this continuum would be whether there are traits of personality that under conditions of stress can act in an abnormal manner but later return to a relatively normal level of functionality if the perceived threat has subsided. Furthermore, there are various shades of social maladjustment and distress potentially induced by certain traits of personality more than others. Their predominance in the organization of behavior determines specific types of personality disorder. The basic difference between the presupposed "normals" and "abnormals" is based on the empirical observation that the same traits apparently belonging to both groups are differing in their degrees of behavioral expression by becoming inflexible and extreme in manifestation in people with personality disorders.

To this clinical dichotomy of personality, insightful clinicians and researchers introduced their models of personality emphasizing a new general behavioral organization of it based on innate factors that characterize its overall direction of responses within one's social functioning. Different clinical researchers have, at different times, observed three general inherited characteristics in the development of personality, assumed as guiding behavioral dimensions that are shaping the environmental influences.

The first one is related to the distinction between subject-object dichotomy, elegantly and imaginatively elaborated by Carl Jung's classification of people as introverts and extroverts. This dimension emphasizes the foremost role played by the interaction between the assumed inherited make-up of one's self versus other people in shaping the environmental responses around him.[15]

The second construct focuses on a model of evaluating the major traits of personality from the perspective of the active-passive polarity of behavior. The displayed behavior in the social inter-action is viewed as taking place within two primary modalities, that is, initiated either by persons who direct events or, on the contrary, reacting to others' actions.

The third dimension used for measuring human behavior emphasizes the physiological stimulus response in the context of the individual's pain-pleasure orientation. From this point of view, based on the individual's temperament, events tend to be viewed by people either as satisfying and rewarding or unpleasant and discomforting. The positive events are pursued and reinforced; whereas, the negative ones are discarded and avoided. An important point to note is that all these three distinctive behavioral components, biophysiologically determined, may be displayed in various degrees by people in dealing with their environment.

These concepts have been partly used by Hans J. Eysenck, a research psychologist, who attempted to correlate traits of personality to physiological and biological factors. He developed a scale measuring what he called neuroticism (anxiety, anger-hostility, depression, self-consciousness, impulsiveness, and vulnerability) and psychoticism that contain items for predisposing factors, which he combined with another scale of extraversion, attempting to separate normal behavior from neurotics and psychotics. In support of this three-factor model of personality, he found a degree of correlation between normals and neurotics with regard to their responses to psychotropic drugs and to suggestibility of the body-sway test.[16]

As already mentioned, new clinical findings further questioned the validity of the assumptions about the decisive role of environment in the formation of personality. A major impetus came from the findings about monozygotic twins adopted and living in different environments having similar personalities that didn't follow the rules of assumed cultural development. Independent of it, two longitudinal studies done later by Jerome Kagan verified the fact that the child after birth presents fixed traits resistant to change. If so, it meant that these traits were genetic. The first study showed that 15 percent of the children have low reaction (ebullient LR) and 15 percent had high reaction (inhibited HR), the remainder of them were mixed. Retested five years later only 3 percent changed the category. The second study confirmed the findings of the first study. He found that the initial traits became more entrenched. Although the HR children by the age of seven and after showed signs of anxiety, they were very successful in school. The conclusion has been obvious: babies have an inborn temperament constant during life time (90 percent of them didn't change their basic traits of temperament).[17] It was found by other researchers that the ones with ebullient risk-taking traits have a risk-taking gene, dopamine receptor D4 (DRD4) which has a large number of variants, one called variable number tandem repeat in axon 3 in long form which is responsible for high-risk behavior. The influence of environment on these high-risk takers could be modulated by environment depending of the variant of DRD4 present in this receptor.[18]

Other temperament inherited traits still required to be defined. This was attempted to be done later by a group of researchers who used a wide-reaching frame of reference to define five broad factors of normal personality identifying neuroticism (propensity to negative affectivity like anxiety, depression, anger, envy, and guilt), which in general would reflect emotional stability-calm under stress versus excitability-tendency to overreact, extraversion, (outgoing energetic versus reserved solitary), openness (curious versus cautious), agreeableness (friendly compassionate versus cold detached), and conscientiousness (efficient organized versus easy going sloppy). They represent clusters of adaptive traits that they have shown to be able to recognize, in liberal terms, various subtypes of personality disorders. In general, each factor representing a set of clinical behavioral traits slides from normal at one pole to abnormal at the other.[19]

Interestingly, high scores of neuroticism have been negatively correlated with problems of health and longevity and risk of major depression.[20]

It is important to note that most of these traits have been linked to some genetic snips of DNA. For instance, a snip from chromosome 20 called SNAP 25 has been associated with neuroticism. It is also associated with mood disorders, attention deficit-hyperactivity disorder, and schizophrenia. Another snip close to another gene is linked to extraversion while a snip, rs644148 is related to extraversion and openness. A few snips close to the CLOCK gene linked to agreeableness. The trait of conscientiousness was associated with chromosome 21 and the gene called DYRKIA. This gene plays a role in Down syndrome and Alzheimer's.[21]

The Neuroticism-Extroversion-Openness Personality Inventory—Revised[22] separates statistically the "normals" from "abnormals," but has been challenged by other researchers on the ground that their concept of personality disorders representing extreme variant of adaptation is not supported by clinical findings. This has weakened its validity in clinical settings. It seems that people with high scores in some categories of the test may not experience subjective distress or noticeable functional impairment.

Temperament and Character

Another group of researchers who have approached the distinction between normalcy and personality disorders have attempted to answer some of these basic issues by using a novel model that took into account general structures of personality described as traits of temperament, that were evaluated together with the acquired ones representing the character. The test of Temperament and Character Inventory[23] attempts to do just that. There are four specific structures of temperament that have been extracted from psychometric and genetic studies of personality and from research of classical and operant conditioning responses of people subjected to pleasant and aversive stimuli.

These temperament dimensions which are noticeable since childhood determine behaviorally the differences between individuals. They were identified as novelty seeking (NS), harm avoidance (HA), reward dependence (RD), and persistence (P). NS is one of the temperament inheritable traits responsible for initiating exploratory behavior, processing impulsive decision making, contributing to quick loss of temper with exhibit of excessive anger, or quick disengagement for avoidance of frustration. Each individual has his own pattern of response to NS. People low on NS are viewed as noncurious, noninquiring, standoffish, displaying low emotions and enthusiasm.

The same analysis applies to the other three temperament traits starting with HA which scores the inhibition or cessation of behavior. Individuals high on HA are likely to be cautious, apprehensive, negativistic, and inhibited in social situations. The ones who score low are more carefree, outgoing, courageous, and confident, displaying optimism in face of danger.

The next temperament dimension RD indicates people who are warm, sensitive, dependent, sociable, and easy going. They are good at maintaining and continuing ongoing relationships. The ones low on RD are practical, tough, aloof, and somewhat socially insensitive. They keep to themselves and disinclined to enter in intimate communication with others.

People high on P are hardworking and determined to complete tasks despite setbacks and frustrations viewed as challenges. Basically, they are ambitious and excessively success oriented. The ones low on P are unreliable, unenthusiastic, slow to start an activity, and give up easily when frustrated or criticized. All in all they are underachievers.

These core personality traits, genetically determined, interact with three selected traits of character described by the authors of the test as related to one's self-concept that have been shaped during one's developmental years. The self-concept is formulated in relationship to the autonomous self, self-directedness (SD) (developed by David Riesman, see Introduction). It interacts with society in cooperativeness (C) and these two factors have been related to individual's view of his spiritual needs of embracing larger goals concerning mankind and the universe (self-transcendence).

The SD people are responsible, mature, goal oriented, and well-integrated socially. They are self-confident and maintain a good self-esteem. Important to note is that they are highly adaptable people according to the circumstances. The potential social downside is that they tend to challenge orders from bosses with whom they don't mind to disagree, thus, making them appear difficult or trouble makers. The people low on SD are somewhat opposite. They are weak, unreliable, irresponsible, and blame others for their errors. They lack direction and purpose, switching from one minor goal to another without realizing anything significant.

The second trait of character, that of C deals with individual's degree of social acceptance, ability to understand, and ability to relate to other people's feelings and situations and to show compassion. Compassion is directly related to the individual's inclination to either help or not, beyond verbal comfort or soothing. Ultimately, it is shown in an individual's conscience to do what's right and avoid taking advantage of others.

ST refers to the individual's ability to go beyond pursuing his egotistic interests and embrace and identify with the society's goals. At the same time, the person transcends himself and strives to satisfy his spiritual needs and values.[24]

These two groups of factors define an individual's personality. Their interaction is based on the assumption that the self-concept acts upon temperament traits influencing and modifying their expression while the temperament traits mold the formation of self-concept. It distinguishes between the core traits of personality identified as the "conceptual-emotional core" and the others as "acquired traits."

The conceptual core goes beyond clinical interpretations, indicating a neurobiological structural system. The authors also created a psychological self-reporting test which when used in clinical setting with patients with or without personality disorders, would allegedly identify the presence or absence of a disorder, based on the received low score on the tested character dimension. When the character score was specifically combined with the temperament score, it identified various subtypes of personality. Their conclusion has been that low scores on the character dimensions may indicate the presence of a personality disorder, while the score of temperament traits helps to identify various subtypes of personality disorder.

The introduction of temperament factors as incomplete as they are, permit us to understand better the variety of degrees to adjustment of people. The fixed temperament factor reduces the possibility for unlimited ability of the individual to adapt to social conditions. It explains why some people deal better with social conformity than others. Certainly, someone high on NS and risk taking would be less inclined to obey social rules perceived as stifling if not harmful. His nonconformist actions would be in line with the main traits of his temperament.

Furthermore, someone clinically displaying an antisocial behavior personality will score high on NS and RD and low on HA. A clinically histrionic behavior which appears as socially nonconformist, according to this model will rank high on NS and on RD and low on HA. The environmental factors could exacerbate or diminish the responses to one style of life.

In general, it seems that these traits act as modifiers of responses to social events. For example, the presence of HA trait will most likely enable an individual to react to new situations in his environment along a behavioral continuum that exhibits prudence and uneasiness at one end and courage and noninhibition at the other. In combination with other personality factors, an event may be perceived as a threat, a potential harm for the cautious individual, while for the courageous one as a challenge to be solved.

The same applies to RD which represents two basic subtypes of personality; one is people who are more impulsive and want immediate gratification, and others who score low, are more reserved and detached, and as such able to postpone the sought satisfaction until the completion of pursued activity.

The NS projected at their extremes of behavioral continuum are either people who look forward to facing new challenging actions or are risk adverse.

More interestingly, a degree of support for these traits came from the identification of some circuits linked to adaptive changes in the brain that regulate successful coping with stress and manage reward, fear, and emotional reactivity.[25]

Some researchers also link these fixed traits of personality to specific neurochemical processes in the brain. It has been suggested that the HA trait is mainly regulated by serotonergic transmitters in the brain, the reward-oriented people by their norepinephrine levels and the NS by the dopaminergic system. It is also hypothesized that the activity of these three neurotransmitters is linked to specific genetic expressions and their dysfunction is reflected in the symptoms and behavior of personality disorders.

Recent research has found a link between optimism and oxytocin receptor gene and other genes related to serotonin transmission, while other research has identified specific brain protein and hypothalamic-pituitary-adrenalin axis genes as linked to resilience.[26]

As we have seen, these traits of temperament influence to a large extent the formation of the individual's personality from birth. They are part of the interaction between mother and child influencing their nurturing relationships. They shape various traits of the child's personality in the course of time. Intricate patterns of behaviors are influenced by genes through chemical reactions of neurotransmitters receptors which respond to environmental stressful events, thereby affecting individual's functioning.

Independent of the above-described traits of personality, there is the American Psychiatric Association's (APA) Diagnostic and Statistical Manual, Fourth Edition (DSM-IV) (to be replaced now by DSM-5) relying on clinical observations that has broadly created three clusters of personality disorders representing a loose combination of social and psychological traits. One is based on the impairment of perception of oneself, of others, and of interpretation of reality (cognitive factor); another cluster reflects the degree dysfunction of their emotional responses and of their impulse control (affective-volitional factor); while the third one is based on their interpersonal functioning (social factor). In total, there are ten different personality disorders, according to APA diagnostic criteria DSM-IV[27] each with a specific cluster of psychological traits and symptoms that are viewed as "enduring patterns of inner experience and behavior which deviates markedly from the expectations of individual's culture." Then, it is obvious that these people are classified as presenting disorders of personality because they have difficulty to adjust to the social requirements of their society. However, it seems that there is a twist in the diagnostic structure of personality disorders according to the preliminary report of the DSM-5 Task Force which is reviewing and updating the nosology of various mental disorders.

The incorporated preliminary report in DSM-5 which became an alternative model in the final version of DSM-5 suggests some significant modifications in the classification of the personality disorders by reducing their number to six. It would be mainly used as a more general model of impairment of personality describing mixed complaints which do not fit in a specific "categorical scheme." The alternate categories would eliminate in time histrionic (hysterical), paranoid, schizoid, and dependent personality disorders. On the positive side, it would require for clinicians to assess the level of personality functioning rating it from 0 (healthy) to 4 (extreme impairment). It is assumed that a score of 1 would represent a neurotic level of organization of personality, 2 mildly borderline, 3 severely borderline, and 4 psychotic.

Another proposed change is a separate personality assessment related to what has been called "pathological personality" of the client broadly described as "personality trait domains"—negative affectivity, detachment, antagonism, disinhibition, and psychoticism. Each category has four to nine "trait facets" to be assessed separately.[28,29]

What is interesting is that established personality disorders like histrionic, dependent, and schizoid personality could be absorbed into other disorders by nosological recasting as if these conditions were wrongly interpreted and diagnosed until now. Be that as it may, still it questions the quality and validity of the psychiatric scientific thinking and its loose nosological policies. Ironically, it reinforces the relativity of assessing correctly whether the alleged emotional conditions are diseases or not (e.g., homosexuality, post-menopausal syndrome) that has plagued the domain of psychiatric thinking and research. It seems to be reflected in the conceptualization of well-adjusted normalcy.

If this alternate changes are intended to be implemented in the near future, should we assume that the histrionic or dependent personality disorders were wrongly considered separate personality entities and people who presented their clinical symptoms had in reality different psychiatric conditions which would meet at best the criteria for personality disorders? This assumption would imply that their traits of personality could be integrated with different psychiatric conditions which would suggest new "dimensional understanding of personality"based on a reinterpretation of their psychodynamics and possible treatment. The clinical and scientific data attempted to support this approach to personality disorders is far from validating these new reclassifications.

Inadvertently, these nosological readjustments imply in one hand that there is not a clear cut distinction between personality disorders and on the other hand it implies that the concept of normalcy is, at most, fluid and arbitrary. One could assume that ultimately, the alleged normals seem better adjusted at a given moment in time than the ones with personality disorders, which could change under stressful conditions; all matter of subjective interpretation.

Let us compare, for example, a conscientious person who is considered to represent a style of normal personality with one who suffers of an obsessive-compulsive personality disorder. The key characteristic of a conscientious person is his perfectionist attitude toward work. He is preoccupied with delivering good-quality work. He is not only a hard worker, but also is well organized and competent in dealing with his work assignments. However, he is unable to overlook details considered by others as nonrelevant, which makes him work unnecessarily extra hours to complete the job. While he enjoys doing a good job, he is over involved with his work and he does not always use his time efficiently. His inability to cut corners when the work requires makes him a less desirable worker for emergency deadlines or overhaul jobs. In fact, when he is pressed by time and he has to ignore details, he feels uncomfortable, uneasy, and dissatisfied. On the contrary, he enjoys and excels in doing detailed, precise jobs, which are time consuming. The same perfectionist attitude he exhibits at home or in his relationship with others, and it often becomes a source of irritation and sometimes conflict in their relationship. If others fail to do things in a precise manner as specified by him, he becomes annoyed, irritated, and is ready to scold them. Basically, conscientious people are intolerant of others' shortcomings if viewed as not meeting their social standards. This might create problems at work with his colleagues who might view him as difficult.

Many conscientiousness persons slip from mild to more serious degrees of compulsiveness which aggravates their position at work. They have to do things in a particular order, check, and recheck specific activities, and they often become obsessed with trivia. They might waste a great deal of time and energy in making sure that the things which preoccupy them are performed to their satisfaction. In this case their compulsive behavior is unproductive, causing problem at work or with others. They might have difficulty getting promotions that affects their confidence and self-esteem. By now their social adjustment has become questionable.

In more severe cases, they cannot stop their repetitive behavior or thoughts unless they go through a ritual, self-developed, that alleviates their anxiety. However, their behavior while troubling them and annoying others rarely reaches the level of being considered socially dysfunctional. They may manage to meet the social standards of functioning but at the cost of great emotional drain and waste of energy.

But the real problem for the more serious cases is coping with their anxiety and depression which is hardly controlled by their rituals. Certainly, they are distressed if their compulsive/obsessive behavior has become a social issue that affects their functioning and compels them to undergo psychotherapy. A few of them, due to the severity of their repetitive compulsive behavior and/or intrusive obsessions become totally unproductive and are considered socially disabled.

Nevertheless, most people with personality disorders are viewed by others as functioning relatively "normal" in society. In general, a moderate degree of psychological distress is not a sufficient condition to affect an individual's social ability to function. What seems to influence one's social functioning is a high level of anxiety—depression inducing a relative degree of cognitive impairment. Under these conditions, the individual's judgment is affected and his social functioning is gradually diminished.

In fact, the notion of conformity-normalcy encompasses those mild personality disorders that can maintain a fair degree of social functioning and integration. Even a housewife suffering from an obsessive-compulsive condition that may interfere with her ability to hold a job because of her anxious state aggravated by her difficulties to meet the pressures and deadlines of work can function quite well at home where her schedule of house chores can be adjusted according to her needs and state of mind. As a result, socially, she can pass for normal.

Moreover, an individual may have a dominant trait of personality mixed with other ones, secondary, that are functioning within the normal range, while at times, displaying some behaviors that are socially questionable or undesirable. For instance, a risk taking individual who is a successful business entrepreneur can also be pleasure—oriented, enjoying gambling for high stakes. Gambling is considered from the psychological point of view a disorder of impulse. However, because our entrepreneur can easily cover his losses, socially his activity is acceptable and he is deferentially treated by casinos as a high roller. If he had lost beyond his means and is unable to pay, his credit line with casino is cut off and he would be treated with the contempt accorded to addicts.

Quite often there is a blurred social distinction between normal and disordered personality that applies to most of the personality subtypes. Ultimately, as long as an individual can leave the impression of functioning under the broader terms of social acceptability, he can pass for well-adjusted- normal. In many cases, a distorted perception of a situation leads to an overflooding of emotions conducive to relative degrees of pseudorational judgment and an incorrect social response that creates a poor adjustment. Though this is more evident in personality disorders, it could occur in the alleged "normal" people making them display temporarily a maladjusted behavior.

And this is one of the problems separating the normal from abnormal behavior. Normalcy, viewed as a balanced approach to one's social functioning underscores an individual's successful ability to negotiate his relationship to his experiential world with less distressful conflicts, which in reality fits in only partially the fluid concept of conformity-normalcy. As long as the concept of normal-well-adjusted personality evolves from the assumptions of the child's compliant responses to the rules of his social environment, it is only natural to assume that the people who learn to adjust to society's prescriptions and regulation should be considered "normal." As such, normalcy has been equated with conformity to the social norms. But where do we place the nonconformists? Certainly, they are not fully adjusted socially to the community rules and as such could be viewed as presenting various degrees of maladjustment reaching the extreme of being social outcasts. However, if we take into consideration the genetic factor of personality another picture emerges.

PART II
The Interplay between Temperament and Character in Redefining Social Conformity

The genetic factors seem to redefine the concept of conformity and that of normalcy. To start with, there are no clear cut boundaries between the behavioral traits of normal and abnormal personalities as long as the person is neither seriously affected by anxiety/depression nor significantly cognitively impaired, or is outright psychotic.

The fact is that some traits of personality could be regarded either within the range of normalcy or not, according to the circumstances and the appropriateness of their behavioral expression. For example, let us consider the trait of NS which could be found in a great explorer, a scientist, a successful business entrepreneur, and so forth or in a reckless adventurer, a drifter, a person unable to hold on to a job, and so forth. It depends on the combination of this trait with other traits like HA or RD-pleasure pursuit. A low degree of HA or a high degree of pleasure seeking would result in a tendency to often function in a manner of ignoring or defying the prescribed social norms of conduct. The person would tend to be overconfident and more likely to attempt to disregard social conventions and as such appear as a nonconformist, not quite socially adjusted. From a different perspective of introvert-extrovert distinction which indicates the social expression of the temperament drives, an introvert and NS would be able to express himself in science, creative endeavors, activities that do not require a high degree of social exposure, while an extrovert will blossom in an environment of social recognition.

Nonetheless, this hypothetical mixture of some traits in higher proportions for the make-up of personality can hardly guaranty normal functioning because of the possible conflict between their strong affirmation on an issue at hand and society's position on it. In a hypothetical case of low HA trait and high NS, assuming that he has a fair evaluation of reality and understands the possible consequences, he might attempt to explore a new uncertain opportunity. He would then be considered a nonconformist. In the same vein, if it is assumed that one would appraise facts dispassionately in a nonbiased manner in order to draw realistic conclusions from situations and events, it still doesn't exclude the fact that a strong pleasure-oriented high RD person would pursue a destructive behavior while suspending any judgment about its consequences. He would act as a nonconformist.

This also explains why an individual who seems to have previously functioned normally becomes emotionally upset to the point of behaving out of character with his regular demeanor when he is suddenly faced with a situation perceived as threatening or distressful to his well-being because of his impression of potential inability to solve it. As previously mentioned, in extreme cases of stress, one's behavior could even approach degrees of irrational or antisocial acting out. In this case, the cognitive processes seem to be overruled by the interference of fixed trait of high-HA and low NS-risk taker, apparently inducing fear and anxiety.

Let us take the case of Danny, a business entrepreneur in his late forties, divorced, and doing fairly well in his field of activity until his life took a turn for the worse. Intelligent, ambitious, street smart, he built a successful business and was enjoying a comfortable life, highlighted by parties and affairs with women. However, all changed for him when his only child, a son of sixteen, died of an overdose of street drugs. The death devastated him emotionally and left him numb and dumb. This incident hurt him even more because he had taken the custody of his son after the divorce. Remorseful, he questioned his supervision whether it was helpful or enough. Though he thought he had been very close to his son, he reproached himself for not having spent more time with him during his growing years. He felt a failure as a father. Distressed and unable to sleep at night, he started to drink heavily while musing over his previous style of fast life as a possible cause to the tragedy. Comparable to his previous functioning, Danny appeared now to be a broken man. His accompanying state of high stress-distress could be related to genetic response induced by" s/s "variant gene, a less transporter of serotonin, combined with the acting up of the snip SNAP 25 under the condition of experienced stress which will also assume a low trait of neuroticism.

Anyway, his business started to suffer badly due to his neglect and mistakes of judgment. He was behaving as a nonconformist. No one would be able to now suspect that he was once a cocky-aggressive person who successfully overcame adverse social and business situations. After being obsessed for years by a sense of failure and inadequacy, he became unable to restore any purpose to his life. It took him years of psychotherapy to get his life at a relatively acceptable level of emotional functioning. Socially, his well-adjusted past life was a reality until he was overwhelmed by events beyond his ability to cope with.

In other cases, individuals exhibit behavior that might be considered undesirable or even antisocial by society only in particular areas of social interaction. These people, who function most often within the socially acceptable range of conduct, may act in an inappropriate manner or be unequivocally antisocial by miscalculating their risk versus possible reward in that situation. From the adaptive point of view, the issue is why should they abandon patterns of behavior proven advantageous to their social existence in favor of a conduct harmful to them? The same personality patterns that previously successfully organized their life seem discarded for a risky and untested behavior. Certainly, primitive emotions that were under control before, have now taken over, imposing their expression on judgment and deciding the course of one's actions. In fact, in these cases the cause seems to be related to an unrealistic risk taking within the framework of an unjustified overconfidence servicing an impulse of an inner drive, most often leading to self-destructive consequences.

A case in point is that of a Supreme Court judge in New York who was caught demanding and taking a bribe of $115,000 from a lawyer in order to approve a settlement in an injury suit related to a car accident. The judge asked the trial lawyer who won the case, and was supposed to get $1.6 million in fees, to pay him $115,000 in order to approve the settlement of the case. Otherwise he would not approve it on grounds of an alleged conflict of interest. The lawyer was stunned but he agreed to pay the bribe with the idea that the judge will come to his senses. Later, pressed by the judge to deliver the bribe, he reported the case to the district attorney office. The judge was caught taking the bribe in a sting operation. Until then, the judge had been a model of "normal" behavior. Let us overlook for a moment the legal implications of his actions and focus on the psychological aspects of his behavior. What compelling emotional processes were at work to drive him toward this reckless behavior? Apparently, he was not under any financial pressure to need extra money immediately. Was greed that powerful to overcome any prudence and ignore his position and background of judicial knowledge? Or was it a miscalculation believing to be entitled to share part of the loot with his friend, the lawyer? Either way, what it is puzzling is the sudden conversion of the judge from an outstanding, respected citizen to an extortionist behaving outrageously and irresponsibly? Ultimately, it means that someone who habitually exhibits a normal personality can switch to aberrant behavior when conflicting needs push him/her to defy elementary rules of social conduct. He was later convicted for three to nine years in prison.[30]

The Conflict between Law and Mental Health in Interpreting Conformity

In fact, the most pertinent issue for the formulation of a social concept of proper behavior is its interpretation by the law and legal process as compared to that of psychology. To start with, there are no explicit definitions of "normal behavior" in the law but only inferences related to its theory of the socially acceptable behavior; normalcy is indirectly surmised from appraising motives, choices, and establishing whether the party was acting reasonably at the time of the alleged infraction. From the legal point of view, normal behavior is inferred from the premise of conformity meaning that all adults acting rationally in their interactions and transactions with others conform to the allowable norms of conduct. This broad concept defines a normal person as one who behaves rationally in the context of a given situation by the standards of the conformity to the community. But, a person is still thought legally normal even when he acts in a situation below the minimal standards of rationality if he was capable to think rationally at that time. This formulation amounts to a normative concept derived from the assumption of adherence to the social-cultural conventional standards of behavior prescribed by society. Conversely, the proof of an individual's inability to understand the nature and the consequences or the wrongfulness of his behavior and actions means irrationality. For instance, let us take a person who in a manic state made unusually expensive purchases beyond his means during a buying spree, that he paid with checks that later bounced. Arrested and brought to court he was held not responsible for his actions, although at the time of court appearance, his manic episode subsided and he was seemingly "normal."

As previously mentioned, in a case of criminal prosecution the defendant is regarded as normal and the defense has to irrefutably prove the legal insanity of the accused by his inability to distinguish right from wrong and to appreciate the unlawfulness and wrongfulness of his act. For example, in the case of a nurse living in Texas, who systematically drowned all her five children and after that called the police to inform them about her crime, her defense lawyer entered a plea of insanity because she was allegedly acting as directed by her satanic delusional system. Yet, the court found her guilty. The decision was based on the fact that she was able to distinguish right from wrong by calling the police after the crime, though the prosecution agreed with the defense that she was mentally ill. However, the decision was changed on a new trial after appeal because of false testimony of a psychiatrist. She was found guilty for reason of insanity.[31]

It is also understood that a person who may act irrationally in a situation under the influence of a delusion or false belief may act rationally in a different situation and may be legally normal. For example, someone suffering of a sexual delusion might feel offended by the statements or actions of a person antagonizing his delusion, and might attack him or her physically while at the same time he or she is able to handle other aspects of his or her life quite well. This was the case of Marty a thirty-year-old college graduate, employee in a company who in the course of working started to make occasional eye contact with a young woman coworker. Sometimes they were exchanging remarks about work. He started to believe that she was in love with him, but he assumed that she was too shy to show it. Meanwhile, he noticed that the supervisor was stopping at her desk, talking, and sometimes laughing together. He concluded that the supervisor, a young man, was flirting with her by abusing his authority. He became progressively enraged until one evening he stopped his supervisor from leaving and shouted, accusing him of trying to get "his girl." Suddenly he took out a previously hidden truncheon and started to hit the supervisor over the head. When other employees tried to stop him, he ran away. Next day he was arrested. Since his statements didn't make any sense and he had a repeated history of hospitalization for psychotic episodes, he was referred to psychiatric evaluation and treatment. He suffered from chronic schizophrenia paranoid type. As previously mentioned, a twist in the insanity defense is offered in some states that permit a defendant to assert an affirmative defense of extreme emotional disturbance at the time of the offense. It is relatively similar to the psychiatric concept of diminished reasoning capacity under severe emotional stress but free of the concomitant presence of a psychotic disorder.

The legal concept clashes with the basic premise of the mental health concept of abnormality, which assumes that the irrational behavior of the mentally ill person is to be expected, since he would be unable to act otherwise owing to his condition. In practice, this doctrine does not always satisfy the legal position toward the adjudication of a criminal act. It leads to conflicts with the legal concept of responsibility for a criminal act in cases of crimes committed under the influence of alcohol or drugs. In this case, one is prosecuted as being sane to the full extent of the law because he or she could have avoided the crime by not using the substance. The defendant doesn't meet the basic condition of "unavoidable" irrationality because his or her irrational behavior was self-induced. At most the defendant can expect from the court is to receive more lenient sentencing. However, this raises the mentioned issue of the role of will in the commitment of a crime viewed within the context of law and mental health.

Mental health identifies disorders of will, known as impulse control as potentially affecting the individual's judgment and impairing his social functioning, whereas the law in many states accepts it only as a mitigating factor, particularly in cases of murder, where it is part of a plea of insanity caused by an extreme emotional disturbance. Furthermore, volitional problems are harder to document legally, hence possible to be abused by defense.

The Broad Interpretation of Social Conformity by the Judicial Activism

Departing further from the basic principles of the penal law that can be reduced to the formula of guilty mind (*mens rea*), forbidden act (*actus reus*), and legislated punishment, the notion of responsibility of the guilty person for the committed crime comes up in the courts' sentencing in terms of its interpretation within its social context. If the law by and large considers the individual as rational unless psychotic at the time of committing the crime, a new dimension was introduced by the defense by attributing to the environmental conditions a causative role in the criminal behavior and used as a mitigating factor in sentencing. This approach has been lately employed by activist judges who tend to interpret the criminal behavior of the accused in terms of societal unfavorable circumstances. In a strange manner it means that the individual acted in conformity to his cultural environment which might justify the crime. It represents a departure from the accepted legal position that the causation of behavior is immaterial to the court and only the identification of it with irrationality counts. The legal position is that, in general, the causation is meaningless since different causalities could lead to the same criminal behavior. People of different social class and of diverse background could commit the same type of crime, fully aware of the intent and desire to do so, while others in the same categories may do the same things owing to their irrational thinking. This approach brings a new wrinkle to the notion of conformity-normalcy by the arbitrary assumption that criminal behavior is in some cases the result of an unfavorable environment to which the defendant is adapted. A new cause—effect obfuscates the notion of social conformity and is supported only by the opinion of the defense lawyer and judge.

In New York, a case in point that aroused the wrath of the media and public is the decision of a federal judge to dismiss the case against four Afro-Americans who were caught transporting bags of cocaine in a van in the value of approximately $4 million. The suspects tried to run when they were stopped by the police for allegedly acting suspiciously. According to the judge, since it was normal for any minority person to be afraid of police and their fleeing led to the search, their case should be dismissed regardless of the possession of cocaine. The judge based his decision on the logic that the search of the van took place as a result of the police's biased actions. However, in response to the public outcry, the case against these drug dealers was later reinstated.[32] This was an extreme case of peculiar attempt to enforce an antilegal judgment.

Moreover, these assumptions of social causations disregard and discard the mental health studies of etiology of abnormal behavior, an important issue for the classification and treatment of mental disorders.

The judicial activists reached these self-serving conclusions by extrapolation from arbitrary environmental theories of maladjustment and assumptions of what would constitute normal behaviors in our dissonant society. Yet, all these manipulations of the notion of normalcy prove only the problems encountered in defining social conformity.

The irony is that what might complicate the courts' sentencing is the gradual emergence of the genetic factor as contributing to the antisocial behavior. A recent meta-analysis of families and adoption studies has suggested that about 50 percent of the criminal behavior seems to be related to specific genes. For example, it was presented that the low activity of allele (met/met)is associated with 40 percent higher rate of crime in individuals with attention-deficit/hyperactive disorder and schizophrenia. The dopamine receptor gene DRD2 with two alleles A1/A2 variant was found to be associated with a higher risk of delinquencies. The genetic argument in law is far from being now settled, but when more research will be able to pinpoint its role on crime, it will present a serious challenge to the interpretation of law.[33] It will redefine normalcy and implicitly the boundary of social conformity

Social Conformity and "Normal Behavior"

From a different social perspective, there are cases where normal behavior disintegrates and conformity collapses due to unexpected actions of the individuals out of character with previous lifelong pattern of behavior. In a sense, this sudden reversal of behavior defies our knowledge about the assumed functioning of a normal personality previously conforming to the rules of law and community.

A case in point is that of a former Goldman Sachs director Rajat Gupta, successful financier with high business and political connections who was frequenting the highest financial and political circles and was known to the last two presidents of the United States. He was recently indicted on five counts of security fraud and one count of conspiracy to commit security fraud.[34] He is the biggest corporate executive charged for illegal security trading in Wall Street. He was also funneling inside information to Raj Rajaratnam, the chief executive officer of a hedge fund, who was recently convicted for eleven years.[35] What made a respectable businessman like him get involved in these illegal activities? Certainly, the desire to get very rich quickly and prove his financial skills had suspended his judgment and blinded him to the possible consequences of his miscalculated actions. With no extenuating circumstances and no justifiable excuses for his actions, his alleged socially well-adjusted behavior vanished.

It should be emphasized that quite a few persons judged as normal in a set of social interactions may be fully nonconformists in other areas of their life being either dishonest, untrustworthy, and self-centered or displaying hidden deviancies ranging from sexual perversions, drug abuse to spouse abuse or child abuse, and so forth. To appreciate the elusiveness of the concept normalcy-conformity, one has to only consider the possible variations in behavior of an average, allegedly normal person.

A bizarre case reported by newspapers is that of a twenty-five-year-old woman, a nurse aide who was recently arrested after failing to help a man hit by her car while she was driving. What is strange about the case is that the man she hit went with his head through the windshield of her car and with the body hanging on the hood, she continued to drive carrying him along in that position even when she reached her home garage. In the garage, she did not help him extricate his head from the windshield, though he was severely bleeding and asking for help. She visited him from time to time, inquiring about his condition until he died. Next day, she dumped him with the help of two female friends in a vacant lot far away from home. Apprehended, she claimed to have been too panic stricken to think straight.[36]

Considering all these facts, it seems that the societal concept of normal behavior fails to include people with poorly identified personality disorders who function at least as pseudonormals. This would suggest that some people could be judged as belonging closer to normal personality while others acting on the fringe of abnormality. As previously mentioned, let us not forget that, by the same token, an alleged normal person is not necessarily free of episodes of behavior belonging to what could be classified as inappropriate, objectionable, or aberrant.

Take the trivial situation of some alleged normal customers who are tempted to steal or not pay for merchandizes. While some are kleptomaniacs who get a thrill from stealing worthless articles, others could be respectable citizens who occasionally under propitious circumstances believe that they can get articles of value for nothing by stealing them. One obvious element is the combination of opportunity and greed. These rational people are calculating their odds for success after surveying the surrounding before appropriating the desired article. They are caught because of miscalculating their chances by not noticing the placement of security or of a hidden camera. It was also speculated that some of these people are risk takers by getting an emotional charge out of their action of beating the odds by cheating the store. This is an interesting assumption that might attempt to present the stealing as a daring nonconformist act. Most likely, the act was prompted by the alleged opportunity to make a quick financial gain while negating the potentially unpleasant consequences. Certainly, it doesn't include the inveterate kleptomaniacs who are compulsive shoplifters.

The mental process facilitating this approach belongs to the magical thinking.[37] Magically, this type of thinking blocks any thought or apprehension related to a possible risk of being caught, reinforced by his unshaken confidence, and his cleverness to beat the system. If successful, he or she serenely walks out of the store with the stolen merchandize.

This is exactly what a young woman, Mary did, an administrator of a business office who was sent by her father to buy a dress for her mother's birthday. The father, aware of the limited financial resources of his daughter gave her $800 for the cost of an expensive dress. She went to a luxury boutique, found a dress for the amount of money allocated, slipped it in a bag and ignoring the line at the cashier, attempted to leave the store without paying. Caught at the door of the store, her defense was that she thought to have left the dress on the rack before deciding to leave because it was late and could not wait on the long line at the cashier. Allegedly, she was afraid to miss the train to her parents' home in suburbia where the celebration was held. Arrested, the judge sent her for psychiatric evaluation. At the interview, she claimed to have been in a state of agitation in the store, afraid of not choosing the right dress, of missing the train, and being late for the evening celebration. However, she admitted to have resented her mother getting an expensive dress while she was modestly dressed. According to her, the relationship with her mother has always been tense because of the mother's critical attitude toward her. After further discussions she also suspected that "subconsciously" she might have wanted to keep the money to buy a similar dress for herself, although she denied being aware of these feelings at that time. Anyway, this was an elegant psychological way to indirectly admit the reason for stealing without taking any responsibility for the act. Important to note, the young woman claimed she never attempted before to steal anything from a store. She received one year probation.

Twisted Conformity in Cases of Sexual Harassment or Rape

And this brings us to scrutinize a wider issue of distorted conformity resulting from the new legal interpretation of some criminal acts in some cases of rape or sexual harassment. As a departure from the rules of law in the case of rape or sexual harassment, the use of the discovery process deciding the conviction relies on the uncorroborated testimony of the alleged victim. This twisted judiciary process has sometimes led to the conviction of the innocent based on the uncorroborated testimony of the alleged raped or sexually harassed victim. In case of rape, we have today other evidence as forensic investigation and DNA to confirm the actual crime which may or may not corroborate the accusations of the alleged victim. Nevertheless, there are cases when the prosecution and the court ignored the facts and still convicted the innocent guy. The issue is more complex in cases of sexual harassment when the alleged crime is perpetrated without witnesses. There is her word against his. In these cases the statements of each party should be evaluated in the context of their previous relationships and her motivation to complain. What is her emotional and financial stake by accusing the guy of improper behavior? Political underlying motivation has tended to ignore these facts by implementing this form of moral relativism within the framework of a political correctness platform.

In many cases, the justice is subverted and left at the mercy of a possible biased testimony of a woman who might unscrupulously take advantage of the law that favors her. But the prosecution and judges posturing as defenders of the new brand of social morality implement arbitrarily a deviant process of law, a "nonconformist law." It was initially pushed by activist feminists and mainly supported by a Supreme Court Justice, Sandra O. Connor to protect a legitimate right of women from sexual harassment or rape. However, the approved law twisted the evidentiary process by accepting the contentions of the plaintiff woman about allegedly having been raped or sexually harassed as truthful even in case of lacking medical proofs or corroborative evidence. It was based on two false psychological assumptions: one, women always tell the truth in these situations and second, men as predators sexually harassed them unprovoked. Since the implementation of the law, these assumptions proved to be often unsustainable. Most often the court rules out without any careful investigation and evaluation the range of possible devious motives of the plaintiff from that of retaliation for being fired or not promoted because of inefficiency and incompetence to revenge for emotional rejection; the result is offering her a unique opportunity to make a fast buck.

This subjective implementation of law has led to unusual abuses of law by some dishonest women. These women, for revenge and humiliation of the accused, in addition to extracting heavy financial settlement from innocent men, falsely accused them of committing the above crimes. A few examples might elucidate this controversial legal and social issue blighting our legal system. Furthermore, this relativistic approach by the law has an impact on the concept of right and wrong and as such on the notion of social conformity-normalcy.

Let us take the controversial and explosive issues related to an alleged date rape. We are not discussing here about a possible misunderstanding of intent in the process of dating which could take place at the first date or even at any subsequent one. We are questioning the claim of a woman who has a date with a man and goes to his apartment at her free will and later complains that he went beyond petting or necking and without her permission attempted to assault her or raped her. There is no evidence for it except her words. What's more, it is claimed that the seduction took place while she was under the influence of alcohol, which affected her ability to defend herself. At best, all evidence is circumstantial because no witness was present at the alleged criminal act.

An interesting case is the accusation of a twenty-nine-year-old paralegal woman, Di Toro who claimed three months later after dating a forty-three-year-old man, Greg Kelly, an anchor at TV program "Good Day New York" of raping her.[38] The issue was whether it was consensual sex or rape. She has claimed of having no memory of the attack since she was drunk, meaning that she was mentally and physically helpless. She realized this only later when she became pregnant and had an abortion. Her story is very twisted since she pursued emotionally after the alleged attacker by texting him seventeen times and only when he was unresponsive to her renewed advances and she had an abortion and decided to complain to the police who referred the case to the district attorney office. The pressure on her to act was initiated after her live-in-boyfriend complained to the police commissioner. Her case was dropped since there was enough evidence that her legal claim was contradicted by their exchange of messages to each other with sex content after the incident. In addition, there were other untrue statements made by her that put her rape claim seriously in doubt. Whatever motivated her to misrepresent the facts shows the possible pitfalls by accepting irresponsible false rape accusations in the alleged rape-date.

In other cases, the alleged rape took place in unusual circumstances but invariably the woman alleged that she was raped, while the man emphatically claimed either that there was no sex or that it was consensual sex. Take the case of Susanna Coetzee who started to exchange flirtatious emails with a man on an internet dating site. They decided to meet each other, had a drink in a hotel, and went upstairs in a room where they were supposed to have consensual sex. Nevertheless, while in bed, Coetzee stopped the sexual act demanding money. The man refused and she accused him of rape. She ran out screaming and asking for help.

Afterwards, Coetzee started to threaten him with court action through email and telephone, asking for $15,000 for not reporting him to the police. Fortunately, he was able to prove that she lied and was an extortionist.[39]

However, more dramatic is the case of Biurny Peguero Gonzalez who accused a man of raping her after meeting him in a random encounter of "girl's night out" of drinking and dancing. According to her story, she was sitting in a car with her girlfriend in front of a restaurant waiting for two other girlfriends to bring some food when a group of men stopped by, started to talk to them and one of them, William McCaffrey jumped in the back seat of the car. Gonzalez's friend got out of the car, expecting her to do the same. Instead she remained in the car when Gonzalez started the car and drove away. She left the car at a nearby garage and got into the car of McCaffrey and his friends who before followed her car. She claimed that she was high on five Hawaiians, got scared and started to cry. Meanwhile her girlfriends were trying to contact her on her cell phone. The guys took her back at the parking lot where she met her girlfriends. An argument started between her and her close friend ending with being grabbed by the girlfriend by the hair. Then Gonzalez made the declaration that she was hit and raped by McCaffrey.

She was driven by her girlfriend to the hospital where she had a gynecological examination which was negative. Next day McCaffrey was arrested and against the negative gynecological examination for rape she steadfastly stated that the guy hit and raped her. He was convicted to twenty years of prison. Four years later while Gonzalez was already married with a baby, she became remorseful about fabricating the story of rape for appeasing her girlfriends. She confessed her fabricated story to a priest who advised her to contact police. After four years of jail for a crime which he didn't commit, he was freed. His conviction was without any legal proof and rejection of physical evidence of nonrape. It was only based on the verbal statement of an emotionally unstable woman.[40] This shows the perversion of the justice which in cases of sex complaints of rape or harassment omits the due process of discovery, relying only on the statements of the accusing woman. And her blatant lies presented as her version of truth become the legal truth.

A different version of accusations of false rape is that of Danmell Ndonye, a eighteen-year-old freshman at Hofstra who accused five men of gang raping her in a restroom at a party of Alpha Kappa mixer at the school on campus club. She stated that she had been raped after being confronted by her boyfriend who couldn't find her at the party. Police arrested four young men who were thrown in prison. She reiterated her story to the prosecutors until she was confronted with a cellphone video made by one of the accused which captured the sex episode showing that she was a willing participant. The charges against the four men were dropped when her blatant fabricated story of rape collapsed. Ndonye was suspended from Hofstra. According to her boyfriend she lied afraid of being called a slut.[41] Most important, it shows the different outcome of a case when there is valid evidence against the accusations and when the conviction is handed down arbitrarily without any corroborating proof.

In passing, an intriguing recent case is that of a sixty-five-year old man who claimed that was raped by a young nurse in twenties while in Temple University Hospital, Philadelphia where he was recuperating from a motorcycle accident. According to him the nurse took him to bathroom to wash him and proceeded to assault him sexually. The administration investigated the case and found no base to support his allegations. However, we don't know on what evidence they reached their conclusion.[42]

Leaving aside this dubious case, the most devastating scandal of an alleged rape which reached national coverage is that of Duke, a lacrosse player's case. In March 2006, an Afro-American student at North Carolina Central University, Crystal Mangum, who also worked as a stripper and dancer accused three white students from Duke University, members of Blue Devils men's lacrosse team, of raping her at a party held in a private house.[43] The prosecutor Mike Nifong called the alleged rape a "hate crime." The players were convicted by the media before any trial. However, under closer investigation the accusations started to fall apart one by one. The case collapsed when it was found that Nifong, the prosecutor withheld the DNA evidence from the defense attorneys which would have exculpated the accused. In April 2007, Nifong was disbarred for dishonesty, fraud, deceit, and misrepresentation. Interestingly, the student stripper was not prosecuted, she didn't face any charges for her false accusations. Independent of it, later on, the stripper showed her true metal. In April 2011, she was charged with assault with a deadly weapon with the intention to kill her boyfriend. He was knifed in the chest and was hospitalized with serious injuries. And finally, in December 2011, she was found guilty of child abuse, in addition to smashing the windshield, slashing the tires of the boyfriend's car, and setting his clothes on fire.[44]

Anyway, under these circumstances, the assumptions about the stripper Crystal or Nifong of being and acting normally becomes highly debatable.

The New Well-Adjusted Normal Behavior as Emerging from the Moral Relativism

Considering these facts, the concept of "proper adjustment" has to be negotiated as part of the controversial and fudged social notions of moral relativism that relies on obfuscating the distinction between right and wrong, by drawing theoretical supported from the pseudologic of multiple truths. Ultimately, moral relativism intertwined with political correctness obscures the difference between right and wrong by invoking the twisted logic of the sophistic theory of multiple truths.

Multiple truths is the brain child of the postmodernists constructivist writers, who revived an old philosophical debate about the social role of subjective truth as an expression of an individual's perception of reality, and came to the conclusion that society has to deal with multiple truths. Their argument has been that truth depends on the individual's specific view of himself and others as developed within the framework of his cultural environment. Since our society is multiracial and multicultural, an inevitable conclusion would follow as advocated by the supporters of multiple truth that we have to deal with formulations of truths based on the individual's cultural background.

Considering the fact that the concept of conformity-normalcy is evaluative, more or less attempting to appraise the successful societal functioning of an individual, then to some extent its validity is linked to one's cultural environment. This would hypothetically mean that different cultural environments operate with different truths (more correctly beliefs), which should reflect the concept of normal conduct in that particular society. The most that could be assumed is that in our pluralistic society, individuals, on one hand, may adhere to their native customs and on the other, they have to follow the societal rules and regulations of the majority that they vowed to obey as representing the law of the country. Then, it should be obvious that people's parochial beliefs cannot be viewed as guiding truth for society's interaction, but just as a specific way of interacting among the members of that particular ethnic group. By the same token, from a legal perspective, most modern cultures have relatively similar view of what may constitute right and wrong. Though there are variations in the interpretation and application of different civil laws, the general concept of reward and punishment remains valid. For example, the obligations of each party within marital functioning or divorce might vary from culture to culture, approaches that reflect the customs and religious precepts practiced in that country, but in the Western countries persistent physical abuse of the spouse constitutes an illegal behavior.

The advocates of the multiple truths in a pluralistic society tend to discard few important factors that question the validity of their argument. While indeed, people perceive reality from a subjective position, influenced by their cultural background, this does not mean that they are unable to appraise and realize that there is an objective reality based on factual data that doesn't support their subjective contention. The subjective truth represents, in reality, either an opinion based on a personal belief or a calculated self-serving statement. Furthermore, the more subjective an individual's perception of significant events owing to his cognitive and/or emotional disorder, the more he tends to slant reality and to arrive at incorrect conclusions about it. In this context, subjective truth is often less a reflection of the cultural customs and belief and more an expression of one's personal interpretation of reality pointing, directly or indirectly, toward a self-serving approach in manipulating human interaction.

Nonetheless, subjective truth has lately become the buzzword for various interest groups that try to promote their stakes and give legitimacy to their dubious actions under the cover of multiple truths. The use of this semblance of truth, relative truth helps these people to pretend to interact legitimately within the social framework of acceptable behavior. In reality, it distorts the societal consensus about the use and meaning of truth in the human communications. Ultimately, it affects people's social intercourse and relationships by making them more equivocal, tricky, and unpredictable. The promotion of relative truth implicitly questions the good faith of people using it in their dealings with others.

Intentionally or not, it has broadened and twisted any concept of conformity-normalcy to the point of including as part of it the gray area of disingenuous social manipulations and prevarication. Under these circumstances, an alleged well-adjusted pseudoconformist person is anyone who is skillful in manipulating others while feigning sincerity and clamoring fairness and forthrightness in his dealings.

After all, society from government to common citizens has always operated with a fair degree of deception and misrepresentation of truth in its regular ordinary transactions. This could be explained by antagonistic interests and conflicts between the leading classes and the governed population. To be able to function successfully, most people have resorted to all forms of manipulations, legal or illegal, to appease the inner conflict induced by their biological drives leading to social warfare because the integration of genetic-biological drives and the socially acquired characteristics of personality have never been fully achieved as to work harmoniously with the social demands.[45] The evolved religious morality attempting to harmonize instinctual drive to the social need for cooperation has been helpful but didn't solve the persistent clash of the inner drives within the individual's personality and between those drives and their societal expression.

Take, for example, the dramatic changes experienced by our society during the last four decades by the massive immigration from the underdeveloped countries which has created a new diversified cultural landscape that has had a significant impact on the concept of enforcing the laws of immigration, people's rights, and on what might constitute conformity-normal behavior. It led to a clouding of the notion of right and wrong, twisted some fundamental values of society, and the previous traits of proper behavior.

The social values, a basic reference point for normal behavior, have been undermined when the concept of job competition based on merit has been replaced with pedigrees of race and/or gender that have nothing to do with offering equal opportunities to all members of society. When students without satisfactory skills of writing, reading, or math, are admitted to college, not only the fair selection of the best is seriously jeopardized but also the whole quality of academic performance is undermined. Not to mention that their admission has blocked the entrance in schools of better students who did not meet the new policies and are deprived of pursuing the desired education. No wonder that the controversial issue of the affirmative action is again before the Supreme Court for reevaluation.

The skewed system of social values that has emerged has twisted the interaction between various segments of populations promoting a moral relativism and an ambiguity of social conformity.

Adhering to a set of ethical values and norms has become irrelevant for defining social-adjustment normalcy as long as they don't conform to the new moral relativism. Adultery, prevarication, perjury, cheating, stealing, all have become explainable, sometimes acceptable if the individual could justify them by claiming extenuating social circumstances.

The moral relativism combined with political activism has made the notion of proper social-adjustment normal conduct a highly debatable issue. At best, it conveys a flexible, fuzzy concept that tends to reflect the prevailing loose social policies and ambiguous attitudes. If in the past the notion of normalcy had relatively well-circumscribed boundaries, now under the equivocal concept of moral relativism has lost its core meaning.

Notes

1. A. Maslow, *Toward a Psychology of Being* (New York: Van Nostrand Company, 1962), 191.
2. E. Durkheim, *Sociology and Its Method* (London: Macmillan Co., 1982).
3. F. Boas, *Race, Language and Culture* (New York: Macmillan, 1948).
4. A. Kroeber, *The Nature of Culture* (Chicago, IL: University of Chicago Press, 1952).
5. Alfred Adler, *Understanding Human Nature* (New York: Fawcett Publications, Premier Books, 1965).
6. K. Horney, *Our Inner Conflict* (New York: W. W. Norton & Company, 1945).
7. E. Fromm, *Man for Himself: An Inquiry into the Psychology of Ethics* (New York: Reinhart & Co., 1947).
8. H. Stack Sullivan, *The Interpersonal Theory of Psychiatry* (New York: W. W. Norton & Co., 1953), 367–82.
9. A. Maslow, *Motivation and Psychology*, chap. 12 (New York: Harper & Brothers Publishers, 1954), 17.
10. R. Dawkins, *The Selfish Gene* (Oxford: Oxford University Press, 1989).
11. B. F. Skinner, *About Behaviorism* (New York: Vintage Books, 1976).
12. J. Dollard and N. Miller, *Personality and Psychotherapy* (New York: McGrow, 1950).
13. W. H. Sheldon, *The Atlas of Men: Guide for Somatotype for the Adult* (New York: Harper & Brothers, 1954).

14. K. Goldstein, *Human Nature* (New York: Schocken Books, 1963), 3–69.
15. C. G. Jung, "Psychological Types," in *Collected Works*, vol. 6, 2nd ed. (New Jersey: Princeton University Press, 1971), 330–495.
16. H. Eysenck, "Normality, Abnormality and the Three Factors Model of Personality," in *Differentiating Normal and Abnormal Personality*, ed. S. Starck and M. Lorr (New York: Springer, 1994).
17. J. Medina, "Molecules of the Mind," *Psychiatric Times*, April 4, 2010, 53.
18. J. Arehart-Treicher, "DNA Study Gets a Snip Closer to Understanding Personality," *Psychiatric News*, August 8, 2010, 15.
19. R. R. McCrae and P. T. Costa, "Validation of the Five Factors Model of Personality across Instruments and Observers," *Journal of Personality and Social Psychology* 52 (1987): 81–90.
20. M. Brodsky, "What Lies Ahead for Neuroticism," *Clinical Psychiatry News*, nr. 23, December 7, 2012, 7.
21. J. Arehart-Treicher, "DNA Study Gets a Snip Closer to Understanding Personality," *Psychiatric News*, August 8, 2010, 15.
22. R. R. McCrae and P. T. Costa, "Personality Trait Structure as a Human Universal," *American Psychologist* 52 (1997): 509–16.
23. R. C. Cloninger, D. M. Svrakic, and T. R. Przybeck, "A Psychobiological Model of Temperament and Character," *Archives of General Psychiatry* 50 (1993), 975–90.
24. N. A. Gillepsie, R. C. Cloninger, A. C. Heath, and N. G. Martin, "The Genetic and Environmental Relationship between Cloninger's Dimension of Temperament and Character," *Pergamon: Personality and Individual Differences* 35 (2003): 1931–46.
25. D. Jeste, "Positive Psychiatry," *Psychiatric News*, June 15, 2012, 4.
26. Ibid.
27. *DSM-IV Diagnostic Criteria* (Washington, DC: American Psychiatric Association, 1994).
28. M. Brodsky, "Changes in the Offing for Assessing Personality," *Clinical Psychiatry*, January 2012, 8.
29. M. Moran, "DSM Section Contains Alternative Model for Evaluation of PD," *Psychiatric News*, May 3, 2013, 11.
30. K. Cornell Smith, "Bribe Judge Will Collect 97G a Year in Slammer," *New York Post*, October 29, 2002, 5.
31. *Wikipedia*, "Andrea Yates, Texas Nurse in Who Drowned Her Five Children," June 20, 2001.
32. H. Baer, "Suppression of Evidence," US v Bayless 913F. Suppl. 232 (1996).
33. A. Levin, "As Genetic Data Increase, How Will Court Respond?," *Psychiatric News*, December 7, 2012, 18.
34. K. Whitehouse and B. Golding, "Indicted Gupta Finds That Greed Isn't Good," *New York Post*, October 27, 2001, 30.
35. N. Popper, "Galleon Hedge Fund Billionaire Raj Rajaratnam Found Guilty of Insider Trading Case," *Los Angeles Times*, May 11, 2011.
36. "Texas Woman Charged with Allowing Hit-and-Run Victim to Die in Broken Windshield," Fox News.com, March 7, 2002.
37. G. Serban, *The Tyranny of Magical Thinking* (New York: Dutton, 1982).
38. B. Hamilton, J. Schram, and T. Perone, "Candid Kelly Accuser Hurting Own Case," *New York Post*, January 30, 2012.

39. "'Victim' Susanna Maria Coetzee is Convicted of Trying Extortion," *False Rape Society*, April 14, 2009.
40. L. Italiano, R. Calder, and K. Sheehy, "Fake Rape Gal's Tale a Wicked Plot to Get Attention," *New York Post*, December 8, 2009, 5.
41. K. Crowley, R. Fenton, and L. Alpert, "Rape-Lie Motive," *New York Post*, September 18, 2009, 7.
42. S. Farberov, "Man, 65, Claims He Was Raped by Young Female Nurse....." Mail Online, http://www.dailymail.co.uk/newsarticle-2300900/Man-65-claims-Raped (accessed March, 29, 2013).
43. "Duke Lacrosse Accuser Crystal Magnum Charged with Murder," WRAL.com, February 22, 2010.
44. "Former Prosecutor Nifong Disbarred," *ABC News*, June 16, 2007.
45. J. Arehart-Treicher, "Propensity to Violence," *Psychiatric News*, July 7, 2008, 24.

3

Stress, Coping, and Social Conformity

Stress, Coping, and the "Well-Adjusted-Normal Person"

The standard assumption is that a well-adjusted person has the skills to cope with overwhelming or adverse conditions triggered by a variety of life events. He should be able to overcome them, but it is quite often not the case. What happens with well-adjusted people when they are unexpectedly hit by an unfavorable situation and fail to cope properly with it? Some of these events are self-induced because of one's own inefficient handling of one's needs and aspirations, but perceived by one as threatening to one's way of living, while others are triggered by external agents not under one's control. Under these circumstances, the stress increases in direct proportion to the threat posed by the personal life event which is perceived as unfavorable and unexpected. The individual tends to feel that his options are either nonexistent or very limited in overcoming that adversity, while he is unable to accept the undesirable outcome induced by that event. Ultimately, the stressors disturb his mental equilibrium by producing worries, anxiety, and a state of either anger or helplessness. Should one assume that he or she has now a maladjusted-abnormal personality?

Confronted with a crisis, someone who previously seemed to have functioned in a well-adjusted way could suddenly display an aberrant behavior in his attempts to cope with those overpowering circumstances. The whole turmoil could have been created by his inner drive to attempt to satisfy a pressing need that overrides the conflict with the acceptable societal norms of behavior.

Self-Induced Stress

Take, for example, the case of a lawyer, Carlos Perez-Olivo, from Chappaqua, New York, who was tried and convicted for shooting and killing his wife. According to his story, while driving home on a secondary road on a late Saturday evening after visiting his friends, their sport utility vehicle was cut off and stopped by "a Toyota Camry driven by a Hispanic gunman with a mustache and baseball cap." The guy stepped out of his car, shot him in the stomach, and shot in his wife's head, the mother of their three children.

Though wounded, Perez-Olivo drove the car six miles to the nearest hospital. His wife died two days later in the hospital.[1]

Under investigation as a witness to the crime, the detectives had difficulty accepting parts of his story like the reason for driving on a secondary road (he was allegedly looking for a gas station) or his ability to describe the assailant quite well when he was supposed to be seriously injured almost immediately. Furthermore, they found the gun used for the shooting with the serial number erased thrown in a lake near the crime scene. He became the prime suspect when the motive for the crime became apparent. Perez-Olivo had wanted to collect $500,000—the amount for which his wife's life had been insured. As a recently disbarred lawyer without a steady income, he needed the money. The insurance company refused to pay since he was a suspect. He decided to sue the insurance company, a fact that inadvertently accelerated his indictment because the police had now the motive for the shooting. According to the police, "it was a compelling circumstantial case, all investigative roads led to one person and one person only." He was convicted, but he maintained his innocence.[2]

Perez-Olivo, a criminal lawyer by profession, recently disbarred for misconduct, and apparently without any steady source of income decided to get rid of his wife to obtain the insurance money. It was a desperate solution to his pressing financial troubles.

Though Perez-Olivo was not a professional criminal with a record, under unbearable self-induced circumstances he became one. He thought he had pulled off the perfect crime, with no witnesses, no gun to be found and with the final proof of innocence: Himself being shot and wounded. Then, what went wrong? Parts of his story were not fully credible. For instance, in addition to the nonsensical explanation about taking the secondary road, his suspicion that the attack was a possible act of revenge of a former disgruntled client was implausible. If someone wanted to kill him, the assassin would have riddled his body with a couple of bullets to ensure his death. The crime scene should have been reversed: he dead and his wife killed because she witnessed the crime.

Obviously, already stressed by pressing financial difficulties that required a fast solution, he had planned the crime in haste. His overconfidence took over. His overreliance on his skills as a criminal lawyer to deal with any incriminating evidence of a crime reassured him of his ability to commit a "perfect crime." The risk factor was ignored by the magical rationalization of his alleged talents which gave him a false sense of security. On the other hand, Perez-Olivo, as a private person and as a lawyer, had functioned before more or less within acceptable normal limits, appearing relatively well adjusted, albeit sometimes dishonest, as long as no major stressful conditions faced him. Nevertheless, ultimately, his veneer of normalcy disintegrated and another self, an antisocial bent one surfaced.

There are other spontaneous reactions to acutely stressful situations in which a person loses control completely and acts irrationally. This happened to a jail guard who went temporarily berserk after the repeated rejection by her ex-lover, another woman, who refused to reconcile and go back to her.

The jail guard, Kim Wolfe, a forty-three-year-old, tried to lure back her ex-lover Stacie Williams, a forty-five-year-old, nurse's aide in the maternity ward of a hospital, by going there to talk things over with her at lunch time. She came to the entrance of the hospital where Williams was working, met her and attempted to talk to her. Thirty minutes later, Williams was shot dead.

According to the news reports, Wolfe drove from there to some of her relatives to whom she confessed to the crime. There she started to argue with her eighty-eight-year-old grandfather allegedly over the recipient of her assets in case she committed suicide. It is unclear why in the course of discussion she grabbed her twenty-three-year-old niece, Mary, holding her hostage at gunpoint. Her uncle who intervened in the explosive situation was shot dead together with her grandfather.

Afterwards, she released Mary with the intention of going to Atlantic City. Police intercepted her and persuaded her to go to her mother's home in Hempstead, LI, where she surrendered without any resistance.[3]

Wolfe worked as a jail guard for the New York correction department for nineteen years and allegedly had functioned normally until the time of the crime when she snapped, apparently reaching her mental "breaking point." Until the shooting she had displayed all appearances of normal behavior, parading as a socially adjusted, integrated citizen. However, her "well-adjusted-normal" behavior evaporated under a dramatic stressful situation, which she couldn't handle. It resulted in her losing control and displaying violent aberrant behavior. We cannot assume that she apparently had an underlying explosive personality, because it is unsupported by any evidence from the past.

Could she have acted differently, assuming that she indeed was normal as she seemed to appear until then? After all, at her age of forty-three it is fair to assume that before meeting Williams she had had her share of lesbian affairs, some terminated by her, others ended by her partners. She coped more or less well with the emotional turmoil of those situations. There was no record of a similar violent explosion induced by disappointment or uncontrollable rage in her past. It is obvious that her perception of earlier break-ups was different from that of the last, the fatal one.

Apparently, Wolfe was too deeply involved emotionally, making the termination of her affair with Williams an unbearable and tormenting experience. It means that she didn't realize the extent of her emotional dependency on Williams and was unprepared and unable to protect herself from the emotional turmoil that was brought on by the separation. Had she realized the dramatic impact on her in case of splitting off she should have kept away from any serious argument in order to avoid any escalation of it leading to separation. Unaware of it, she mishandled the relationships with a devastating emotional result as unable to handle it. Caught off guard by the termination and rejection, she became obsessed with her lost love. Unable to win her back, Wolfe's frustrations gradually changed to anger and hate. Unsuccessful in her very last attempt to reconcile, she became enraged and exploded with rage. Blinded by fury, tormented by memories of her former intimacy with Williams, with her judgment "suspended," she shot and killed her. This apparently was her road from a relative normalcy to temporary insanity. Should this aberrant behavior seriously question her previous mask of normalcy? Our limited scientific knowledge doesn't allow any firm conclusion. What we know for a fact is that the emotional brain (the old reptilian brain), is not fully integrated with the more recent cortical brain which tends to explain the weak control of the latter over the former.

More simple situations are the ones where the stress is induced by societal conditions viewed by the individual as unfair, abusive of his rights, or outright harmful. Regardless of whether one's evaluation has been correct or not, one experiences the emotional pains provoked by the situation as real. One tries to cope with this state of affairs, to overcome any negative outcome either by succeeding in nullifying its effect or changing it to one's favor. However, it is difficult to nullify its effect. There are too many factors contributing to the troubling situation, some of which could be very important and beyond one's ability to control. To determine where one stands versus the perceived threatening event, one has to evaluate it dispassionately in terms of one's ability to deal properly with it. The event is difficult to evaluate objectively, because of possible miscalculations created either by the lack of enough information about it or due to the inherent tendency of the individual toward subjectivism. It means that the person has not only to evaluate correctly his knowledge about the situation but also to be aware of his penchant toward self-righteousness that might hurt him in solving the issues raised by the event. The more subjective the person is, the harder it will be for him to find the right solution to the problem. To find the most appropriate solution, he requires to hold back any bias or negative emotions and to weigh in a detached manner all known elements involved in the troubling situation in order to decide whether they favor him or work against him.

Can an alleged normal, who might have a narcissistic bent expressed by his belief about his superiority of judgment and his sense of righteousness to exclude any possibility of being wrong, or with a penchant for histrionics, that tends to dramatize and exaggerate the consequences of any act, be cool and detached enough to appraise an unfavorable situation?

These factors of personality bring us back to the basic traits of temperament which play a distinctive role in the make-up and expression of one's individuality. For instance, genetic traits like the strong combination of a high level of reward dependence and of harm avoidance, part of the narcissistic or histrionic personalities, reinforced by one's experiential world, play a role in the way one evaluates any problematic life event. Not to mention that in attempting to find a solution, other factors, like one's cognition enter into play, deciding the degree of one's awareness about one's stakes in that event or of one's ability to control the gamut of strong negative emotions triggered by the crisis. Ultimately, the ability to solve the problem depends on all these factors—level of intelligence, knowledge applicable in that situation, biased or unbiased judgment, temperament and the capacity to appraise unemotionally the real possibilities for finding a meaningful solution to the problem.

Let's take the famous case of Samuel Richard "Sandy" Berger, former national security adviser in the Clinton Administration and later, adviser to Senator John Kerry's presidential campaign. He was caught stealing classified documents from the National Archives. He had been seen by an employee removing the documents from the files and hiding them in his pockets and even in his socks. He denied the charges for almost a year pretending to have committed an "honest mistake," but after being confronted with evidence, he admitted that he intentionally stole the classified documents that compromised him and the Administration and cut them to shreds with scissors. Apparently, he did it because the stolen documents related to the lack of action by the Clinton Administration against a possible terrorist attack in 1999 by Al-Qaeda. The documents would have contradicted his official testimony made to the 9/11 Commission. It was obviously a cover-up to protect himself and indirectly the former Administration, from the blame of a possible security failure that led to the 9/11 attack. Believing that he would succeed in his fraudulent attempt, he lied to the 9/11 Commission, but when he realized that he would be discovered and accused of perjury, he committed the petty burglary. He pleaded guilty to a misdemeanor count and he got a "slap-on-the-wrist," with only a $10,000 fine and loss of security clearance for three years.[4]

Was this the activity of a conformist-normal? Obviously, legally it was not, but socially it was viewed as acceptable or not according to one's political beliefs.

Another unusual example is that of a prominent New York criminal lawyer, Robert Simels who according to the newspapers hired a hit man at the request of his client, a boss of an international drug dealing ring, to eliminate the principal witness who would testify against his client. The lawyer was caught on tape by the Federal Bureau of Investigation (FBI) giving $1,000 to the alleged hit man who was a police informer. And from defense lawyer he himself became a defendant involved in a criminal deal.[5]

It is obvious that he wanted to win the case at any cost to get more money from his client and to advance his legal reputation. The consequences of ill-thought activity had exactly the opposite effect on his career.

What do these two last cases have in common beyond manipulations and calculations that went wrong? It is evident that their overconfidence about their ability to pull off their deals did them in. Overconfidence is ultimately an intrinsic part of undue risk taking; a trait of temperament, which is itself servicing the need to satisfy his craving for recognition, success, and power—all part of his reward dependence trait. One can say that in Berger's case the problem was created by his gross miscalculation in carrying out his reckless scheme. He failed to assume the possibility of being discovered by the National Archives' employee because he thought of himself as being above any suspicion. As such, he didn't take any measure to control any potential risk.

The second man, the lawyer "Simels," was convinced of his high-operative skills as a criminal lawyer and didn't check either the background of the hired gun or the safety of the conditions under which he tried to implement his plan. This was self-induced stress which, regardless of his alleged high lawyerly skills and clever manipulations, might not be enough to beat the rap. Even if he succeeds in doing it, his reputation is tarnished.

But what happened to their alleged ability to overcome any self-induced situation like those in the past that made them appear socially well-adjusted-normals?

In the first case, Berger was fighting to save his reputation and his political career at any price believing to be able to outwit the authorities. Any admission of his lying to the 9/11 Commission would have been a blow to his overinflated ego. From his perspective, his lying was safe as long as it couldn't be verified. But he didn't know that John Ashcroft, the Attorney General, would have read the damaging memorandum and would unmask him. Resorting to the criminal act of stealing and destruction of the documents was necessary to repair his reputation, but because of his overconfidence he didn't take elementary precautions to protect himself from being caught.

In the second case, the uncontrollable drive to succeed combined with greed overcame reason leading him to pursue actions out of character with his previous professional conduct. To consider them normal by psychological and legal standards is stretching it to the point of meaninglessness.

In fact, there are numerous cases of so-called normal people inflicting emotional wounds on themselves. Some successful politicians destroyed their political careers by pursuing personal activities contrary to the social, moral, or legal expectations of the represented community. The relatively recent cases of Eliot Spitzer, ex-governor of New York[6] or of George Ryan, the ex-governor of Illinois[7] or Rod Blagojevich, ex-governor of Illinois[8] are self-explanatory. One showed poor judgment because of unmanageable lust which led him to hire hookers, the second one, for unchecked greed that led to the acceptance of gifts from contractors, and the third one, among other illegalities, for irresponsibly trying to sell the senate seat previously held by Barack Obama after his election as president for $1.5 million in campaign cash or for a high-paying job. Spitzer was forced to resign and ended a successful political career, while Ryan and Blagojevich came out worse, being sent to jail for corruption. Their alleged well-adjusted normalcy was only a social mask, a smokescreen hiding a duplicitous conformity that was torn apart by their irrepressible inner needs; needs which used reason to rationalize their illegal or inappropriate behavior by giving them the illusion of safety under the cover of the power of high office. They never considered that they might be caught red-handed.

Another recent case of political abuse of power has been that of ex-congressman from New York, Anthony Weiner who emailed sexually suggestive pornographic pictures to a young woman. The pictures showed him naked except for a pair of briefs which bulged with an erection. It became known as the "battle of the bulge!" After a period of denial, when faced with more damaging evidence he was pushed by his party to resign from Congress. He has been described as a "self-obsessed, arrogant and self-righteous sex-deviant."[9]

Indeed, the distorted thinking found in all these cases is a modified remnant of the magical thinking of the early childhood, when the child fails to distinguish between cause and effect and hence confuses reality with fantasy. This explains a child's belief in his omnipotence, metaphorically expressed in the idea of "reaching for the moon."[10]

If this type of thinking is not gradually replaced with logical judgment it becomes integrated into one's reasoning and is reflected in the handling of events during adult life. The result is that rational judgment becomes distorted by the introduction of pseudological premises in support of his emotional needs. In response to the specific inner drives and needs of personality, the solutions found express or avoid frustration by taking refuge in a world of make-believe. In this world, things would take place according to his wants and he would overcome conflicts with society and outwit those who could check on him. The testing of reality becomes replaced with the magic wand of his invincible power. As a result, the individual displays patterns of behavior rooted in his distorted logical thinking which relies on pseudological premises containing elements of his magical thinking that alters his judgment to accommodate his immediate emotional needs.

This warped logical thinking is part of our basic duality of thinking, namely logical and pseudological, present in various degrees in all of us. It helps most of us to justify our peculiar actions in accordance with our emotional needs.[11] When satisfying pressing socially deviant needs, the aberrant pseudological behavior obliterates, suspends, and discards the objective reality. Depending on the extent to which the individual's thinking is based on real, objective data combined with fancy, slanted personal beliefs, it will become his interpretation of the reality and truth. It is important to note that this complex mental process of mixing logic with pseudological thinking (based on their personal convictions, internalized emotional experiences, and inculcated subcultural beliefs), is used by most people to evaluate their social surroundings and subsequently to create a duplicitous formulation of subjective moral judgments.

Furthermore, this mix of logic and pseudologic becomes evident either when the person attempts to cope with stressful conditions or when this logic is used to justify the dubious solution found for satisfying a set of burning emotional needs that conflict with the existent social norms. It could decide the outcome of important events of his life. The extent of its presence and intensity of its control over the thinking of an individual categorizes the person as "neurotic" or not. What is important to note is the degree to which pseudological thinking has become a corrupting component of an individual's personality. It defines one's degree of normal behavior, and facilitates ambiguity of conformity. The pseudologic tends to surface in situations where no logical explanation could justify one's behavior controlled by a burning set of emotional needs which can't find a normal social outlet.

From this point of view, the ex-governors mentioned in the example could be considered to have had "neurotic" streaks to start with. They functioned socially within acceptable limits as long as their narcissistic traits and aggressive drive didn't come into conflict with the norms of society, and until they reached the public office which kept a closer eye on their behavior. This only proves the elusiveness of the concept of conformity-normal conduct which could hide various degrees of abnormal behavior as long as they don't seriously handicap the social functioning of these allegedly well-adjusted individuals.

Other people are assumed to be well adjusted till they perceive a situation as unfair to them, violating their rights in one way or another. Then their frustration and anger could affect their emotional state and social behavior seriously.

An example of self-induced stress with unpleasant consequences is the case of Heidi Jones, a weather reporter at WABC channel. She reported a couple of months back that while jogging in the Central Park, Manhattan, she was attacked by a Hispanic man in his thirties or forties who grabbed her from behind and dragged her into a wooded area where he attempted to rape her. She claimed that the would-be rapist ran away when two passers-by stopped because of the fracas. Furthermore, the same man allegedly approached her two months later and threatened her. Certainly, the staff of news channel expressed their sympathy and compassion for the scary incident. However, they were flabbergasted to find out months later from the press that she made up the whole story![12] Three months later, she confessed to the police that she had filed a false report about the alleged rape attempt. Her explanation was that she was under "emotional and professional pressures" lately, and had wanted to gain "sympathy" from the news staffers. Jones was suspended from the job and the station started to conduct an internal investigation. An internal source said that she would be fired.

Jones had had a distinguished career as a journalist until she broke out the story of the attempted rape. By all standards she was considered to function within the normal range of behavior until the fabricated incident. If it is true that she was professionally unhappy as reported by a co-worker, she tried to cope with the stress induced by the job situation in an unusual and risky way. In her attempt to get the sympathy of her colleagues, she made up a story that achieved her goal over a short period until she was ensnared by the police interrogation. In dealing with the police she showed poor judgment. Her alleged harmless fib told to the co-workers became an official matter for investigation after she filed a police report. Under heavy questioning she proved to be a poor liar since her story started to fall apart. It wasn't credible. Worse, instead of holding her own ground for better or for worse at the police interrogation, she confessed. By doing so, she compounded her troubles. She was not only prosecuted for providing false claims to the police, but she was also on the brink of losing her job.

Jones cooked up an outlandish scheme which backfired because it was beyond her ability to handle the foreseeable and unforeseeable consequences. In fact her handling of the whole situation showed that she never thought it through and was unprepared to fend off the possible negative consequences of her story. And as such, her previous conformity becomes highly debatable. If one could question her social adjustment at the time of the incident arguing that she might already have been "neurotic," but free of noticeable emotional symptoms until she displayed her aberrant and foolish behavior under alleged social pressures, another case of wild fabrication by a policeman would dispel any doubt.

A blatant case of duplicity of conformity as reported by the media is that of a school policeman. Jeffrey Stenroos filed a report with Los Angeles police about having been shot in the chest by a gunman while on patrol outside a suburban high school. He had allegedly confronted the gunman who he had seen breaking into cars and was shot by him in the chest. Stenroos was saved by his bulletproof vest.

This prompted a massive dragnet operation by hundreds of police officers of the Los Angeles helped by state and federal agencies. They combed a seven-mile area around the shooting site, searching for the gunman. They were supported by helicopters, SWAT teams, and K9 units.

After investigating over 350 tips and talking to hundreds of people, the police was unable to confirm the story or to trace the gunman. In fact, nobody from the area heard any shot at that time. The investigators concluded that the gunman's story was an outright lie told by the policeman. They arrested Stenroos for filing a false report and released him on $20,000 bail. Was the policeman a normal-conformist person, prior to the occurrence? We don't have any evidence to the contrary until this incident.[13]

What prompted his deviant nonconformist behavior? Since he didn't appear to show any sign of irrational or psychotic thinking, his behavior was triggered by some personal motives, regardless of how unrealistic they might have been. The personal gains that he hoped to realize by concocting this scheme were important to him and drove him to take this risk. As a policeman, though, he knew quite well how thoroughly the police investigate any shooting, particularly against one of their own. He thought that he had taken all the precautions to succeed, except one. Nobody in that neighborhood heard any shot at that time. His calculated risk misfired because of a very damaging error of judgment. Basically, his well adjustment collapsed because of his poor judgment. It means that his attempt to cope with whatever situation created by his realistic or unrealistic needs was hindered by an inefficient thinking that was unable to properly meet the demand of the situation. The discrepancy between the satisfaction of his need and his ability to implement it by acceptable social means, created a stressful situation which he tried to overcome by an irregular approach. It shows again how fragile and unreliable is the concept of normalcy-conformity.

An intriguing case of nonconformity is that of Mary Turcotte, a twenty-six-year-old nun who reported to the police that she had been assaulted by a stranger on January 2011 while walking on a street in Brooklyn, New York. She was attacked and choked into unconsciousness by an Afro-American between forty and fifty years old. When she regained consciousness, she found herself seminude, lying in a snow bank. Under closer scrutiny, she admitted to the police that she had made up the story to cover her tracks after bringing a lover into the convent for sex. Later, a nun at the convent stated to a reporter: "It was all proven to be false. It wasn't her fault. . . . We are going to give her some help."[14]

The case seems simple: Lying for self-protection. The harder part to understand is that she was a nun who had allegedly renounced the temptations of the flesh and vowed to devote her life to the Church's teachings and God's worship. However, apparently, her judgment was suspended, overwhelmed by her strong emotions for the man who she had met at a bodega, that led to an uncontrollable desire for sex with him. Yet, she didn't want to take responsibility for her frivolous actions and to cope with the conflict, she lied. We don't know whether she was mentally "normal" when she decided to become a nun or during her tenure as a nun, her mental state changed to her present deviant behavior.

All things considered, we can see the poor coping of these people under perceived unfavorable or stressful conditions because of their twisted, inadequate judgment in appraising the risks they are exposed to by their actions. This doesn't change the fact that somehow they felt secure with the idea of inventing heavy lies to try to get what they wanted or to avoid unwarranted consequences. Lying was the common denominator in all their solutions. This devious way of dealing with troubling events using ad-hoc and strange solutions was facilitated in part by the new social acceptance of these confabulatory social defenses, which are justified as "relative truth." Lying peddled as relative truth has become part of the routine interaction among people with a fair degree of social currency and it is thriving in the new moral ambience that promotes loose societal norms of conduct.[15]

Important to note is the fact that by the standard definition of conformism-normalcy, their inability to cope with adverse events within the social constraints make them socially deviant or simply temporarily maladjusted, though otherwise their routine functioning could remain within normal limits. Only a regular pattern of social poor functioning might qualify them as presenting a maladjusted personality.

Attempting to Conform to the New Equivocal Social Values

Furthermore, some of these aberrant behaviors have become intertwined with the significant changes in the moral values which have created new relative norms of conduct, some legislated by the court or decreed by the government that have challenged the previously held standards of acceptable social behavior. It has slowly evolved over the last four decades as part of the moral relativism that has gradually pushed aside the traditional set of social beliefs-values negotiated by people as guiding principles in the organization of their lives in the community. Ultimately, these new ethics, unintentionally or not, have led to the justification of opportunistic, self-centered, and self-serving norms of behavior. Ideologically, the concept of moral relativism has derived its strength from the notion that absolute truth is part of relative truth which itself is part of multiple truth that could explain the same set of facts in different ways. This type of opportunistic reasoning has opened a Pandora's box for the interpretation of reality and morality. It has promoted a lax, unprincipled view of morality that has spread like a brush fire and has permeated all types of human social intercourse from dealings in the financial market and corporations to private transactions. From the ethical point of view, the new loose morality slowly evolved either by the necessity of survival, euphemistically translated as official persuasion or because of the relentless pressure of authorities to accept the new values, forcing people to acquire a different mode of relating to each other in society.

In a strange way, the behavior of Berger, Jones, and Stenroos is the unintended outcome of the new unprincipled morality with its prevailing controversial ethical values. Certainly, the prime examples of blatant social misconduct going unpunished are those of US President Bill Clinton having oral sex with an intern in the Oval Office while running the international affairs of the country or of Congressman Rangel, who omitted to pay income tax on his personal assets for years even while he was Chairman of the Ways and Means Committee, which dealt with taxation legislation. The new message of society's leniency toward acts of transgression has never been clearer. The pattern of ambiguity toward truth and subjective interpretation of laws has become part of the social norm of conduct creating the present ambiguous conformity.

As previously mentioned, these relativistic social values have slowly crept into the financial market to become prescriptions for organized fraud and deceptions as plotted by devious executives of mighty corporations, disingenuous bankers, analysts, and investment bankers of Wall Street. Stealing, lying, cheating, or operating Ponzi schemes to defraud the public has become part of doing business in the financial markets. All these crooks were topped by Bernard Madoff, the Ponzi king, and "genius" swindler, the supercrook who cheated institutions and private investors of approximately $65 billion.

The problem is that not all people have been able to discard the old set of social values in favor of the new social-political norms of conduct. This has created grave moral or social conflicts affecting their well-being. There are two categories of people poorly adapted to this moral ambience: One is the gullible and naive investor or consumer who has trusted and believed, in the integrity of the federal and state regulatory systems that would protect him from financial or business sharks. Unfortunately, the system has let him down. These people, sadly, seem to have failed to accept that the fabric of the establishment with its old social values of honesty and integrity has been gravely impaired for some time now. One way or another, a new alleged "respectable elite" hiding under a mask of normalcy has participated, accelerated, and patronized the moral and economic collapse of our society.

The naive and gullible are the victims of the crooked politicians and financiers whose social status of adjustment-normalcy has been questioned by the stressful events that have threatened their peace of mind, social status, or often their livelihood. We had recently witnessed the drama of thousands of victims of Bernard Madoff, the gigantic Ponzi schemer. The cheated ones were not only banks, foundations, celebrities, and rich people, but also widowers, elderly, and ordinary hardworking citizens who entrusted their life savings or retirement money through their financial advisers to Madoff. Some of the older ones over seventy were not only wiped out financially but also lost their houses. They had to go on food stamps, had to move in with relatives, or had to look for work hoping to get a job. A case in point was Abby Frucht from Wisconsin, who was eighty years old, in poor health, and lost all his life savings in Madoff's fraud scheme. He and his wife were forced to sell all the assets that they owned in order to survive. Pretty soon, they will run out of money and they don't know what will happen to them. They have become destitute and the impact of the fraud has been emotionally devastating. They are frightened and wonder for how long they would be able to resist emotionally and physically. Their life has become a nightmare with no power on their part to control or modify a terrible outcome. No wonder then, that they live in a state of anxiety and depression because their ability to cope with the situation is minimal and their prospects of a livelihood are nil.[16]

To what extent will they still be able to function "normally" when they live in constant turmoil, uncertain whether they will survive tomorrow? Their lives have reached the level of an unbearable crisis in which their coping mechanisms have become overloaded to the point of exhaustion. As a result, they have developed an emotional condition that has replaced their normal sense of well-being. They live now in misery and anguish like hundreds of Madoff's clients. At the same time, their previous sense of well-being has evaporated together with their normal responses which couldn't survive the relentless erosion of integrity politically sanctioned within the framework of moral relativism with its obfuscation of true and false or right and wrong.

The External Stressor of Affirmative Action and the Ambiguity of Conformity

There is a second category of people whose concept of conformity-normalcy becomes extremely confused when they are in a conflict with the government's political policies. They have a perception that they are abused or feel that their civil rights have been violated by laws and regulations that affect their lives. This state of affairs has been brought about by the novel and disputed interpretation of social values by opposing groups, which is sometimes confusing and at other times controversial and frustrating to some segments of the population.

Whereas some of the old beliefs-values have been specific to our democratic-capitalistic society, and others have been part of the popular wisdom promoting a desirable mode of human interaction, the new values tend to overreach themselves by trying to meet the diverse needs of a pluralistic, multicultural society. The new societal code of behavior and ethics, legislated as norms of social interaction, reflects the political-social changes undergone by society requiring the whole population to adjust, though in some areas its main beneficiaries have been the previously disenfranchised segments of population. This has created serious conflicts of adaptation for the ones who feel unfairly treated by the newly imposed rules. These newly dissatisfied segments of population feel deprived and robbed of their legitimate civil rights in favor of the previously socially neglected minorities, now the beneficiary of the new advantageous social laws. They view it as "discrimination in reverse," as compensation for past discriminations for which they do not feel responsible in any way. However, it affects their livelihood and their self-esteem. The ones who view themselves as "progressives," have created a moral and social conflict with the other who are proponents of a fair approach to social inequities. In this context, one of the highly controversial and debated issues is that of meritocracy.

The rules of social competition have been, to a large extent, turned upside down. The factors of race and gender, included as preferential factors in the equation of social competition, have changed in part the concept of merit based on desirable qualifications for admission in college, hiring, or promotion at work. While theoretically the presumption is that the job credentials of the candidate selected on the basis of the preferential treatment are in line with the requirements for college admission or specifications of the job position, most of the time the reality is different; the candidate's qualifications are mediocre or below par. This seems to have created problems for society. The lowering of the standards for admission and training, based on race or gender in law enforcement agencies and other public sectors have already created resentment in the rank and file with what many have considered an unfair dealing and a violation of their civil rights. The preferential systems for school admissions and promotions have led to legal actions against governmental agencies from time to time.

One of the latest cases of promotion-based job conflicts is that of Danny O'Connor, a Memphis police officer, who was twice denied promotion for sergeant after passing the examination and being ranked among the top seventy-five on the list of successful candidates. However, the list was revised according to the race quota requirement. Since only twenty-six Afro-Americans were on the original list as having passed, another nineteen Afro-Americans with scores below the passing score were moved up, and the whites were denied promotion.

O'Connor tried the next year with the same result. He was qualified for promotion, but was dropped to make room for the promotion of twenty-three Afro-American who had failed the examination. The issue raised by O'Connor and his colleagues was that of fairness versus political interpretation of exam used for arbitrary promotions.

The main issue raised by the arbitrarily rejected candidates was how these officers who didn't meet the standard for passing were more "socially deprived," as compared to a good number of Afro-American officers who successfully competed in and passed the examination. Another question was whether these political promotions served the interest of the community.[17]

Against the social-political controversy about the validity of arbitrary implementation of affirmative action, the authorities said that it wasn't a matter of personal injustice for O'Connor and his deprived colleagues but one of public policy. The reality has been that it can be easily translated into a loss of income and emotional well-being in addition to loss of self-esteem. Certainly, this twisted interpretation of meritocracy provoked the resentment and anger of all whose promotion was denied. It affected their sense of well-being and as such their emotional balance of normalcy. O'Connor's case together with those of a number of policemen in the same situation has reached the Supreme Court of the United States.

Important to note is the fact that this is not an isolated case of discrimination in reverse; there have been thousands of public employees who over the years went to the courts asking for remedy against the injustice of the employment system that practices official nonconformism.

An intriguing case of abuse of affirmative action by taking illegal advantage of it is the case of Elisabeth Warren, professor of law at Harvard University, and staunch social activist, who in order to advance her professional career shamelessly claimed an alleged Native American Cherokee heritage. The impeccable political credentials of being a social activist woman and belonging to a disfranchised minority guaranteed her swift promotion to the top of her profession. Her shenanigan was discovered when she stood for the post of US Senator from the State of Massachusetts. Unperturbed, she dropped her native claim as a nonevent, a regrettable slip up, which should be forgiven considering her alleged achievements.[18]

Unfortunately, most of the cases of affirmative action affected innocent people resulting in undesirable financial and emotional consequences. The great majority of the cases of discrimination never reached the court because either the affected ones didn't find an organization to fight for them or they became resigned to the situation, if they were unable to find a job in the private sector. For many of them, the emotional damage has been the same. They see the rules as discriminatory, as duplicitous conformity since they feel punished for past historical racial injustices or conflicts for which they think they were not responsible whatsoever.

The latest salvo in the battle of affirmative action for college admission has been fired by Abigail Fisher, a student who was denied admission in 2008 because of her race. The case is currently before the

Supreme Court: *Fisher v. University of Texas*. The college has argued that taking race into consideration for admission decisions fosters diversity as decided by the Supreme Court in 2003.[19]

Political Correctness versus Social Conformity

There is another social issue that has altered our norms of evaluating social adjustment. As we know there is a general social pressure to act politically correctly as interpreted and monitored by vigilantes and activists who claim to uphold legislations or rules of new social conduct. Most of the people agree that no one has the right to offend others by verbally abusing them because of their race, sex, or sexual orientation. On the other hand, the unsettling fact is that anyone can be offended by someone who disagrees with his political or social point of view about racial or gender issues. The problem is complicated by the fact that the First Amendment and the Bill of Rights give the citizens the inalienable right to disagree, to argue, and to express their thoughts without fear of government censure or worse, retaliation. Then, who is to decide what is politically correct or not? Should it be a prosecutor or a judge, political appointees with vested interests according to their party affiliation or an ignorant jury afraid of being viewed as politically incorrect? As a matter of fact, many politicians, activists or media representatives use political correctness to suppress voices of dissent which might dare to question the methods used by these activists to advance their careers. Society is struggling to deal with the attempts to condition it to accept too many distorted social ideas about the alleged verbal offenses addressed to particular segments of population. Most verbal statements or behaviors are arbitrarily interpreted as offenses and are not supported by any objective documentation to prove their validity. They further confound the ambiguity of conformity.

Let's take the example of the administrators at a high school in California, who sent five students home because they refused to remove their T-shirts with a design of an American flag on the Mexican Day of Independence. The assistant principal, Miguel Rodriguez told the students that they could not wear the T-shirts because it would offend the people of the other nation! Apparently, later the students complied but were anyway taken to the principal's office for a chat because it was politically insensitive to wear the country's flag when the Mexicans were celebrating their national holiday.

The administration used the pretext of political correctness to send a subtle message that part of California was once Mexican territory.

Reported by the press, the superintendent considered the incident "extremely unfortunate" but no action was taken against the administration. What was the message being given to the teens about right and wrong within the context of national identity?[20]

In other instances, the interpretation of political correctness could be quite harmful. All of us are familiar with the Duke lacrosse case discussed in the second chapter. It is amazing to see the opportunistic approach of Duke's University administration. It gave in to some politically active members of the teaching faculty working together with an unscrupulous, crooked district attorney, who without investigating the case, indicted the students in the name of political correctness. Without any verification of facts, without waiting for the court's decision, they indicted the students for forcible rape and kidnapping. No one considered that the stripper who changed her story five times during the investigation could lie. Certainly, the rogue prosecutor shamelessly used political correctness as a weapon to advance his career, knowingly lying, and withholding crucial evidence like DNA without any compunction. He was fully aware that the DNA would have absolved the defendants. Most of the faculty and the administration at Duke University afraid of being associated in any way with alleged racism tried to show blind allegiance and irresponsible adherence to the prosecutor's political correctness. When the case was dismissed, they tried to settle the suits against the university and blame the prosecutor. In the name of the same political correctness, the stripper who brazenly and shamelessly lied was not prosecuted for perjury. However, this flagrant abuse of the rights of the students would have affected their sense of justice after being faced with a morally corrupt university staff and perverted process of justice.[21]

Another case where the use of political correctness had fatal effects is that of Nidal Malik Hasan, an army major and psychiatrist, who shot and killed thirteen people at a military base in Texas, in the name of jihad. What is important is that the Pentagon knew about the email correspondence between the major and the radical jihadist Imam Anwaral-Awlaki, in Yemen. Moreover, his email was read in 2008 by FBI experts on terrorism who found it "consistent with medical research." Hasan never did any research in the area of terrorism, except for displaying a poster (found in his apartment after the shooting) comparing suicide bombers with kamikaze pilots. Hasan was known for expressing extremist views and he was seriously conflicted about being a Muslim and serving in the US army. However, his superiors and colleagues ignored these signals apparently "afraid of being accused of racially profiling a Muslim," something that would have been politically incorrect. After the shooting, various hypotheses for explaining his action were put forward by the army mainly to cover up their negligence and politically misguided judgment. However, the answer was given by Hasan who shouted "Allahu Akbar" before he started shooting. This is the usual slogan of suicide bombers and of other jihadis. No wonder that Al-Qaeda called him a "mujahid brother, a trailblazer and a role model." From a different perspective, it shows the nefarious effect of some of the tenets of political correctness when it is approved automatically without any critical evaluation of facts. Did the employees of army and FBI, indoctrinated with these set of biased political beliefs imposed by self-serving political activists, act properly, or were they prejudiced or afraid of being reprimanded by superiors in case they did not accept them uncritically?[22]

It is interesting that political correctness has been vaguely and hypocritically associated by disingenuous political activists with human brotherhood, part of the universal love for each other which is demonstrated by mutual respect and tolerance regardless of race or sex. This empathy has been equated in its broadest sociological sense with a feeling of like-mindedness and support experienced by people participating in or defending a common cause or confronting a common distress. In this sense, it is part of the social bond of solidarity with a touch of empathy that is an extension of primitive feelings of belonging to the clan or group. It could be extended to a whole society or nation as it happened after 9/11 or after the tsunami that hit Indonesia. Unfortunately, this preachy "brotherly love" is contradicted by the concept of political correctness which uses its own policies that tend to reinforce the social strife.

Some cases of political correctness reported recently by the press take the cake. It reaches the highest level of absurdity or of dumbness depending on how you interpret it. However, the problem is that it inflicts emotional pain on the victim and his family.

A nine-year-old boy in Gastonia, North Carolina, was reported by a substitute teacher to the principal of the school for "sexual harassment." The substitute overheard the boy remarking to one of his friends that the teacher was cute. According to the mother of the boy, the principal suspended the boy from the school for what he considered to be a sexual harassment![23]

This is an example of the degree of misguided political indoctrination of our school system. The number of such examples is legion.

Take, for example, the ridiculous action of Los Angeles County affirmative action office that decided to ban any computer equipment labeled "master" and "slave" because the terminology was offensive. They wanted to change the labeling. By doing so, these activists were disregarding the fact that these terms identified the primary and secondary drives of computers and had been in use for decades. These ignorant zealots backed off only after strong negative publicity and the refusal of suppliers to do business with them.[24]

A New Perspective on Love and Intimate Relationships from the Viewpoint of Conformity

Another social value that is highly debated is the expression of love between sexes. It has undergone drastic changes with the result that it has altered the stability of intimate interaction between people and affected the sense of well-being of many people. Free love with or without cohabitation has been advocated as an alternative to marriage in response to the criticism of the institution by the women's liberation movement. It is regarded allegedly as a panacea for the conflicts of intimate male-female relationships. Somehow it was felt that this new approach to the relationship would permit each partner to maintain his or her independence while operating within the ideology of the women's liberation movement, that emphasized the emotional and economic liberation of women from the social constraints imposed previously by men. Indeed, the feminist liberation ideology fulfilled the prized desire in most women to be free and compete socially and economically with men but at a price, that is, the destabilization of their relationships with men. However, it legitimized their social demands by trying to minimize the existent differences in personality make-up and social interests between the sexes and stressing their similarities. To justify the new social position of women, the old psychological differences between the sexes were reinterpreted, like the expression of aggression, logical abstraction, and so forth, attributed now to the socialization process. All in all, the conclusion pushed for by the feminists was that sexes are basically the same, except for the biology of reproduction. Obviously, the biological-hormonal differences didn't disappear, though they became inconsequential for women's access to job opportunities. This was because the new technologies blurred the distinctions of work roles between sexes. The technology that made the housewife's work almost obsolete has opened up vast areas of employment for women.

Issues of the Modern Marriage and Social Conformity

The new social role of woman has today created confusion and conflict in their marital interaction. In this new level of social interaction, men and women convey ambivalent or contradictory messages to each other about their wants and desired roles. Their ability to meet their expectations of each other falls woefully short of their hopes. While men have welcomed women's sharing of the economic burdens of the household, many of them have problems dealing with the women's independence and their demands that are at cross purposes with their expected role in the marital interaction. Most men tend to see modern women as assertive if not aggressive, critical, demanding, and socially competitive.

The assumption that their differences would be solved by promoting a true partnership between the couple hasn't panned out in most marriages. Most of the relationships have become limited, guarded, and mainly oriented towards sex with men quite often cautious and mistrustful of any excessive personal sharing. It explains why so many spouses pursue independent social pathways after love brought them together. It seems that after the first wave of passion has dissipated, the women's need for self-assertion is reaffirmed by their demand for their own personal space with many either asking for a regular time-out with friends, separate bank accounts, or the pursuit of personal interests. These demands create conflicts of personality in many cases, which slowly erode the initial uncritical acceptance of the spouse. Many find it progressively difficult to strike a balance between closeness, intimacy, and the maintenance of their separate identities, which requires the satisfaction of their unshared needs. In addition, job pressures clash with marital obligations which leave both parties mutually frustrated and disappointed in each other. When they realize that their needs do not quite coincide, the marriage changes into an arena of confrontation where each partner attempts to win the argument and impose his or her priorities on the other. The wife feels overworked with her dual role, pursuit of the career, and involvement with the care of children, while the husband feels caught between the obligations of a developing or demanding career and responding to the emotional needs of the wife and participating in the household chores. Battered by these day-to-day conflicts, most couples struggle to maintain a true marital partnership. Both the man and woman are too egotistic and self-involved to make meaningful compromises.

Slowly, they drift apart. No wonder then that close to 50 percent of the American marriages end in divorce.

In this context, the question is who is more likely to get divorced, the ones who are allegedly well-adjusted-normal or the ones with personality problems? Usually, it should be the ones with personality disorders since they would have more difficulty coping with a variety of conflicts created by the interaction with a spouse who has similar disorders. However, this is not necessarily so. Even if someone is allegedly "well-balanced emotionally" he or she might have difficulty reaching a compromise with an intransigent, rigid spouse who considers any concession a sign of weakness, a surrender of his or her independence viewed by either one as affecting his or her self-esteem negatively.

A good example of marital problems spilling over during divorce procedures, in which at least one partner has a disturbed personality is the recently reported case in Orange County, California. A married woman, Catherine K. Becker of Garden Grove was charged with "aggravated mayhem, false imprisonment, assault with a deadly weapon, administering a drug with the intent to commit a felony, poisoning and spousal abuse." According to the same police report, the woman puts a poisonous substance or drug in her husband's food to make him sleepy. While the husband was sleeping, Becker allegedly tied him to the bed and when he woke up, she cut his penis off with a knife and threw it into the garbage disposal. Later, she called 911 for emergency assistance and told the responding officer, that he "deserved it." The married couple was going through a divorce.[25]

On the other hand, the well-adjusted person influenced by the new concept of loose interaction between sexes might be less inclined to repeatedly negotiate the relationship with a critical spouse who doesn't meet his or her emotional needs. According to the latest statistics of the Census Bureau, one in twelve couples will start divorce proceedings after twenty-four months of marital life. This puts the median duration of the marriage at 7.2 years.[26]

Alternative Solutions to Marriage

We now have a pretty good picture of the difficulties encountered by the sexes attempting to live together within the framework of the new set of social values. If one condition for social adjustment is considered to be one's ability to adapt and cope with unfavorable situations, it means that the marital failure of a large number of the couples entering into this contractual agreement is caused by their inability to function and adapt to it. If 80 percent of failed marriages have been provoked by irreconcilable differences according to the census bureau, this fact questions the assumption that well-adjusted people represent the bulk of the individuals getting married. However, someone might argue that the emotional and social interaction between sexes is so twisted by the new social values that many people, well-balanced emotionally, prefer to reduce the relations to the basic biological expression of sex in noncommittal affairs with a socially perfunctory interaction and communication. Both sexes, particularly men, tend to postpone the marriage in favor of serial affairs while others prefer to settle for long period of cohabitation. These arrangements can be terminated on short notice or without warning; a switch of feelings, a change of mind, a promise of more fun, or the hope of a better life could terminate a love story or a cohabitation which had appeared solid and indestructible.

The result has been that romantic love has become interchangeable with erotic love. This approach to intimate relationships between sexes could work for a while, since the lovers pay little attention to the other's true personality and thereby avoid possible conflicts provoked by their dissimilar needs. However, passionate love is short-lived and melts when one of the lovers loses interest after starting to know the other better. Most marriages based on passionate love tend to suffer because of the partners' inability to switch from pure physical attraction and sexual possession to mature love which presupposes enjoyment of togetherness and of each other's personality. Thus, it ends in divorce when the incompatibility of their personalities becomes self-evident. The children might become a true casualty.

The children may end up psychologically shortchanged and sometimes handicapped when pulled emotionally apart by the acrimonious divorce of their parents. One problem is that quite often since neither of the divorced parent wants to be thought of as authoritarian and punitive, they tend to overlook the misbehavior of their children. In this way, the children grow up with a faulty sense of discipline and tolerance to frustration, which, in turn, means that as young adults they might have problems in adapting socially to unfavorable conditions. But the worst situation is when they grow without any adult supervision because of the working mother who is overtaxed by her job's obligations or emotionally unable to discipline them. In many cases, the children's socialization is then left to their peers and to the lawless street culture which may result in their becoming social delinquents.

The socially promoted idea that children become better adjusted to society by spending more time with their peers than their parents is not only farfetched but also harmful. This might explain why the ability to act properly is so difficult and complicated for many people since they don't have a clear point of social reference. Nevertheless, this is only a relatively minor aspect of the problem contributing to the poor adjustment of many young adults, hence affecting their understanding of what constitutes acceptable behavior in society.

Conformity Confronted with Judicial Subjectivism and Cultural Relativism

In general, the issue of social conformity takes a new twist within the framework of meeting the imposed legal terms of the acceptance of some social conflicting issues like an infringement of one's rights created by arbitrary law or alleged incorrect social conduct as interpreted by biased authorities or an activist judge. As mentioned, many decisions are taken by both sides of the bench, the judge, and the prosecutor by often using pseudological arguments to rationalize their position strongly influenced by their political creed. Faced with this situation, how could a plaintiff who by definition was acting as a nonconformist, be cool and collected when arbitrarily bypassed for promotion because he did not belong to the preferred gender, race, or political organization? And how could a judge or prosecutor be objective when their future careers depend on serving his political affiliation or the government?

A so-called normal-conformist may act in a detached manner in situations in which he is not personally involved, but if he thinks that the event represents a threat to his well-being, then he will exhibit negative emotions whose magnitude depends on his ability to grasp the facts correctly, and on his awareness of his own built-in biases. At the same time, the intensity of the conflict will be decided by many variables starting with the significance of the dispute, his degree of expectations, and the power of the adversary. Furthermore, the conflict could be exacerbated by people's cynical view of the justice system which made them lie, cheat, or try to influence the jury, or to do anything that might alter the outcome in their favor. The subjectivism of the implementation of the new social policies dictated by the moral relativism has further heightened the conflict and the resentment against the arbitrariness of the courts which inadvertently or not often practice an ambiguous conformism.

Take, for example, the legal interpretation of the definition of what might constitute a hostile environment at work. It is loose enough to include a variety of actions allegedly unfavorable to the victim. A woman, Cecil, hired by a company in Louisville to handle drafting deeds of easement and purchase agreements claimed that she was discriminated against because she didn't receive any training as compared to her male co-workers. She was treated unfairly by the supervisor who set her too ambitious targets. She accused her company of canceling one of her field trips as part of the same discriminatory attitude toward her. In addition, she complained that her boss on one occasion made derogatory remarks and acted violently toward her. By the nature of her complaints, it seems that she sued for financial gains taking advantage of the laws referring to hostile environment at work as a member of the "protected class." All what she had to claim was that the alleged harassment was severe or pervasive enough to create hostile or abusive work environment. As one might remark, the issue of hostile environment is a subjective view depending on the biased perception of the plaintiff, not to mention that the appraisal of the body of evidence in support of the claims is based on the assertions of the same party. Quite often it relies on the self-serving statements of the alleged victim supported by hearsay and witnesses, who happened to be acquaintances or friends of the plaintiff. The argument of the plaintiff is that most of the acts of real or alleged harassment take place in very private situations without witnesses. This leads to frivolous suits. In this particular case of Cecil, the court decided that the actions weren't so pervasive and severe as to constitute a hostile environment.[27]

Quite the opposite, is the case of a jury which awarded $6.8 million in a sexual harassment suit initiated by a woman, Kendra Lynn, who claimed that in 2003, her night supervisor commented unfavorably about her body or made sexually suggestive remarks on five occasions within a two-month period. She also complained that her boss struck her buttocks with a belt while making inappropriate remarks. She was transferred to another shift but the shifts overlapped with one handled by her previous boss. The company didn't follow up the status of her complaints. Any cursory evaluation of her complaints shows that the acts of harassment took place in private situations. We don't know whether there were witnesses to all or some of his inappropriate behavior. Nonetheless, the jury was subjective and irresponsibly generous.[28]

But even assuming that she could have proven the harassment which took place over a two-month period, was it so emotionally harmful that it entitled her to $6.8 million punitive damages? Certainly, the woman made the money using the one-sided law of sexual harassment, but the decision of the jury was out of whack or deliberately malicious. From a psychological point of view, it questions their common sense.

A more unusual case is the award of $15 million in a harassment suit against Flushing Hospital, New York. A nurse of fifty-five year-old sued a physician after she allegedly suffered years of torment that ended with being sexually assaulted by him. According to her, he was well known in the hospital for dirty jokes told at the nursing station but the hospital tolerated it. She claimed that on one occasion the doctor grabbed her by force at a nursing station and tried to push his tongue down her throat. The director of the hospital saw the attack but didn't intervene. Apparently, things got out of control when in September 2001 the same doctor chased her through the halls until he cornered her in a room with two heavily sedated patients and aggressively groped her below the waist. The doctor was not reprimanded until the nurse lodged a written complaint. After the attack on her, the misconduct board suspended his license for two months and put him on three years' probation. He also lost his admitting privileges at Flushing Hospital. However, the court awarded her $15 million for the sexual harassment.[29]

The case is very bizarre considering that he was allegedly behaving inappropriately for years and nobody else from the staff of the hospital complained of being sexually harassed. In fact, the nurse had been "tormented" for years and didn't complain until he allegedly attacked her. It is strange that while she was running from him through the halls of the hospital she didn't ask for help from a nurse or guard. Furthermore, the alleged attack took place in a room with two heavily sedated patients who obviously could not testify about what really happened. One could assume that it was her word against the doctor and she won based on the legal concept of harassment which implicitly favors the alleged victim. The issue is not the verdict per se, but the anxiety and stress induced in the loser who can't win because the normal judicial process relies on self-serving statements of the "protected" plaintiff which have been well documented by now.

In other cases, the deception is motivated by the desire to avoid a situation viewed by them as either embarrassment and loss of face (Peguero admitted false accusation of rape), Hofstra student afraid of being considered a trump or as revenge for being fired from the strip job (Crystal Magnum—Duke University lacrosse case, proven false accusation of rape). Either way the assault on the truth was ruthless while a reprehensible moral attitude was displayed, severely harming innocent men. Though their behavior was rooted in the dishonesty and turpitude of today's social climate, it also indicates a strong streak of psychopathy. And their lies were believed by the police, prosecutors, and juries without any critical appraisal of facts because they appeared to be in line with our social policies. For example in the Duke University case, who acted "properly normally," the phony plaintiffs, the crooked prosecutor, the inept police, or the opportunistic enforcers of the University's administration? Obviously, none of them, though most of them were previously viewed as pillars of morality of the community.

There have been valid cases of sexual harassment and hostile work environment but they have been eclipsed by the many unjustified court decisions related to the same issues based on exaggerated or unsubstantiated claims. The game of sexual harassment is not about establishing truth and delivering justice, it is just about the legal "loot," the money which the lawyer and the alleged victim get. No wonder that the cases of sexual harassment have become routine court claims of people and in particular of some women, who attempt to solve their problems at work by complaining of hostile work environments. There are complaints of sexual harassment which never reach the court and are settled by the lawyers. An interesting case of alleged sex harassment has recently surfaced because of the high political profile of Herman Cain, Republican front-runner and presidential candidate for the 2012 elections. He had been accused by two women employees at the National Restaurant Association in the late nineties of "alleged conversations filled with innuendo or personal questions of sexually suggestive nature." The vagueness of the allegations resulted in a financial settlement with the company without court intervention. Cain denied the allegations and of any involvement in the settlement. For "x" amount of dollars the allegedly dented self-esteem of the employees caused by the allusions of the alleged perpetrator, was fast reestablished.[30]

A more blatant case of apparent sexual harassment is under investigation now at Homeland Security where under the leadership of Janet Napolitano, a hostile work environment was allegedly created for men. A high-ranking immigration aide Suzanne Barr took a leave of absence after being accused by two men of engaging in lewd and hostile behavior with subordinates. One of the accusations was that during a trip to Colombia she directly solicited sex from an Immigration and Customs Enforcement employee.[31]

Faced with this moral relativism, many people have a hard time to cope morally with these officially lopsided situations that assault their common sense, test their fair judgment, and their integrity. Their sense of fairness, a part of normal behavior, is under siege by an ambiguous morality and judicial system which often legislates from the bench.

Ironically, the latent social conflict between sexes instead of being attenuated by the new legislated social policies has been exacerbated by the numerous suits of unsubstantiated hostile work environment claims and/or alleged offensive treatment of people at work. In the new politicized working climate, attention on issues of poor job performance or incompetence has been shifted by inefficient employees to claims of abuse and mistreatment, conjuring up a hostile work environment. If some unscrupulous women or men add to their complaints some derogatory statements made about their sexuality or alleged attempts to having been touched physically, then they are winners since the burden of proof of innocence falls on the defendant. As part of this shell gamer, some of the plaintiffs to reinforce the veracity of their testimony, will use a friend with whom they allegedly talked about the incident in order to confirm their complaint. After all, the case in court is worth hundreds of thousands if not millions depending on the largess of a biased or irresponsible jury. Ultimately, the taxpayers are footing the bill.

An intriguing case of a court decision regarding a marital rape has questioned the soundness of our judicial system and impartiality of judges. It has been recently reported by the press that a Californian wife who won a case of marital rape against her husband based on recorded documentation of the sexual assault resulting in his conviction was ordered by a San Diego judge to pay her ex-husband a spousal support of $1,000 a month after release from jail next year. In addition, she has to repay $47,000 to her ex-husband, the money spent on divorce lawyers to win the alimony. The argument of the judge was that she has been making $120,000 per year during the marriage while her ex-husband was earning only $11,000.[32]

The decision of the judge is baffling considering the fact that a sexual assault victim is forced by the court to support her ex-husband who is the convicted attacker. The judge defended his biased decision against the public outcry by relying on a loophole in the Californian divorce law which excludes alimony only for attempted murder of the spouse. It is more likely that the judge took advantage of the law's flaw to implement his version of law in this case with total disregard for its particulars. The ex-husband, a graduate of college with major in math, stayed temporarily home to take care of the two small children by an arrangement with the wife. His potential earning would be much higher than $400 per month, now that the children have remained with the ex-wife since that frees him for full employment. It seems these facts were too complicated for the judge to evaluate properly in order to arrive at a common sense decision. His judicial acumen is questionable for leaving the woman stuck with these payments plus the care of their two children.

The issue is whether the "conformist-normals" can function properly or maintain their social adjustment in a lenient and twisted judicial system which directly or indirectly by its legal inconsistencies or subjective implementation of law inadvertently tempts people to cheat, lie, and take advantage of others. The ability to navigate socially while being aware of the pitfalls surrounding any social interaction is the difference between getting hurt emotionally and financially, or overcoming the hindrances set by others. This is not an easy task considering that the conflict could emerge from unexpected places because people in this climate of moral relativism try to do what they think will benefit them, ignoring the rights of others leading to legal confrontation.

In this respect the recent conflict among the members of the wealthy Pritzker family, a Chicago dynasty, is quite revealing. The whole conflict had been about the fair distribution of the inheritance of Pritzker's family wealth to their members. To come to the point, one of the fourth generation Pritzkers, Liesel sued her father and other members of the family for restitution of over $1 billion taken from her trust left by the great grandfather. In addition, she asked for $5 billion in punitive damages. Liesel also accused her estranged father and cousins who had run the Pritzker Foundation of misappropriating $480 million over several years. She contended that her father "systematically emptied" her trust fund and her brother's trust fund to benefit other members of the family and sold some assets at below-market values to other relatives. From the details of the story reported by the New York Times, in 1994, her father tried to stop Liesel and her brother from changing their family name in court to that of their stepfather and he was alienated from both siblings. He felt ethically justified to use their trust fund but not that of her cousins for a variety of donations in tens of million dollars, since in his opinion they were not Pritzkers anymore. The case was recently settled out of court. The case is more interesting from the moral point of view of a family plagued by years of devious and acrimonious interaction, yet presenting a mask of proper social adjustment and propriety to outsiders; a mask that was covering an internal drama culminating with acts of revenge, greed, lies, illegal financial manipulations, court actions, and so forth.[33]

There are situations when the higher courts succeed in redressing the imperfections and abuses of the lower courts, but for a stiff price. One of these is the famous Florida sex abuse case which started in the eighties as a policeman's act of revenge against another policeman. Small children testified as alleged victims under the influence of an expert witness who took advantage of their suggestibility. A highly politically motivated prosecutor pretending to be a defender of morality and social justice jumped onto the bandwagon for advancing her career. She was supported by some biased media reporters who made explosive statements without any valid proof. Did these public accusers and self-promoters believe in their arbitrary findings or were they outright opportunistic liars? This case became a "cause célèbre" because of the strange ways in which the politicized judicial process upheld conviction of an alleged sex abuser. It also showed the irresponsible manipulation of the justice system for personal gains in particular, by the prosecutor.

Grant Snowden, a policeman, was initially accused of molesting a three-year-old boy who was under the care of his wife. She was running a small baby-sitting service. Two years later when he was brought to trial, the prosecutor charged him with molesting two other children, after the first charge was dropped for lack of evidence. The jury acquitted him because there was no evidence that they knew each other. With her prestige severely damaged, the ambitious state attorney, Janet Reno, brought other charges against him, as already being in the file system for alleged sexual abuses and succeeded in obtaining his conviction on dubious grounds. Instrumental in his conviction had been the testimonies before the jury of the prosecution's expert witnesses in child abuse. One expert had a degree in speech therapy and was falsely introduced by the prosecution as a psychologist. Furthermore, the speech therapist confirmed the made-up allegations about alleged sexual activities using leading questions which had been again and again repeated to the children in rehearsals before the trial. (Example: Isn't it true that on such and such a day Snowden did so and so to you?) Another expert in child abuse brought in by the prosecution, a psychologist, ended her testimony to the jury with the absurd statement that 99.5 percent of the children making accusations of sex abuse are telling the truth, whereas the unreliability of a young child's testimony is well known. It is usually the subjective recollection of facts. The unholy alliance between an unscrupulous prosecutor hungry for notoriety and political power and some outright dishonest or incompetent expert witnesses led to a man's conviction to life in prison.

However, the crusade of a dedicated investigative reporter who documented in articles published in the New York Times the injustice committed by the politically perverted trial bore fruit when the Eleventh Circuit of the US Court of Appeals reopened the case and reversed the conviction of Snowden. Meanwhile, he had spent twelve years in jail to feed the political ambitions of the State Attorney, Janet Reno who gained national prominence by successfully prosecuting this case to become Attorney General of United State under then President Clinton.[34,35]

This case reminds us of the earlier one of the rogue prosecutor, Nifong of the Duke University lacrosse students' case who, apparently inspired by the Florida conviction, tried to withhold crucial information proving the innocence of the defendants from the court.

Most people go to court to resolve disputed issues under the assumption that justice will prevail. This is a risky conclusion, suggesting that someone is either misinformed about our legal system or believes in divine intervention to ultimately protect his interests. Society has always tried hard to indoctrinate the citizens with the idea that the law is impartial, objective, and rational, which happens to be an unreachable goal. Unfortunately, the administration of the justice depends on too many known and less known variables. Ultimately, justice is heavily influenced by the moral climate of the society that can pervert and manipulate its interpretation and execution. And this is exactly what has happened now to our judicial system. The assumption that the truth will emerge and be self-evident to the judge and the jury, since facts speak for themselves, is at best naive. In reality, between the facts and establishing the truth there are too many intervening factors brought in by the intermediaries of the judicial process: The witnesses, the expert witnesses, the lawyers, and finally the jury and the judge—all of them more often intentionally than not, distort or pervert the facts to fit their own beliefs or interests. The jury may be biased or inept (like in the recent Florida murder case of defendant Anthony Casey), or the judge a politically motivated activist, who tries to legislate from the bench and not to apply the law on the merit of the case; or the expert witnesses could be corrupt or incompetent. Add to it the lawyers, who by definition are manipulators of facts trying to shape the evaluation of the case and the judgment of the court because of their ambition to win the case at any cost, and one will get a full picture of problems encountered by the plaintiffs in their attempts to secure justice.

It is naïve to assume that the court participants in various capacities at the trial are functioning and acting more or less honestly until proven otherwise. Behind their façade of integrity they might lie, cheat, or abuse others without any compunction. In fact, they are trying to win against their opponents by using whatever means are available to them, legally or not, as long as they are not discovered and convicted. And this is part of successful coping, one of the conditions of "normalcy." On the contrary, honesty may be counter-productive and harmful for the individual.

An example is Jeffrey W. Baird who worked as an undercover investigator for the New York Mayor's Commission that investigated allegations of police corruption (Mollen Commission). Baird was instrumental in exposing corrupt police officers and practices. After termination of his work at the Mollen Commission he was reassigned to New York Police's Department of Investigation. Here, he experienced retaliations from his superiors. They refused to give him the necessary support to conduct his investigative work, not to mention that among other acts of harassment were verbal abuse, destruction of the headset of his telephone, repeated change of his assignments, and denial of promotion. After repeated complaints, he gradually became anxious and depressed and went on sick leave. Since his condition didn't improve he decided to retire on disability with diagnosis of posttraumatic stress disorder caused by "intense campaign of harassment, isolation, and defamation resulting in a hostile work environment." His request was rejected by the police department. In reply, Baird sued and won.[36]

The story of Baird is important for two main reasons. First, it shows that the humanist concept of conformist-normalcy is self-contradicting. If indeed the idea of "normalcy" presupposes that the normal individual is well adjusted to the prevalent social condition, Baird didn't pass the test. Though he performed successfully in his job for Mollen Commission by exposing the secret file with the corruption in the police and the Department of Internal Affairs, he didn't receive any praise and promotion. On the contrary, he was transferred to another department that exposed him to reprisals. Doing a good job and being honest didn't pay off by the theoretical standards of normal community conduct. On the contrary, it induced emotional distress, and it slowly destroyed him. He had functioned normally until the stressful conditions instigated by the bosses brought him crashing down. The daily stress became unbearable even for a tough cop, and in due course, the anxiety and depression took its toll on him.

It means that conformist-normalcy, describing a state of emotional equilibrium maintained by an individual's capacity to handle the stressful events encroaching on the organization of life, without inducing overt distress, is illusory. In reality, the cumulative effect of events, if too powerful, could bring about the breaking point of one's functioning, impairing one emotionally. One develops an emotional condition which could be transient or chronic. In these cases we have at best a relative, flexible normalcy. It is a dynamic concept of adjustment in which normalcy, at best, might define a moment in time in someone's life.

The adjustment in a relative, dynamic proper social functioning indicates that an individual could maintain a state of emotional equilibrium with his environment as long as it is not drastically modified by overwhelming events surpassing his capacity to cope with them. This notion presupposes that the well-adjusted person in a society operating under ambiguous conformity should function while continuously changing according to the interaction between his handling of his emotional needs and the pressures exerted by the social environment. As long as his drives, needs, and aspirations are in harmony with the societal rules and regulations, he functions as what is called as a conformist. But if the situation changes overnight by either society altering some rules of conduct like an arbitrary enforcement of a new law that affects him or other conflicts created by the arbitrary prohibition of his rights, it might force him to act as a nonconformist. The result is a destabilization of his previous sense of emotional equilibrium and introduction of a different mode of dealing with unfavorable situations.

By the same token, the confrontational attitude might change again if there is favorable resolution of the conflict. And indeed this happens when the stressful situation created by what seems at the beginning to be uncontrollable forces, turn out to be controllable by manipulations. The threat which at the beginning appeared as insurmountable, gradually, with the use of the new found counter forces becomes manageable and negotiable.

However, equating normalcy with conformity to the norms of society and its correlate of social adjustment represents only one part of one's possible social functioning; there is another category of "normal persons not socially adjusted" who present various degrees of nonconformist behaviors that ignore, reject, or oppose the social norms of conduct. They might function quite well emotionally and cognitively but for many reasons which will be discussed in the succeeding chapters, they depart from the common acceptable behavior of the community, to the point of working against it or wanting to destroy it.

Notes

1. R. D. McFadden and F. Santos, "Westchester Lawyer Charged in Wife's 2006 Shooting," NY Times.com, December 21, 2007.
2. Ibid.
3. K. Crowley, L. Mongelli, and IKimulisa Livingstone, "Lover Rampage," *New York Post*, June 17, 2010, 25.
4. M. Sherman, "Ex-advisor Berger to Plead Guilty," *Sun-Sentinel*, April 1, 2005, 3A.
5. S. Cohen and C. Lisi, "Lawyer A 'Hit'-Feds," *New York Post*, August 11, 2008.
6. *Wikipedia*, "Eliot Spitzer Prostitution Scandal," 2010.
7. "Ex-governor (Ryan, G) Convicted of Racketeering," NBCN news.com, April 17, 2006.
8. "Rod Blagojevich News," *New York Times*, 2012.
9. A. Soltis, "Weiner's Rise and Fall," *New York Post*, June 17, 2011, 2.
10. G. Serban, *The Tyranny of Magical Thinking* (New York: Dutton, 1981).
11. J. Schiram and D. Kaplan, "A Cold Front at Channel 7," *New York Post*, December 16, 2010, 7.
12. Ibid.
13. T. Richards, "LA Officer Accused of Shooting Himself, Filing False Report," Aolnes.com, January 28, 2011.
14. D. Lohr, "Nun Allegedly Lied About Rape to Hide Affair," Aolnews.com, January 2, 2011.
15. G. Serban, *Lying: Man's Second Nature* (Westport, CT: Praeger, 2001).
16. "Victims of Madoff's $65 Billion Ponzi Scheme Speak Out," *Haaretz Daily Newspaper*.
17. Terry Eastland, *Ending Affirmative Action* (New York: Basic Books, 1996).
18. S. Mandel, "Elisabeth Warren and the Tragedy of the Modern Liberalism," *Commentary Magazine*, May 3, 2012.
19. A. Liptak, "Justice Take Up Race as a Factor in College Entry," NY Times.com, February 22, 2012.
20. "Ridiculous Case of Political Correctness," Listverse.com, October 26, 2010.
21. Ibid.
22. D. Tillotson, "Case of Political Correctness Taken to an Extreme," *The Daily News*, February 20, 2011.

23. M. Ramraj, "Sexual Harassment: 9 Year Old School Boy Suspended," *Truthdive*, December 5, 2011.
24. "Ridiculous Cases of Political Correctness," Listverse.com, October 10, 2010.
25. "Catherine Kieu Becker Accused of Cutting Off her estranged Husband's Penis," *Huffington Post*, July 12, 2011.
26. "Divorce Statistics-Divorce Rates 2000," USAattorneylegalservice.com; "Single Parents Statistics Census 2009," About.com, February 26, 2010.
27. A. Alitowski, "Louisville Hostile Work Environment Claim-Gender Based," Kentucky personalinjurylawyblog.com, March 1, 2010.
28. M. Kind, "Jury Awards $6.8M in Sexual Harassment Case," *Kansas City Business Journal*, January 17, 2006.
29. N. Bode, "Flushing Hospital Nurse Gets $15M Award in Sexual Harassment Suit," *New York Daily News*, February 23, 2009.
30. K. Markovicz, "Why this Guy?," *New York Post*, November 1, 2011, 25.
31. N. Chiles, "Obama's Homeland Security Dept. Engulfed in Sex Scandal," Atlanta blackstar.com, August 25, 2012.
32. N. Miranda, "Marital Rape Victim Challenges Alimony Pay," abc7news.com.
33. A. Dunn, "Pritzker Heirs Settle Family Feud over Inheritance for $560 Mln," Bloomberg.com, January 7, 2005.
34. D. Rabinowitz, "The Pursuit of Justice in Dade County," *Wall Street Journal*, October 28, 1996, A18.
35. "Review & Outlook: Reno Overturned," *Wall Street Journal*, February 20, 1998.
36. Supreme Court of New York, NY, *Jeffrey W. Baird against Raymond Kelly*, Index 101889/03, March 29, 2004.

4

Conformists versus Nonconformists

The view held by psychosocial researchers that a normal individual is one who is well adjusted to societal rules and is as such implicitly conformist, doesn't fully take into account the new rules of normal behavior. While the process of adaptation helps people to function within the parameters of social rules and regulations, there are individuals who ignore or reject many of society's norms of conduct, while still being considered "normal." The true conformist accepts and follows the rules imposed by society even as he grumbles when they negatively affect his sense of fairness or justice, whereas the nonconformist fights them. While the conformist may participate in civilized debate held within the acceptable rules of social protest, the nonconformist demonstrates publicly against them. Any contemplation of open disobedience makes the conformist feel uneasy; any thought of publicly challenging the rules induces discomfort, while the nonconformist doesn't mind attacking and rebelling against them. This doesn't mean that most conformists don't attempt to protect themselves from personal social conflicts either by devious manipulations or in the last resort, by legal action. Even if they question the existing socially imposed conditions and even when they disagree with some aspects of them, they are not inclined to actively disrupt the public order by acts of defiance or outright insurgence as some nonconformists would do in order to try to force social change. The majority of conformists tend to follow the public consensus since it gives them a sense of comfort and security. From a socio-anthropological perspective they have a strong herd instinct. While most of them try to function within the limits of the laws imposed by the establishment even when displeased by them, the slickers attempt to manipulate them in their favor. Though they tend to accept or tolerate their leaders, they become frustrated and complain when there is a flagrant discrepancy between the leader's political promises and actions. The imposed policies are viewed as detrimental to them, and blatantly incompatible with the platform on which they were elected.

And here starts a serious problem for many conformists faced with new social and moral laws enacted in accord with the changing political and social landscape. While most conformists don't feel at ease to attack these laws which are seen as violations of their social rights at public demonstrations, other, less conventional conformists attempt in various ways to resist by arousing the public awareness from writing against them in the press, bloggers, etc to challenging in the courts what they think to be arbitrary if not unconstitutional.

In fact, under adverse sociopolitical conditions, even those conformists regarded by society as responsible, reliable, and law-abiding citizens, and who customarily subscribe to the social order decreed fit by authority, will not accommodate a government which they perceive as prejudicial to their rights. New official policies related to jobs and education or affecting their standard of living and well-being create discontent and resentment, unless they succeed in reorganizing their lives outside of the discriminatory rules. Nevertheless, this forced redirection of their lives is not easily achieved emotionally or socially. The dilemma for the conformist is a very trying one: To submit to the government policies often might result in a heavy emotional and social price; to oppose it, it would require reorienting their thinking and life to a different conceptual framework in order to deal with it. The individuals who bitterly try to comply with the perceived injustices of the government, particularly concerning their livelihood, try to survive by pretending to conform while attempting to manipulate their environment. There are other conformists, who are more opportunistic and switch their allegiance to the political-social trend trying to take advantage of the benefits offered by outright support of government policies.

Nevertheless, some conformists prefer to discard their mask of conformity. They refuse to accept in varying degrees, the disingenuous policies of the government and protest, changing their position from conformity to outright dissidence. Some move to the other extreme of nonconformity and become staunch opponents of the government. Are they still normal by the psychosocial criteria of well-adjustment?

The Eccentrics

There are various shades of nonconformism. There are nonconformists who while functioning more or less within the parameters of the law, exhibit behaviors that don't follow the standards of the community. Known as eccentrics, they take liberties with fashion by dressing extravagantly to attract attention, or behaving in an unconventional manner or organizing their personal life in an unusual style that put its imprint on their social interaction.

A celebrated case was that of Greta Garbo who retired from her successful Hollywood career at the age of thirty-six to live a reclusive life shunning limelight or publicity, until her death. Her new mysterious style of life, surrounded only by a few female friends and occasional walks in the city, was baffling to the press and public.

Another more recent case reported by the media was that of Huguette Clark, the heiress to a mining fortune, who left behind a $400 million estate, but lived the last twenty-three years of her life as a recluse in a secluded apartment on a floor of a New York Hospital. This was even though she was in relatively good health until her death at the age of 104. For seventy-five years, she shunned opulence and led a life of self-induced isolation under an assumed name. For decades, she didn't visit her multimillion-dollar properties in California and Connecticut. Anyone who wanted to visit her, even former friends or relatives, was refused entrance or direct communication. Her only companions were her private nurse and her collection of French dolls. Her lawyer could speak to her only from behind a closed door. Withdrawn into her own constricted and protected world she preferred to play with her dolls and watched cartoons on television.[1]

Was she acting as a normal conformist? Apparently, the authorities thought so, but psychologically, her infantile behavior indicates that she probably had serious emotional handicaps, which she managed to conceal from the world at large by building a buffer of wealth. Her case is similar to another famous reclusive millionaire, Howard Hughes. After his death, it was revealed to the world that he suffered from a severe obsessive-compulsive disorder mixed with traits of paranoia.[2]

Other eccentrics are fully integrated into society while still displaying benign odd behaviors. They are undeterred by society's criticism of their comportment or convictions. Many well-educated and intelligent people have displayed behaviors defying the conventions of the society. In fact, eccentricity has been associated with creativity and originality and eccentrics are viewed (often with admiration) as being fearless and unconcerned about public opinion. An amusing anecdote about Albert Einstein relates that he was seen picking up discarded cigarette butts off the street, allegedly because his doctor had forbidden him to smoke his pipe![3]

There are countless such examples of unconventional behaviors by both the famous and not-so-famous people.

However, there are eccentrics who deliberately pursue behaviors or express beliefs that are different from those around them to attract attention and gain recognition. Under the shield of eccentricity, many young women dress themselves in a provocative manner by revealing as much as possible of their bodies to attract attention, but not always to their intended benefit. Recently, the police in Brooklyn, New York, was forced to tell women walking on a street close to a park to cover up because of a string of sexual assaults on women after dark. The attacker(s) apparently targeted women wearing short skirts.[4]

The Hobos and Hippies

There are other nonconformists who have difficulty holding regular jobs, observing the internal regulations of the company, meeting deadlines, or taking orders from bosses who they don't respect in principle. They are more than simple eccentrics, because they have difficulty functioning properly in society. They are only marginally functional. However, there is another group who, in addition to functioning marginally, go one step further by attacking the sociopolitical structure of society and acting as extremists. Let us see where do they stand vis-à-vis the concept of normalcy.

This group consists of two loosely defined variants of nonconformists, the hobos, who are viewed as social outcasts, and the hippies who display a mixture of eccentric behavior, unconventional appearance and prefer to live on welfare, abuse street drugs and boast a mild brand of unpredictable extremism by rejecting conventional values. They are in a way the vestiges of a subculture that emerged as a by-product of the social-cultural revolution of the sixties. These people live a life free of most societal constraints while taking advantage of the state welfare systems. One may regard them as social freeloaders, footloose and fancy-free, who justify their style of life by criticizing and ridiculing the societal organization. Are they just marginally adapted to society because of their unwillingness to fully integrate in the community and as such a burden to it, or are they, by and large, psychiatric cases who suffer from relatively minor to moderate personality disorders that contribute to their dysfunctional life? Should hippies be regarded as a subgroup of marginally normal people, or people presenting a mixed bag of mild personality disorders who are not interested or refuse to treat their psychological conditions even when treatment is offered? From the legal point of view their widespread use of street drugs automatically makes them breakers of the law. By the same token, because they live off various forms of social assistance, it could be assumed that they either have physical or emotional conditions that preclude their ability to hold down a job or that they are cheats claiming fictitious disabilities. While they would like to think of themselves as regular people who detest authority and who show it by their acts of social noncooperation and by their sustained protest against societal hypocrisy and inequities, the reality is that it is a ruse to cover up their social failure. Their unrealistic aspirations of achieving significant levels of social recognition are apparently subverted by their personality problems resulting in their negative social reactions. Frustrated, but unable to accept their limited capabilities, they attack society as directly or indirectly responsible for their unfulfilled life. Reluctant to settle for a life viewed by them as drudgery, they pretend to pursue their so-called creative activities while resorting to abuse of the social system which helps them to survive under the most beneficial conditions.

A large number of them give the impression that they are aspiring writers working on blockbuster novels or screen plays, or would-be actors or actresses, social activists, reformers, film or video makers, or even spiritualists! Interestingly, their careers are perpetually in the making. They are merely waiting for the "big break." Their present situation is "transient" and it justifies the dutiful filing of papers for receiving social assistance, food stamps, or other forms of financial help. Yet, they don't see this public assistance as contradictory to their contempt for the social system that feeds them. Their attitude of bravado and nonconformism is more of an outright opportunism.

After examining these variations in nonconformist styles of behavior and life, the customary understanding of well-adjusted-normalcy has become quite vague and ill-defined, mixed in varying degrees with marginal abnormal behavior. Nonconformism represents a poorly defined mode of interaction in society which comprises the odd behavior of the eccentric, the inappropriate and annoying social actions of the hippies, and the controversial category of the violent actions of radicals or dedicated extremists.[5]

The issue that is hotly debated today is whether the radicals and the terrorists could be considered normal, a special subgroup of "militant-normals "people or according to some psychologists, outright criminals.

To a large extent it depends on the definition and interpretation of their activity within context of their ideological goals.

The Ambiguous Conformity of Religious Radicals, Political Extremists, and Terrorists

The radical extremists embrace various social, political, or religious causes, and all share in common the drive to convert others to their religious beliefs or political ideology with the final goal to control them and society. All of them proclaim in their rhetoric to know the magic formula that would improve or advance the life of people and the means to build a better world if only people followed their religious or political prescriptions.

The religious extremists try feverishly to promote their brand of religious belief as the true message of God. They combine exhortations with veiled threats of celestial retribution, particularly in their pursuit of proselytism. Most religious extremists attempt to work more or less within the framework of social legality, although some of them resort from time to time to murder, arson, or bombing that target facilities which operate contrary to their beliefs and interpretations of the Holy Scriptures. The attacks on and destruction of abortion clinics are well known. These religious extremists tend to think that their actions were inspired by God and they were implementing the divine order as expressed in their religious precepts. Yet, nonconformist as they are when relating to society, they are highly conformist within their religious sect-entities.

On the other hand, political extremists are determined to change the structure of society at any price by switching quickly from rhetoric to various modes of coercion, including torture, assassination or other acts of physical violence. Most political extremists believe that social change should come about through violent acts that would induce fear in the population and force it to accede to their demands of taking over and restructuring society according to their ideology. They dedicate their lives to the calculated destruction of the existing social order by using terrorist acts. Could terrorists be considered normal or because they commit antisocial acts, we have to assume that they have disturbed personalities?

Some social researchers have separated those who used antisocial methods as part of the fight for the independence of their countries as being normal. A psychiatrist in Belfast who worked with IRA terrorists described them as "fairly normal individuals" who regarded themselves as freedom fighters. A psychologist later supported this finding by stating that there was "no psychological evidence that terrorists are diagnosably psychopathic or otherwise clinically disturbed."[6] The Sinn Fein/IRA movement and the former Stern (Lehi) and Irgun Israeli Groups were included in this category. As a matter of fact, the IRA negotiated the peace treaty for Northern Ireland with the British in 1998 and became part of the leadership of the country. An IRA's splinter group didn't accept the peace settlement and has continued sporadically to kill British policemen or place bombs in government buildings.

Talking about the Lehi group, among other acts of terrorism, it was responsible for the assassination in 1948 of Lord Moyne, the resident British minister in the Middle East and of Count Folke Bernadotte, the United Nations mediator. The Israeli Government declared the organization a terrorist group but also instituted a military decoration named the Lehi ribbon. Later, one of the Lehi leaders, Yitzhak Shamir, became Prime Minister of Israel in 1983.

A special case is that of Joschka Fischer, foreign minister of Germany in 2003. He was the leader of the Greens Party, a leftist and a sympathizer of the revolutionary Red Army Faction. In 1976, he participated in a street demonstration in Frankfurt when he was arrested but not charged. He had a close friend who was put on trial in 2001 as an underground soldier of the revolutionary cell and at whose trial he testified.[7]

Not the same attitude is held toward the terrorists of the Gaza strip, Hamas, the Islamic Resistance Movement. Hamas is viewed by the US as a terrorist organization that controls the local government. Likewise Hizbollah in Lebanon, another political organization attacking Israel is now part of the government. In the same category are included FARC, the Revolutionary Armed Forces of Colombia considered a terrorist organization and LTTE, the Liberation Tigers of Tamil-Eelam that assassinated a former prime minister of India, a president of Sri Lanka and a former prime minister in Colombo. The LTTE was fighting for the independence of the Tamil-majority provinces in Sri Lanka.

A terrorist organization in Japan, Aum Shinrikyo, representing a cult, was responsible for the sarin gas attack in the Tokyo subway. It is considered as a special terrorist organization, the first one to use a weapon of mass destruction.

But the most powerful terrorist politico-religious organization is Al-Qaeda. It indisputably meets all the criteria for terrorism using extreme violence to reach its goals of restoring the power of the Muslim fundamentalists throughout the Arab world and the weakening or defeat of the USA and its allies. Al-Qaeda has many affiliates worldwide. It tenaciously pursues a policy of attacking the interests of America and its allies after 9/11. Was Bin Laden, the architect of this vast terrorist organization, a businessman from a rich family close to the Saudi Arabian ruling class, abnormal because he didn't go by the acceptable rules of society? Bin Laden was a religious-political radical, a Muslim fanatic turned against his country and the Western world, fighting for his religious and political utopist ideals with all weapons of unconventional warfare available to him. He was convinced of the righteousness of his cause, regardless of how illusory it might have seemed to others. Do his beliefs and actions show that he was mentally ill? Judged by his terrorist actions, his antisocial one can say that he was a ruthless revolutionary and a fanatic religious extremist.

From the psychological point of view, what might strike an observer as strange is the fact that some terrorists have been treated as normal, "respectable" citizens fully accepted by their societies and by and large by the international community, while others have been branded as ruthless criminals. It seems that the ones who succeeded into reaching a position of legitimate power in their countries after the fall of the old regime have become respectable and are accepted as part of the political-social process.

In this context, the terrorists appear to be radicals who defy the established order and resort to criminal acts ranging from murder of those who oppose them to destruction of government properties. Once they come to power, their previously rejected cause automatically gets legitimacy making them not only normal but also visionaries! After they impose the new social order and have liquidated everyone who opposed them from the old regime, the ones who still resist are either ostracized or their antigovernmental actions win them the badge of "terrorists." Life has come full circle!

A famous example of a revolutionary bandit-terrorist-turned-chief of state and statesman is Joseph Stalin. In June 1907, Stalin masterminded and organized the biggest bank robbery of the time in Tblisi, Georgia, with a gang of twenty comrades. It was an armed attack on a stagecoach carrying around 275,000 rubles (about $3.5 million in today's money). About forty people died in the battle between the thieves and the police. It made international headlines and except for knowing that it was the work of revolutionaries, no one was caught.

Most of the money was gradually taken out of the country to help Lenin and other revolutionaries to carry out their political work. Because the needle of suspicion pointed to Stalin, he left town two days later for Baku and didn't return again to Tblisi.

He continued to fund the revolution with other acts of robbery like the attack on September 1907 on the steamship *Tsarevich Giorgi* which was on its way from Odessa to Batumi. He and his twenty-five comrades-pirates, armed with guns and grenades, took over the ship when it reached Cape Kodori and left after they bagged about 16,000 rubles for the cause of revolution. Nobody was hurt and they left on a lifeboat taken from the steamship.

After committing other criminal acts in the name of revolution, Stalin became the main financier of the Russian Bolshevik Center. Stalin, the admired Georgian poet, the would-be-priest, the extremist revolutionary, the bandit-pirate, the executioner of suspected enemies, became the feared "Red Tzar" of the Soviet Union. History condemns him as paranoid because of the large-scale liquidation of all his real or imagined political enemies. The total number of people murdered by his secret police, the NKVD, on his orders, was around 1.5 million. But it was he, together with Winston Churchill and Franklin Delano Roosevelt who decided the fate of the world at Yalta in 1945. So much about questioning the fine line between terrorism and normal behavior.[8]

One might then say that a terrorist from a psychological and legal point of view is a normal individual who defies the existent social order because he is convinced of the rightfulness of his political or religious doctrine. At the same time, he rejects any democratic form of protest as powerless and ineffective. The only option for winning against or at least revenging himself on the prevailing social order, from his social-political perspective is to disrupt and disorganize the functioning of society by inducing fear and terror. In reality, most of the terrorists embrace an antigovernmental, antisocial doctrine as a vehicle to vent their dislike or hate for the social system which they see as unfair and prejudicial to their life or the minority class to which they belong.

Theories about a Terrorist's Personality

It is assumed that the fuel sparking terrorist actions is the need to redress the social imbalance or for the more radically inclined ones, the need to avenge the social inequities and alleged personal abuses of the authorities. But these social conditions, when they do exist, are supposed to be experienced by the whole minority that should also harbor feelings of hatred and vengeance. Then why is it that only a small fraction of that minority turns to terrorism? It means that the hatred-revenge hypothesis doesn't fully explain the range of motivations leading to terrorist acts.

A variant hypothesis is what has been called "negative identity," inspired from Erickson's psychodynamic formulation of the damaged self-concept and assumed to be embraced by the potential terrorist. It claims that the motivation of the terrorist is his alleged inability to attain a highly desirable social role. It was further elaborated by Jeanne Knutson, who postulated that an individual with a damaged self-concept induced by a failure to meet his social aspirations because of what he perceives as social oppression, channels his feelings of rage and helplessness toward revenge and annihilation of the oppressors. In reality, this hypothesis, a variant of the frustration-aggression theory, has very limited clinical applicability since it could at best be applied to a small number of uneducated, unemployed, impoverished people from a ghetto or refugee camp that lack a social identity. It can't be generalized to all terrorists.[9]

Another speculative variant of the damaged self-concept theory is that of narcissism-aggression. Put forward by Jerrold Post and John Crayton, this theory allegedly applies to narcissistic individuals with grandiose egos, sociopathic traits, and poor reality testing who vent their rage and feelings of helplessness.[10,11] This hypothesis fails to explain the motivation of hijackers and suicide bombers who commit acts of terrorism paid with their life for satisfying the political goals of their organizations.

However, other researchers like Martha Crenshaw or Maxwell Taylor concluded based on her studies that "the outstanding common characteristic of terrorists is their normality."[12,13]

Furthermore, we know by now that many terrorists have belonged to middle-class families or themselves were professional people like doctors, engineers, businessmen, and so forth who neither had an oppressed social upbringing nor experienced a sense of inadequacy or weakness. Familiarizing ourselves with the process of how someone becomes a terrorist might help to understand how the selection of potential terrorists is made by the terrorist group or organization.[14]

What are the desirable qualities that recruiters of a terrorist group or organization look for in a potential terrorist? It starts ideologically with the commitment of the candidate to the cause espoused by the group of destruction of the existing political and social system by whatever means are available. Psychologically, a recruit should be possessed with rage at the alleged injustices experienced by him or his perceived minority class. In fact, these two conditions are not enough; it could make him at best a radical activist. To become a terrorist, a personality with a particular mindset is required that motivates him to commit violent antisocial acts. The consensus among researchers is that the personality profile that forms the terrorist mindset varies widely from one case to the other.

For example, one group is represented by people alienated from society who might have some traits close to borderline personality. They have little education and see a bleak future ahead of them without any prospects for betterment, in a society they perceive as rejecting and oppressing them. Joining a terrorist group gives them a reason for their social existence and a sense of contribution to a worthy cause. They may have started as sympathizers or initially joined thinking it was a social support or religious group, but unbeknown to them, the group was actually feeding candidates to a terrorist organization. They end up as followers, or foot soldiers of the organization, the ones who ultimately execute orders according to the group's terrorist agenda to prove they are worthy of its acceptance.

Another group of the more educated ones might become motivated after being politically and/or religiously indoctrinated with the idea of liquidation of the present social system which is projected as the source of oppression of their ethnic group or religious sect. Furthermore, from a marginal social position of nonrecognition by their powerful "oppressors" (their country's government), suddenly, as part of the terrorist group, they are catapulted to national importance! The government acknowledges them by responding to their actions of violence, murder, reign of terror and destruction of property. In this twisted context, they do believe that their method of terror will bring down the societal system and they justify their antisocial acts as being fair and legitimate.

Taking their enemy down with them in the name of a noble cause is a sacred duty of any enlightened "holy terrorist warrior." For these self-sacrificing soldiers to die in this "holy war" is an act of martyrdom bestowing on them the highest patriotic and religious honor, and they are treated as heroes for their acts of ruthless violence. It is immaterial that their religious or political cause is viewed by outsiders as discriminatory, unjustified, unfair or absurd, because for the terrorists it is real and meaningful. After all, didn't the Communist Chinese or the North Vietnamese fight wars of liberation in their countries which were considered by their enemies as wrong wars? Didn't their soldiers die willingly for their noble cause even without gaining heroic glory? However in the end their sacrifice proved to be for the right cause.

In this case, the terrorists are the vanguard of a full armed rebellion and die because they want to die for a cause close to their heart, regardless of how convoluted a reason it may seem to others. It has given meaning to their lives, and it has become the reason, the essence of their existence. They wonder whether their enemies can go beyond fancy psychosocial explanations and gauge the true meaning behind the "daring" acts of the Pakistani-English physician-terrorists who sacrificed their careers, family and freedom in their attempt to blow up Glasgow airport.[15]

Certainly, outsiders are more likely to assume the possibility that either they are naive and misguided by the indoctrination of their religious or political leaders or that they labor under the illusion that they are fighting for a brave new world that will never come. These assumptions are no deterrent for the suicide bombers who knowingly die as part of a successful mission which in reality might turn out to be a futile sacrifice made in the pursuit of an illusion, even with regard to their celestial expectations.

Psychology of the Suicide Bomber

The idea circulated by some research psychologists that suicide bombers have depressive traits of personality because of their death seeking behavior is based on the false assumption that only depressed people commit suicide. The suicide bomber's motivation to set the bomb and kill himself seems more likely to be the result of the hate and revenge he feels for the authorities who he sees as perpetrators of oppression and abusers of his ethnic group. From his biased perspective, the only way to ameliorate the group's miserable social status and feelings of impotence in fighting the authorities for his rights is revenge, to get even with them. The encouragement of the terrorist group gives the final push to commit the fatal act. Palestinian and Iraqi suicide bombers have different motives. The Palestinians are fighting the Israelis, while the Iraqis' battle is against the domination of the Shiite sect that came to power after the US removed Saddam Hussein. The common trait of both groups of suicide bombers is their inability to see any future for themselves either because of enemy occupation as in the case of the Palestinians or economic and political deprivation by the majority Shiite group in Iraq.

Some social researchers have tended to label them as fanatics because of their unwillingness to compromise instead of showing hate and contempt for the government or for the dominant and opposing political faction. This intransigence in dealing with the existing state of affairs or inability to accept coexistence with a more powerful opponent pushes them against the wall. The result is the rejection of any compromise or negotiation from a position of weakness that leaves no other alternative except the use of force to inflict casualties on the enemy. In this case suicide bombing becomes a weapon of choice. Many Palestinian suicide bombers have been young women who wanted to avenge a relative or a lover killed by the authorities or to vent their hate against the occupying forces perceived as responsible for their bleak life and future. They believe that they will be compensated in the afterlife with divine rewards. According to Ben Eliezer, ex-Defense Minister of Israel, the Palestinian suicide bombers are motivated by "misery" and "hopelessness." He went on to say that they are "seduced" by terrorist organizations.[16]

Among Muslims, the suicide bombers are seen as martyrs and their bombing act is called *istishad*, which is a religious word meaning "to give one's life in the name of Allah with the reward of entering the eternal Paradise." In contrast, suicide committed because of unbearable personal suffering induced by emotional or physical problems is called *intihar* and is not pardoned by the religion. Then, how could one support the idea that all suicide bombers have disturbed personalities?[17] At best, one may consider the suicide bombers as representing a subgroup of fanatics with their particular standards of twisted values.

While in psychological terms, the word fanatic implies a personality disturbance in view of his violent actions leading to self-destruction, in reality the religious-political fanatic holds to a set of religious and/or political beliefs considered by him as highly noble and honorable that are reinforced by the terrorist group to which he belongs and with whom he totally identifies. This also helps him to reject and fight against his undesirable social condition and being a terrorist gives meaning to his existence. Therefore his mind is closed to any other avenue of evaluating his social condition because any admission that it's possible to change his life using other means, will increase his insecurity and make him more anxious. This focused mindset gives him strength to act coolly and calculatedly in the execution of his irrevocable and ruthless task. Any doubt or any emotional hesitation could compromise his mission and it could lead to a situation worse than death—that of being arrested by authorities. The issue to be debated is not his fanaticism is an expression of his strong adherence to religious / political beliefs, but his readiness to die for them. It presupposes a mental attitude which is disturbing by our present cultural standards. As controversial as this issue might be, the believer's sacrifice of life for a higher cause is well known since antiquity. Didn't the first Christians prefer to die on the cross as Jesus Christ did? Weren't the Japanese pilots ready to die for the Emperor and their country by committing kamikaze? Were they "crazy" or did their religious or cultural milieu make their sacrifices desirable? It reinforced their faith in their religious cult and in the case of the Japanese, their patriotic death was the ultimate act of love for their country, making them national heroes.

The Role of the Group in Terrorist Activity

In the above context, the suicide bombers seem to be the product of a cultural ambience which glorifies suicide for patriotic or religious reasons. Add to it a rigid personality prone to strong convictions and you have the motivation of a suicide bomber. The stressful circumstances of its execution crown the sacrifice with an aura of martyrdom. Furthermore, one has to realize that the terrorist groups are more or less similar in their organization to religious cults, which explains why the terrorist who belongs to a group has to subscribe to its ideological convictions and accept its rigid code of behavior. To act differently, will mean to dissociate himself from the very reason of joining the group. Not to mention that member-terrorists who dare to question the group decisions or ideology or want to drop out for any personal reason expose themselves to very strong retaliations. In reality, the decision to be part of the group is seen by the members as irrevocable. In fact, the terrorists have to submerge their individuality into the collective judgment and behavior of the group as espoused by its leader.

From this point of view, group psychology gives us a better understanding of the motivation and participation of the members in terrorist activities. Certainly, this presupposes that the would-be-members of the group join the group for the pursuit of their personal political and religious needs which are supported by the group. Ultimately, any potential terrorist joins a terrorist group to be able to perpetrate terrorist actions. Conversely, if the terrorist group is inactive, it cannot justify its existence and ceases to exist.

As strange as it may sound, the terrorist, viewed by society as a nonconformist, a dangerous rebel attacking and attempting to destroy the establishment, is in the context of his terrorist affiliation, a conformist. He faithfully follows the rules of conduct of social interaction imposed by the leaders of the organization and dutifully executes any task required for the successful implementation of their cause. There is pressure from the group for conformity promoted by mutual interdependence and trust that forges the cohesiveness of the organization. In a roundabout way, the terrorist switches his allegiance from the existing social order against which he vehemently rebels to join a subversive setup dedicated to the destruction of the existing order where he acts in conformity with the ideological and social norms of this group. Could he then be considered mentally disturbed as some psychologists have suggested?

The Hypothesis of the Mental Illness of the Terrorists

The argument of J. Post, a psychologist, in support of the mental illness hypothesis is that the terrorist might think logically, but that his logic is twisted by his "inner psychological forces" that rationalize his actions. This argument is vague, poorly documented, and unconvincing.[18] According to him, the psychological inner forces are identifiable as representing the inculcation from generation to generation, from father to son of hate as would be the case in Northern Ireland or the Basque country. Post's argument is speculative and unsupported by facts.

Another argument in support of the mental disturbance theory has been the argument about a terrorist's eagerness to accept committing violent acts against civilians. However, the terrorist justifies his attack of civilians by taking responsibility for his criminal act in an attempt not only to advertise his "fair cause" but also to warn the population that by collaborating with the regime they expose themselves to further violent acts from the terrorist group. In this way they try to shift the responsibility for the acts of terror to the victims who didn't do anything to change the present injustice carried out against the cause which the terrorists are fighting for.

The data available amply indicates that terrorists are by and large people drawn from the ordinary population who for emotional or ideological reasons hate the established order that they perceive as corrupt, unfair, and oppressive. In contrast to other people who in various degrees might feel the same way but don't rebel, the terrorists are ready to bring down the existing order by acts of violence. This might raise the question of whether there is a "terrorist personality," ready to commit serious antisocial acts culminating in murders and ultimately death for their cause. Their violent acts indicate their readiness to face the risks of exposure and other unforeseeable and mortal dangers. For them, these risks are the price they are ready to pay for the success of the cause. The outstanding feature of the terrorist as a risk taker is just an expression of his held beliefs which give meaning to his life. The existing psychological evidence indicates that their personality traits vary from individual to individual with the overall assumption of being temperamentally high on(NS) novelty-seeker, low on (HA)harm avoidance and relatively high on(RD) reward dependence. All these hypothetical traits are used to loyally serve the common ideological or religious cause and the terrorist's group conformity, which decides the course of their lives.

The Wide Range of Conformist and Nonconformist Behavior Including Normal Behavior

What is important to realize is that the notions of normal behavior and terrorism while socially poles apart, in reality represent opposite and antagonistic views of society where normal people have different modes of coping or relating to it in order to pursue their aspirations and goals. In this context, take for example the outright antagonism between two individuals: one, an FBI agent and another, a terrorist. The FBI agent is informed about the plans of a twenty-eight-year-old terrorist of Pakistani origin to bomb a New York City subway station during rush hour, one of three coordinated suicide bombings. The FBI agent tried to gather evidence to uncover his plans, while the terrorist, a young high-school educated man fully aware of the risk of being caught, operates as secretively as he can. Both protagonists are logical people fighting for differing political ideologies with all available means to further their cause. Certainly, the FBI agent uses all the legal means at his disposal whereas the terrorist uses all the illegal means of unconventional warfare and pseudolegal ways to achieve his goal. The FBI, relying on tips from its network of informers was able to identify the terrorist, monitor him and before he could act on his plan to explode the device at a subway station, to arrest him. During his interrogation, the terrorist took responsibility for attempting to blow up the subway station, admitted attending an Al-Qaeda training camp in Pakistan and disclosed his connections with three other would-be terrorists with whom he had previously traveled to Pakistan. At the same time, he attacked the American involvement in Pakistan and Afghanistan. The authorities indicted him for possession of explosives to commit mass murder and attempt to destroy public property, among other charges. Obviously, the terrorist lost the battle, although he was able to carry out the plot to almost the final stage of its execution. Has he a significant personality disturbance that will explain his actions, as some alleged experts at terrorism would like to assume?

Analyzing his actions, one might conclude that he was not cautious enough in the pursuit of his fight against the government by purchasing large quantities of chemicals for preparing the explosive. It is also possible that he unwittingly gave some personal data about deliveries of the stuff to the suppliers that made it easier for authorities to track him down. His operation was apparently pursued alone. However, we don't have any evidence to prove that his actions were in any way the work of a disturbed person. Most likely they were dictated by the ideological imperatives to which he heartily subscribed and for which he was ready to risk his life. It is important to note that the antisocial behavior of the terrorist doesn't make him a sociopath. And this brings us to the variety of profiles developed by some clinicians to identify nuances of personality traits among the special subgroup of antisocials, the "political assassins."

The Question of Social Functioning of the Political Assassins

The concept of "normal behavior" in terms of conformity-nonconformity becomes even more controversial when applied to political assassins. For example, Lee Harvey Oswald shot and fatally wounded J. F. Kennedy in 1963 in Dallas, Texas. The story is well known and the reason for the assassination seems to have been political. The evidence which we have is mostly circumstantial and the information about Oswald's personality is incomplete. We know that he was a leftist, had been for a couple of years in the Soviet Union, but when dissatisfied with his life there he came back to the US and married a Russian woman. Here, he drifted from place to place holding various low-level jobs, trying unsuccessfully to get a visa from Mexico in order to go back to Russia. He finally ended up with a small job in Dallas, at the Texas School Book Depository from where he shot the president.

What we know is that he didn't have a history of mental illness and he carefully planned the assassination. Obviously, the planning of the shooting was rationally done and he thought carefully about escaping without leaving traces after assassination so as to avoid the consequences of his crime. We don't have a clear picture about what he wanted to achieve by killing the president. He wasn't either a radical communist or a fanatic anarchist that would justify his action, regardless of his rambling dissatisfaction with the capitalist system. His assassination by Jack Rubin complicated even more the finding of motives for his act. All in all, the evidence suggests that he functioned within relatively normal social limits, though his life story showed some traits of personality disturbance suggesting the possibility of a borderline personality disorder with mild paranoia.

A different picture emerges about John Hinckley Jr. who attempted to assassinate President Ronald Reagan. His motive was clearly stated by him, that is, to impress the actress Jodie Foster with whom he was infatuated for years and who persistently rejected his advances. He relentlessly stalked her, sending numerous letters, enrolling himself at Yale University to be able to meet her, but only succeeding in talking with her a couple of times without any success in convincing her to date him. Hinckley Jr. who identified himself with Bickle, the main character of the movie *Taxi Driver* where the protagonist attempted to assassinate a senator, believed in a twisted manner that his act of shooting the president would make him a national figure and put him on par with Foster. His past history showed a young reclusive man with poor social skills, unable to pursue a college degree or to stick to a job, and who was getting progressively more frustrated and depressed. Certainly, his thinking was unrealistic, pursuing magical solutions, triggered by his impulsive and destructive actions that suggest a socially maladapted individual. He finally snapped when he lost the emotional and financial support of his family and couldn't cope any more with the stress of his unsolved serious emotional problems. Hinckley was found by a jury nonguilty by reason of insanity.[19]

This brief comparison of two people committing similar acts of murder or attempted murder show that the distinction between a relatively normal and fairly abnormal personality is a question of evaluating the degree of social adjustment: It was marginal for Oswald and full maladjusted for Hinckley as interpreted by the standards of the community. Could Oswald's actions be considered within normal range as compared to that of Hinckley Jr.? In fact, both had a twisted perception of reality and various degrees of personality problems expressed in different contexts.

Using the same criteria how would one categorize the behavior of the famous terrorist Ilich Ramirez Sanchez, a.k.a. "Carlos the Jackal" famous in the seventies for his bombing attacks that killed eleven people and who is incarcerated in France? He still considers himself a professional revolutionary. Is he a rebel nonconformist or an outright sociopath?[20] There is another category of normal-nonconformists whose actions are considered, in general, to be criminal behavior.

The Imposter as Nonconformist Acting in a Conformist Manner

The imposter is a person who adopts a different social identity while his personality remains unchanged. Most often they fraudulently identify themselves with a career, an expertise for which they don't have professional qualifications. The skillful imposter misrepresents himself as being someone he is not. The gamut of misrepresentations varies according to their goals. There are the thieves of other people's personal identities which they use in phony financial transactions to get money for themselves by pretending to be the impersonated person. Others are con artists who temporarily impersonate a legitimate profession or person in order to get credibility and authority to execute their fraudulent scheme. And there are true imposters who fabricate for themselves a new identity and profession which represent their new community identity and status until they are caught. They try to play highly lucrative social roles as lawyers, physicians, financial consultants, psychologists, and so forth, as if they possess the necessary degrees and knowledge. In general, these people are smart, intelligent, creative, audacious, and clever. They are the risk takers and looking for immediate reward satisfaction, who function well within the boundaries of the impersonated profession without committing any social infraction, except that unknown to the community, their social adjustment is a fraud.

One of the most unusual cases is that of Ferdinand W. Demara, a phony Canadian surgeon who operated during the Korean War. What was remarkable about this imposter was his success in treating Korean War casualties such as serious physical trauma related to the combat action, which required difficult surgical intervention. He was able to perform complicated operations, sometimes extracting bullets lodged near vital organs, without having acquired any formal surgical training. Before this activity, he successfully impersonated other professions. Regardless of his unusual skills, legally he was a fraud. He admitted in his own biography to being a brilliant liar.[21] As a departure from most imposters, he showed by the nature of the profession that he chose to masquerade in, a compassion and a desire to help people. When he was caught, in recognition of his outstanding medical work and services to the country, he wasn't prosecuted but summarily discharged from the army.

What is fascinating about many imposters viewed as "normals" by the community until caught practicing a profession without valid credentials, is the fact that they use their above-average intelligence and skills to fabricate or steal a professional identity instead of applying themselves to get it on their own merit through legal channels. The psychological hypothesis is that they are narcissistic people who don't have the perseverance and discipline, and who become easily frustrated by the regimentation in schools and colleges. Unable to deal with these irritating conditions, they prefer to freelance in any career they can dream of. They are also audacious, adventurous, and imaginative in creating ways of representing any chosen career like actors on the stage with the difference that the stage is the real world. They play a risky game and they rely on their cleverness to overcome issues of credibility and legality or to rescue them from any tight spot created by their professional activity. Their unbounded confidence plays a crucial role in creating a veneer of professionalism.

There are other imposters who take on a different identity to infiltrate illegally a foreign business or government agency. The live under an assumed identity in a foreign country, and they are a genre of imposters known as spies. There is the famous case of the Soviet spy, Colonel Rudolph I. Abel of the Commissariat for Internal Affairs who lived in Brooklyn, New York from 1948 to 1957, when he was caught posing as a photographer while in charge of the Russian spy network in the USA.[22]

More recently a network of seven "dormant" Russian spies living in the USA under assumed identities and holding regular jobs, married, and so forth was unearthed. The most famous was Anna Chapman, a young attractive Russian whose job was to try to extract information from her highly placed American boyfriends.[23]

There are other alleged normal people who secretly live a double-life, one very conformist and another one nonconformist if not illegal. Take for instance the case of "Deep Throat," who supplied information to an investigative reporter that contributed greatly to the downfall of President Nixon. What is shocking about him is the fact that he was an enforcer of law and order as Deputy Director of FBI, the ultimate conformist, who was giving official information about Nixon in order to bring him down. What was the real reason for this objectionable and inappropriate activity by a high-ranking FBI officer? It was an act of vengeance for not being appointed Director of FBI after the death of Edgar Hoover. Certainly, if he wanted to act properly according to the regulations of his job, and not to violate the oath to keep the nation's secrets, he could have gone with his information to the grand jury and not leak it to the press. Well, by our social standards, he was a model of normal behavior until it was proven otherwise.[24]

The Overlapping of "Normal Behavior" with Personality Disorders Thereby Distorting Conformity

A popular presentation of various "normal" personality profiles which has followed quite closely the DSM-IV personality disorders of the APA is that of Oldham and Morris.[25] As the authors emphasize, normalcy represents one end of the behavioral spectrum identified by a constellation of adaptive traits of personality, while the other end of this linear projection indicates distinctly deviant behavior representing various degrees of poor or maladjustment "from the expectations of the individual's culture," considered to belong to psychopathology.

It means that the same traits of personality could function within the socially acceptable range and be part of the alleged normal personality or if twisted or suppressed under the influence of environmental and genetic factors, could become lasting patterns of deviate behavior that generates serious suffering and impairment of societal functioning. Then, one can say that under strenuous social conditions viewed as stressful and irresolvable, the same traits of personality considered to function within the normal social range, now are out of control. Furthermore, unable to cope with the crisis or to alleviate the pressure of it, the person could reach wrong conclusions about handling the stressful event and adopts inadequate, frustrating solutions that might even interfere with the possibility to adapt to the new conditions created by that event. Under these circumstances the stressful condition doesn't subside, and after a while a deviant coping mode inducing maladaptive behavior sets in. As previously mentioned, under favorable conditions the causative stressful condition could subside and the individual returns to his regular patterns of behavior. He acts more or less again as a conformist.

This notion of flexible, wide range of responses to stressful situations reflecting a relative adjustment seems to be more in line with clinical and social experiences. We can see "normal people" acting in socially objectionable ways under harrowing circumstances which are hard to overcome, switch back to "normal behavior" when the conflict subsided or a favorable solution was found.

The "abnormal" response depends on many psychosocial factors from lack of experience in dealing with adverse situation to the quality of cognitive processes related to a constellation of traits of personality which do overreact when faced with situations considered as damaging. Think of a narcissist who has a high regard of himself and is unexpectedly faced with a critical situation at work or in an intimate relationship where he feels put down, ridiculed, mistreated, or possibly rejected. Confronted with a situation seen as out of his control, he gets upset, and might mishandle the crisis by losing his cool and misbehaving. This could happen when his judgment becomes overloaded emotionally under stress resulting in an inability to find the proper, appropriate response to the conflicting situation. Already distressed, in other situations also perceived as unpleasant, he acts somewhat unsure and tense since he doesn't feel that cocky and self-assured any more. His confidence is shaken and he feels miserable.

With his self-concept shattered, he may find it difficult to regain his high self-reliance, self-esteem and above all self-confidence. However, to succeed in restoring his old self, he has to experience new favorable social circumstances that spur his ability to rationalize the previous failures by blaming others, fueled by a self-deceiving attitude about his unique talents not fully noticeable to others.

Nevertheless, as previously mentioned, there are other people whose overblown or constricted traits of personality are enduring and inflexible, interfering with what is considered a conformist, well-adjusted pattern of behavior. Many people develop inconsistent or inadequate adaptive patterns of personality in their youth in response to specific circumstances of their lives. They are the ones known to their friends and intimate partners as being sensitive to particular issues which if inadvertently mentioned, trigger automatically negative reactions that upset them. With a mindset that is sensitive to specific social stimuli and interactions and a limited capacity to cope, some of them might display social inadequacies or inability to maintain a smooth equitable relationship with their close ones. They are what is popularly known as neurotics, functioning within a framework of ambiguous conformity.

As strange as it may sound, there are people who are able to harmonize their dominant traits of personality considered by cultural standards to be outside the range of normalcy with a specific social function or niche of activity and could become or are outstanding leaders in that particular field. Moreover, the ones that are skillful in manipulating other people within the framework of moral relativism which they practice without any qualms are socially successful. Under a veneer of superficial conformism they cleverly hide their dubious nonconformist actions, also functioning in the twilight zone of an ambiguous conformity. Take for example a successful politician who exudes unlimited confidence about his ability to solve the complex problems of the city, state or nation, convinced of his superiority over the constituents in deciding what it is good and bad for them by showing his unwavering readiness to lead them. Does he question his political aspirations as being fueled by his big ego that tends to dismiss any of his shortcomings as irrelevant for his candidacy to the elected position? To win at any price he tends to be unscrupulous, ready to make dubious political compromises if he thinks that they are advantageous to him even if they go against his previously professed beliefs. Flip-flopping on a hot social-political issue when circumstances change is a basic method of manipulating the electorate. Unabashedly, he will promise whatever the constituents want to hear for gaining the craved power as long as he believes that he can manipulate them later. Is he a social conformist or rather a clever opportunist who skillfully handles the social norms of conduct?

An intriguing example is that of John Edwards, ex-US senator and twice candidate for the presidency of US, but who settled in the 2004 campaign for vice-presidency with John Kerry as running mate for president. However, his second 2008 campaign faltered, when he was charged after an investigation by a grand jury for allegedly using more than $1 million in illegal campaign contributions to cover up expenses incurred in his love affair with a videographer with whom he fathered a child during the campaign. Part of the covering up was done with the help of his former chief aide, who falsely claimed paternity of the child. It was claimed that the campaign money was used to support and seclude his lover and her newborn baby. Two years later he admitted to the paternity of the child, claimed that the money he received from two wealthy supporters were gifts, and that he was unaware that the money had been used to provide a luxurious life to his girlfriend who he wanted protected from the media and public scrutiny. However, at the same time he lied to his wife who was his closest political adviser during the campaign, and who was also struggling with terminal cancer. Ironically, at the same time, he was publicly professing his high moral standards emphasizing his strong faith in God, "Whom he was asking in his prayer for guidance in order to make the right decision." And this man used his populist bait to try to become Vice President by hook or by crook. He was tried and acquitted because it was unclear whether the contributions from his two rich friends were personal gifts or campaign donations. Both friends were dead by then.[26] Before and during the trial, he was considered a slick politician who broke the campaign laws blatantly to satisfy his personal needs. After his acquittal, he again became an upstanding citizen, who functions according to the social rules of moral conduct.

Keep in mind that he hasn't been alone. Many elected or appointed officials get carried away by the power they gain and fancy themselves as above the law by abusing the power of the office and the trust of the constituents and of citizens. The list of congressmen and senators who took bribes from lobbyists and contractors or received excessive campaign donations from corporate executives for favorable business treatment is impressive. No wonder that most politicians are seen as opportunists without any scruples in their quest to pursue or maintain power most often for their own benefit. A great number of them are outright demagogues using the political ideology which they embraced as a ticket for access to power. This explains why when they feel that they can't reach their goals within one party, they switch party allegiance claiming to be either independent or joining the rival party outright. They have total disregard for the members of the party, who voted to put these opportunistic politicians in high office as their representatives. They try to convince the public that their flip-flop actions are perfectly legitimate and morally right, done to serve better the interests of the constituents. It is part of the usual cynical political process. Its questionable legitimacy is an arbitrary consideration, based on the parties' tacit understanding that the switch could be mutually beneficial to the politician and the newly adopted party. The issue of morality is a personal matter left to the constituents to judge. Are their actions normal in conformity with the social expectations? Certainly, by our social standards it is our ambiguous conformity intertwined with moral relativism that makes them "normal" regardless of how unscrupulous their behavior is.

They have company in the world of dishonest corporate executives. An interesting example had been that of a Dunlop, ex-chief executive officer (CEO) of Sunbeam-Oster, who in 1998 organized a massive accounting fraud at the corporation in order to inflate its revenue. He was known as a turnaround specialist, successful in streamlining weak companies. He did it in the past at two other companies, Scott Papers and Crown Zellerbach, and as a result he was known as "Chainsaw Al." For his accounting irregularities he was sued by the Securities Exchange Commission and he settled the charges for $500,000. He was banned from serving as an officer or director of any public company. In 2009, Conde Nast Portfolio named him the sixth worst CEO. What made him run a fraudulent account operation, besides greed? Well, the problem seemed to have been his concern about his reputation of turning around the company which was at stake. He needed a buyer of the company and to get one, he thought that the inflation of revenue will help. He had to save his reputation in the corporate world. His failure was the miscalculation about the massive sale of out-of-season products to retailers which made industry insiders suspicious. And from here onwards it was a debacle. He was a respectable executive, admired by many for his management skills until he tried unsuccessfully to pull a fast one.[27] He was an outstanding skillful executive considered functioning normally in a climate of moral perversity until his blatant fraudulent acts were discovered.

There have been other CEOs who either looted their companies in an organized way like John Rigas, CEO of Adelphia Communication, who together with his son Timothy Rigas as CFO defrauded the cable franchise company of millions of dollars, ending with their conviction for twelve and seventeen years, respectively in prison.

Another high-profile CEO, Dennis Kozlowski of Tyco was sentenced to twenty-five years in prison for spending the company's money lavishly. He was accused of looting tens of millions of dollars of company funds. What is interesting about Kozlowski is the fact that from a humble beginning, he worked his way up to the top of a Fortune 500 company. It seems that his newly gained powerful position overwhelmed him with the "sweet smell of success," distorting his sense of reality and making him act in an extravagant manner like paying $6,000 for a shower curtain or organizing an outlandish birthday party for himself that cost about $1 million.[28] What happened to the common sense, integrity, and responsibility that had helped him to reach the top position? Granted that he had a narcissistic personality, high on self-confidence and risk taking, yet they can't justify his new behavior which was very likely symbolic of bipolar disorder.

Another highly successful hedge-fund manager was Raj Rajaratnam, a Sri Lankan native who started his career at an investment banking boutique, Needham & Co as an analyst in 1985. By 2008 he became a self-made billionaire in charge of the Galleon Group. However in 2009 he ran out of luck when he was arrested for insider trading. In 2011, he was found guilty of conspiracy and security fraud and convicted to eleven years in prison and fined $92.8 million. It is odd considering that this man was featured the previous year as one among the elite US money managers. The common assumption would be that he committed these illegalities because of greed. This is a problematic hypothesis, if one considers that out of $60 million made out of insider trading, theoretically only $12 million before taxes would have been added to his fortune of billions.[29]

Though greed played its role, it seems that his performance as a hedge-fund manager wasn't a fraud, since it wasn't based on regularly receiving tips for buying the right stocks. More likely his transgressions were attempts on his part not only to take advantage of the available profitable situation but also to maintain a high performance. Anyway, he took an unnecessary risk, miscalculated his chances of winning, and ended up paying dearly.

Certainly, there have been other investment bankers who were convicted of insider trading: Hafiz Naseem of Credit Suisse, Zvi Goffe, an ex-Galleon trader and the most famous of all, Sam Waksal of Imclone. All were convicted for security fraud and in all these cases the motive for the fraud apparently was greed. The issue is the extent to which they can be considered "normal-conformists." Based on their pattern of behavior they were acting normally, in a conformist manner in running their companies while nonconformist in their illegal activity, in a way showing duplicity of conformity. They were convicted as white-collar criminals who were having problems of playing by the social rules. In this context the common usage of concept of well-adjustment doesn't quite apply to them, which places them at best in a special category of "pseudo-normal," nonconformists.

If we keep in mind the ambiguity of social conformity, we are confronted with the fact that insider trading has been permitted until now to the members of the Congress. To trade and enrich themselves on inside information obtained in the course of taking actions on various industries or legislating the investment banking business, it has been perfectly legitimate for congressmen. Their insider transactions have been done legally while maintaining the veneer of social conformity, while outsiders using the same information, if detected or caught, have been labeled as criminals. This has been a selective approach to legality only to add to the confusion about the arbitrary sense of proper social adjustment.

The same sense of pseudonormalcy can be found among the social elite of other professions like actors/actresses of Hollywood. For example take the baffling crime of shoplifting committed by the successful Hollywood actress Winona Ryder. What prompted her to try to leave the Saks Fifth Avenue store in Beverly Hill with merchandise worth thousands of dollars without paying for it? She wasn't a professional shoplifter or a poor woman in desperate need of clothes. Was it unadulterated greed that drove her to risk her reputation or a calculated operation that went wrong? She was arrested and convicted to three years' probation. But her career was seriously damaged. She seems to belong to the category of pseudo normals with a volatile approach to conformity. But she is not alone, as there are many others. The case of O. J. Simpson is well known.

An intriguing case is that of actor Robert Blake indicted in 2001 for murdering his wife Bonnie Lee Bakley, who had been previously married ten times. She was shot waiting in their car in a street near a restaurant where they had dinner. He was tried for shooting her, but the evidence was insufficient to convict him, though it was found that he wanted to hire two men to kill her.[30] Anyway, he was sued by her children in the civil court and sentenced to pay $30 million. He declared bankruptcy.

More intriguing is the fact that a great majority of people with tolerable levels of personality disorders are considered to be well-adjusted as long as their symptoms do not seriously interfere with their societal functioning. All these people display various degrees of nonconformist behavior which contribute to their success or failure.

Notes

1. M. Schudel, "Huguette Clark, Copper Heiress and Recluse, Dies at 104," Washington Post.com/local, May 24, 2011.
2. R. Brewster, "The Eccentric Howard Hughes: A Wealth of Madness," Yahoo.com, March 3, 2010.
3. *Wikipedia*, "Eccentricity Behavior," November 5, 2012.
4. J. Schram and L. Calabrese, "Looking for Cover Girls," *New York Post*, October 1, 2011, 12.
5. W. Rasch, "Psychological Dimensions of Political Terrorism in the Federal Republic of Germany," *International Journal of Law and Psychiatry* 2 (1979): 79–85.
6. K. Heskin, "The Psychology of Terrorism in Ireland," in *Terrorism in Ireland*, ed. Y. Alexander and A. O'Day (New York: St. Martin Press, 1984), 88–105.
7. M. Kelly, "A Thug Protests," *New York Post*, February 12, 2003, 23.
8. S. Montefiore, *Young Stalin* (New York: Vintage Books, 2008).

9. J. N. Knutson, "Social and Psychodynamic Pressures toward a Negative Identity," in *Behavioral and Quantum Perspectives on Terrorism*, ed. Y. Alexander and M. W. Gleason (New York: Pergamon, 1981), 105–52.
10. J. Post, "Notes on a Psychodynamic Theory of Terrorist Behavior," *Terrorism: An International Journal* 7, no. 3 (1984): 242–56.
11. J. Crayton, "Terrorism and the Psychology of the Self," in *Perspectives on Terrorism*, ed. L. Z. Freedman and Y. Alexander (Wilmington, DE: Scholarly Resources, 1983), 33–41.
12. M. Crenshaw, "The Causes of Terrorism," *Comparative Politics* 13 (July 1981): 370–99.
13. M. Taylor and E. Quale, *Terrorist Lives* (London: Brasssy, 1994).
14. Ibid.
15. *Wikipedia*, "2007 Glasgow International Airport," August 27, 2012.
16. "Israel Admits Bombes Motivated by 'Misery,'" *The Times of India*, June 21, 2002.
17. M. Taylor and E. Quale, *Terrorist Lives* (London: Brasssy, 1994).
18. J. Post, "Notes on a Psychodynamic Theory of Terrorist Behavior," *Terrorism: An International Journal* 7, no. 3 (1984): 242–56.
19. K. Collins, G. Hinkebein, and S. Schorgl, "The John Hinckley Trial: Key Figures," http://law.umkc.edu/faculty/projects/trials/hinckleyinsanity.htm (accessed November 9, 2011).
20. BBCNEWS, "Carlos the Jackal Faces New French Bomb Attack Trial," http://www.bbc.co.uk/news/world (accessed November 7, 2011).
21. R. Crichton, *The Rascal and the Road* (New York: Random House, 1961).
22. N. Polomar and T. B. Allen, *The Encyclopedia of Espionage* (New York: Gramercy Books, 1977), 3.
23. P. Thomas, J. Cloherty, and J. Ryan, "How FBI Busted Anna Chapman and the Russian Spy Ring," *ABC News*, November 1, 2011.
24. Associated Press, "Ex-FBI Official: I'm Deep Throat," NBC news.com, June 1, 2005.
25. David Kuo, "John Edwards: My Faith Came Roaring Back," www.beliefnet.com/News/Politics (accessed March 12, 2007).
26. Ibid.
27. J. A. Byrne, *Chainsaw: The Notorious Career of Al Dunlap in the Era of Profit-at-Any-Price* (New York: Harper Business, 1999).
28. K. Crawford, "Ex-Tyco CEO Kozlowski Found Guilty," *CNN Money*, June 21, 2005.
29. N. Popper, "Galleon Hedge Fund Billionaire Raj Rajaratnam Found Guilty of Insider Trading," *Los Angeles Times*, May 11, 2011.
30. G. Cadorette, "Robert Blake Acquitted of Murder," Hollywood.com, March 5, 2005.

5

The "Normal" Psychopath

> By right means, if you can,
> but by any means make money
> Horace, Epistles I i 66
> All these elite citizens

Part I
The "Normal" Psychopath ... Master of Duplicity
They are intelligent, friendly people who can make a decent living without boldly deceiving others by hatching sophisticated fraudulent schemes. Most of them take advantage of the lax social-moral climate by using their professional or business expertise as a launching pad for their financial scams. Since our ambiguous mores convey an air of relative neglect toward unlawful nonviolent behavior as a by-product of the significant social and political changes, such people sense it as an opportunity for making easy money by cheating and swindling. They seem to come out in droves to take their chances for scheming, as long as they perceive their operations relatively defensible in the court of law or, more likely, hard to detect. The temptation of taking advantage of these special situations has been too great to let them go. These people have been driven among other motives, by greed and thirst for power that brings admiration and respect.

These nonconformist-opportunist crooks also get emotional satisfaction by proving that they are cleverer than others. However, they are remorseless because they justify their deceptions as provoked by unusual circumstances which compelled them to do such acts.

Let us take, for example, the business of Wall Street that most often has fostered a culture of corruption and deception. Its business flourished to a great extent due to the deceptive practices of many investment bankers, brokers, and stock analysts; all of them competing for a quick enrichment. The game played by these rogues has been simple: they have deftly advertised themselves as market experts while unscrupulously cheating the investors who naively believed that they were protected by what amounted to be loose or nonenforced securities laws. These stock market operators belong to a special category of "respectable" opportunistic fraudsters who display identifiable psychopathic traits. As a matter of fact, a British professor, Clive Boddy, in his recent article in the *Journal of Business Ethics* came to the conclusion that Wall Street corporate psychopaths have had a major role in bringing the financial meltdown of 2008.[1] Another recent article estimates that about 10 percent of the Wall Street employees are definitely psychopaths.[2] What does it mean to have psychopathic tendencies or to be an outright psychopath?

Robert Hare, a psychologist, describes specific traits of personality of such devious people.[3] Among the outstanding attributes are a display of an exaggerated sense of self-worth, shallow affect, irresponsibility, impulsivity, pathological lying, conning, phony charm, and lack of remorse and empathy. Some of these traits like narcissism, lying, conning, or callousness are more ominous than others. However, it doesn't mean that there are no nuances and degrees of exhibiting these attributes which make many of them appear to act within the range of what is considered normal behavior until their criminal acts are discovered.

Considering these facts, one should not be surprised if his new neighbor, the Wall Street investment manager or advisor who wears expensive suits, drives a luxury car or owns luxurious homes in the Hamptons is a successful fraudster with a psychopathic-tainted personality passing for what we loosely call normal.

How many of the hefty bonuses paid yearly to investment bankers or managers by Wall Street firms are not indirect compensations for pushing dubious stocks or risky investments? Not too long ago, the Securities and Exchange Commission and the New York State attorney general investigated the stock market practices of the analysts at Merrill Lynch, Solomon Smith Barney, or Credit Swiss First Boston that amply proved their deceitful practices of misrepresenting the true value of the analyzed stocks. The analysts' cynical attitude toward clients by recommending them stocks at inflated values which they privately ridiculed is unconscionable.[4]

The best testimony to this state of affairs is offered by the recent letter of resignation of Greg Smith, an executive director at Goldman Sachs, the largest investment house in Wall Street, who accused the chief executive officer (CEO) Loyd Blankfein and the President Gary Cohen of promoting a "toxic and destructive" culture of ripping off clients. He wrote: "The interests of the client continue to be sidelined in the way the firm operates and thinks about making money." As a matter of fact, Goldman Sachs was sued by a German bank for misrepresenting the value of a collateralized security. The company settled for $550 million.[5]

The bottom line is that the new ethical ambivalence toward lying, cheating, and other types of manipulations of truth has favored the proliferation of charlatans, truth spinners, or self-righteous liars. Amazingly, since lying and cheating have been subtly blended in the process of social or business transactions, the clever deceivers who are able to convey credibility and integrity have reached social position of prominence. Most often, these liars when exposed had shown either no shame and remorse or hypocritically and perfunctorily had expressed regrets to incur the favor of the court for a lighter sentence. Not unusually, some of them had justified their dishonest actions as part of the new ways of helping business to grow or to compete in a crowded market. Inasmuch as this ambiguous ethics tend to blur the distinction between right and wrong, it has helped people with the unscrupulous and greedy proclivities to operate their devious schemes with impunity.

These persons, who, by and large, successfully manipulate the truth, abuse, and cheat others, always flash self-assurance and a self-righteous air of honesty. Although they usually try to stretch the interpretation of the law or at least to operate within the confines of its loopholes, if caught, they do not always succeed to beat the rap. Cynical, ambitious, and confident, these social climbers use imaginative but dubious scams to advance or maintain their status by trying to beat the system. Most of them believe that they have found the right formula to get away with murder. These sanctimonious people, psychopathically bent, succeed for a while to give the public a feel of respectability by apparently giving the false impression of socially functioning within the acceptable framework of society.

Take Frank Gruttadauria, a star stockbroker, the manager of a now defunct Lehman Brothers branch office in Cleveland, Ohio, and a man-about-town. He lived a high life, belonged to the most exclusive clubs, co-owned a jet, and was a friend of prominent businessmen and politicians, until one day, in January 2002, he vanished. Unfortunately, along with his disappearing act, tens of millions of dollars went missing

The Mask of Normalcy

from the accounts of his clients who trusted him with their fortune or life savings. His swindles, practiced for a long time at different firms where he worked, were carried out by selectively falsifying the monthly statements of a few accounts of either rich clients or the ones who seemed neglectful in reading them. It worked as long as it was a bull market. Gruttadauria was an example of a successful investment advisor, loved by his clients, and respected by the community.[6] When he was arrested, he justified his actions by claiming that he had the intention to put the money back into the accounts but the bear market conditions made it impossible. He was superficially remorseful, but without a true empathy for the distress caused to others. In short, he exhibited traits of a psychopathic organization of personality, seemingly successfully integrated for a while in society.

Another good example of Wall Street operation by misrepresentation is the systematic manipulation of the investors by the alleged proper businessmen who omit, twist, and misstate facts within the area of their specialized work. This has been to some extent the case of J.M., a manager of three hedge funds, Ascot Fund Ltd. and Ascot Partners, Gabriel Capital L.P., and Ariel Fund Ltd., who had funneled over the years more than $2 billion given to him by investors and fifteen institutions to Bernard Madoff, now the convicted global hedge fund manager, the ultimate Ponzi fraudster who cheated institutions and the public of approximately $65 billion. Mr.M instead of actively managing the money entrusted to him by investors was feeding Madoff's Ponzi scheme in exchange of getting fees that totaled $470 million. Obviously, the investors lost their money. He was sued by the New York State attorney general and finally in 2012 they apparently settled the suit for about $400 million to be paid by him. Another major suit by the US Bankruptcy Court for recuperating over $500 million is pending. He was forced to sell his unique collection of Mark Rothko's paintings for $310 million.

Mr.M, a graduate of Columbia University and Harvard Law School, has been for a long time a prominent investment advisor and a philanthropist in New York area. He was a trustee of Yeshiva University, member of the board of Levy Economics Institute at Bard College, President of Fifth Avenue Synagogue, and on the board of other prestigious nonprofit organizations.

His father, a very rich businessman and a well-known philanthropist, gave him the introductory credential to the financial world to become a member of the New York business elite. He lives in Park Avenue in an eighteen-room duplex in the same building where Jacqueline Kennedy grew up and John D. Rockefeller once lived. It has also been the home of financial moguls like Ronald Perleman, Saul Steinberg, Henry Kravis, and so forth.

Connected to Cerberus Capital Management through personal contacts, he invested a portion of his Gabriel hedge fund in this private investment fund and ended up being appointed as the nonexecutive chairman of General Motors Acceptance Corporation (GMAC). All in all, he amassed a fortune from collecting management fees from the money of his funds invested through other hedge funds like that of Madoff.[7]

What compelled this "respectable" businessman, financially secure, a prominent member of community to use dubious and risky financial transactions that finally did him in? Was it classical greed or the need to be successful in his social group? For whatever reason, he decided to take a short cut to financial managing, apparently oblivious to any active fiduciary responsibility. It amounted to a self-serving way of doing business reinforced by this climate of moral relativism. The opportunity to make easy money in a corrupted Wall Street environment fitted well with his disregard for any fiduciary responsibility that would have at least required him to control closely the unrealistic high performance year after year regardless of market conditions of Madoff to whom he entrusted his clients' money. Apparently, he neglected his professional obligations toward clients. He was confident in his skills of persuading his client-investors to trust him and was self-satisfied with his alleged market performance and his financial achievements.

Certainly, his operation as "money-feeder" for Madoff's hedge fund was minor as compared to the vast international elaborated fraud of his business associate, Madoff, the skilful money manager of Wall Street who was a true psychopath in a class by himself.

In a different category has been the master of outright deceit R. Allen Stanford, a Texas financier and cricket mogul, who was once worth about $2 billion, placing him among the richest men in America. His business stretched across the Caribbean to South America through his Stanford International Bank in Antigua which lured investors with high-interest rates on CDs never issued. He was also the owner of multiple homes, private jet, a cricket team, a restaurant, and a newspaper in Antigua where he was knighted by the government. He was accused of lying to investors about the security of their investments held in Antigua. He was tried and convicted by a Houston court for defrauding the investors and using the money to maintain his lavish style of life. At his trial, a retiree investor testified that he lost all his life's saving of $1.6 million on CDs and now to get by he is selling his possession on eBay and eating burgers and cheese. However, apparently, at the time of conviction Stanford held about $300 million in thirty accounts in various countries.

He was running an estimated Ponzi scheme of $7 billion, second only to that of Madoff.[8]

Stanford appears to have been a smart financier who could have made a good living without blatantly cheating his customers. However, he preferred the risky way of making big money with the reward of beating the odds and proving his smartness by pulling off relatively well-devised fraudulent schemes. Charming, friendly, and unscrupulous he built his fortune relying on his skills of false advertising, manipulating investors, and spinning the facts while fully aware that he was wrongly pulling out money from unsuspecting investors. No pangs of conscience, no remorse. The investors deserved to be cheated since they were gullible to believing bank's advertising without checking it. This demonstrated the typical thinking of a psychopath who knew how to hide his true self.

As we see these alleged "normals" are systematically cheating people in a variety of ways in order to supplement their high style of living or to gain the admiration of others. Most of them take their chances only occasionally, in special situations perceived as unique and seemingly safe. Although it sounds oxymoron, these respectable psychopathic-bent people are part of the main stream of society until they make a wrong move that exposes their frauds. As lawyers, doctors, businessmen or politicians, they enjoy the social status of trustworthy members of the community. We hear about their devious or fraudulent activities only when they break the law with impunity due to their own miscalculations mostly triggered by their overblown ego. Until then, they are our charming and honorable neighbors respected by our community. Certainly, we are all familiar with the case of Sam Waksal, the jetsetter, the ex-CEO of Imclone, Corp., who was convicted in 2003 for bank fraud, insider trading and obstruction of justice. As if it was not enough, the Internal Revenue Service (IRS) found that he did not pay the state and federal income tax for 1999 and 2000 amounting to $23.3 million.[9]

The fraudulent schemes of executives at Enron Company, such as Michael Kopper, former managing director of global finance or Andy Fastow, former chief financial officer had made headlines due to their sophisticated methods of inflating the earning of the company by half a billion dollars and by manipulating its debts with the use of personal offshore partnerships. To make things worse for the shareholders, David Duncan, senior audit partner at the big accounting firm Arthur Anderson approved and certified their fraudulent dealings as a novel way of doing business. We can also add to the list names of other fraudsters, such as David Meyers, former controller and Scott Sullivan, former chief financial officer at WorldCom; John Rigas, founder and former chairman and his son, executives at Adelphia Communication. All robbed their companies of hundreds of millions of dollars before being indicted and brought to trial by the federal or state prosecutors. There are other executives who have been recently convicted such as Bernard Ebbers, ex-Chairman of WorldCom,[10] Dennis Kozlovski of Tyco, and so forth. Their number is legion. What is important to note is the fact that all of them were successful on their own, and they did not need to commit frauds.

Why did they do it? With total disregard for the right of shareholders and convinced of their ability to circumvent the law, they treated their company as their own private business using various financial gimmicks including forgivable loans in order to support an opulent life and enjoy the public admiration brought by it. They recklessly inflated the companies' earnings in order to increase the value of the stock and hence of their options which they cashed in and manipulated the companies' balance sheet which was supposed to inform the shareholders about the health of the respective company in order to justify the exaggerated bonuses paid to them based on nonexistent profits. For instance, the chief financial officer at WorldCom had manipulated for years the balance sheet of the company by classifying ordinary expenses as capital expenditure and surprisingly, the quarterly earnings of the company were in line with the Wall Street expectations. But when the books were audited, a fraud amounting to a staggering sum of $11 billion was discovered. As a result, the shareholders and pensioners lost fortunes.

Other executives have been more ingenious and more successful in maintaining a frame of legality. They took advantage of some absurd accounting rules that permitted them to legally calculate as profit unrealistic projections of the earnings from its pension plans that never materialized. A good case is that of Verizon Communication that reported an income of $1.8 billion from the pension plan in the year when in reality the plan had a loss of $3.1 billion. Yet the bonuses of the executives were calculated based on this nonexistent profit. This might be considered a legal form of cheating based on bizarre but self-serving rules of accounting.[11]

There are other forms of blatant deception widely practiced by corrupt financiers who have developed sophisticated fraudulent financial operations for fleecing the naive, as subtle and convincing as gospel truth. The main difference between these opportunistic crooks and con artists is ultimately a question of interpretation. It seems that where the opportunistic crooks (executives or professionals) who exude respectability, cheat occasionally and only under conditions viewed as safe, the con artists take unrestrained risk, and rely on their imaginative scams and skills of persuasion to make a living out of cheating. Most opportunistic crooks use believable schemes resembling legitimate projects and, backed by their prestige and status in the community act more like the investment "guru" Reed Slatkin. He was a multimillionaire, a former bishop in the Church of Scientology, who made a legal fortune by providing start-up funds for the internet service of Earthlink, Inc. In April 2002, he pleaded guilty for swindling eight hundred clients out of about $600 million. After filing for bankruptcy, the multimillionaire surrendered to authorities in Los Angeles. Basically, he operated a Ponzi scheme using money from new investors to pay off the old ones. Before the indictment, he was considered a wizard financier, a smart investor with contacts among Hollywood and TV entertainment crowd, in addition to the network of Scientologists. He lived well and enjoyed the prestige and esteem of people who mattered in his community. What drove him from an upright citizen to the path of self-destruction? Did he fancy being a smart investor because of his luck with the first investment? Apparently, yes. To maintain his good name and fame after losses started to pile up, he slowly slipped into swindling. It is reported that the initial investors reaped profit of about $151 million representing the money of the later ones. The rest is history.[12]

These "honorable" psychopathic-bent people seem to believe that they could get away with their booty and enjoy their success. Their overblown egos refuse to consider that they may be caught and punished. Support for this magical thinking comes from the CEO of Imclone Sam Waksal, convicted for insider trading, who in an interview given to "60 Minutes" after his conviction, justified his plight by stating that "I was arrogant enough to believe that I could cut corners, not care for the details or consequences." He went on to say that "I did not think that I was going to get caught at all."[13] Unfortunately for him and others like him, when they are caught the emotional high price paid may transcend the financial benefits reaped from the crime.

The unanswered question is whether these cheaters are impulsive, unable to control their emotional drives, or are misguided opportunists who gamble for high stakes in special situations, hoping to make fast money allegedly free of risk. Let us take the case of Sotheby's CEO, Diana Brooks, convicted and sentenced to six months house arrest, in addition to other penalties for price-fixing of art auctions. Judge Daniels, who convicted her, told her that she "substituted fame for shame." Her boss Alfred Taubman, Chairman, a real-estate multimillionaire received one year in jail for his role to mastermind the price-fixing plan.[14] It is fair to assume that they coldly calculated the risk involved in pulling off their design and any possible conflict with the law and still decided to proceed by either ignoring the consequences or believing to be able to beat the rap. Then, their failure was due to a gross miscalculation. In this context, they acted like gamblers, albeit unscrupulous ones, who believed in their skill to beat the odds. Most of these opportunistic cheaters are narcissists, belonging to a subtype described as "unprincipled narcissists" with psychopathic traits, who defy social conventions and show a disregard for the truth. Part of their psychopathic-bent traits is that of having a minimal or nonexistent sense of guilt and social conscience, although they try hard to keep their shady activities within the confines of the law. No wonder they enjoy outwitting and defrauding others.

If, in general, one's social proficiency and ability to achieve success is measured by one's skills to negotiate social transactions in one's favor within the rules of acceptable competition, these psychopathic-oriented minds attempt to outdo others by altering the rules through discreet and subtle deceptions.[15] They are the ones operating not always successfully within the realm of the ambiguity of conformity.

Naked greed may lead to patterns of deception even in occupations that apparently rely on high moral values and/or scientific knowledge. Take, for instance, the case of a Brooklyn, New York Supreme Court Judge Gerald P. Garson who was convicted together with two other officers of the court on charges of running a bribery scheme "to rig the outcome of divorce and child custody cases." He was betrayed by his accomplice, a lawyer called Paul Siminovsky who cooperated with the Federal Bureau of Investigation (FBI) in taping his incriminating conversations of bribery with the judge.[16]

An unusual elaborate, massive fraud of about $42 million was masterminded by Semen Domnitser, an overseer of two compensation funds of the Conference on Material Claims as reparations to Holocaust survivors. His accomplices were Dora Grande, a notary public and five other employees, who together systematically falsified the applications for over 5,600 people for fraudulent compensations. The schemers submitted bogus information for alleged victims of the concentration camps or incarcerations. This led to $18 million paid as "hardship" money to almost 5,000 ineligible recipients. Another $245 million were paid to more than 650 applicants as pensions of $411-a-month for allegedly spending at least six months in a concentration camp or eighteen months in a ghetto. The applicants were recruited through advertisements in Russian language newspapers. The schemers were sending applications with false dates of birth before the World War II, since part of the applicants were born after the War, with the photo attached to more than one application but under different names, bogus ID cards and places of birth and dramatic stories about their life during Nazi occupation. All documentations were certified by Grande, the public notary. The scheme with pensions went on for sixteen years. They were regularly receiving generous kickbacks. The fraud was uncovered by an audit of Claims Conference which notified the feds.[17]

But what about clergymen and rabbis who are supposed to be free from the temptation of greed and deception? Think about the famous scandals of embezzlement of certain great fundamentalist preachers or rabbis who have systematically cheated the faithful, abusing their trust while pursuing their lucrative goals of enrichment.

Among professionals, allegedly dedicated to integrity, we find some using deception to gain recognition, as in the case of Dr. Shaul Debbi, an ophthalmologist, who was reported by press of having cheated Medicare of hundreds of thousands of dollars by performing unnecessary operations on residents of adult homes. He was sentenced by a federal judge to short-term prison and surrender of medical license.[18] Did he really need to do it for a living?

By the same token, many lawyers have too much of a psychopathic inclination not to become victims of their own devious fraudulent designs. An unusual and foolish case is that of a general counsel of the New York City Civil Service Commission, Mario Vasquez, who, when passed up for a raise, fabricated a new memo with the copied signature of a mayoral aide who was supposed to approve the increase. He was charged with forgery in the second degree, and attempted grand larceny, both felonies.[19] Another political appointee-lawyer behaved even worse, as chief counsel for the New York State Assembly Speaker Sheldon Silver, Michael Boxley was charged with raping a legislative aide. After months of denying any wrongdoing, faced with new evidence he entered a plea bargain and pleaded guilty only to sexual misconduct after admitting in court to have had sex without her consent. This happened after unsuccessful attempts to use his position to win her over. He was placed on probation. Unfortunately, the Assembly Speaker, though informed after the attack by the legislative aide who officially complained, did not bring the case to the attention of the police, which fact led the aide to file a suit against the Speaker.[20]

Respectable Politicians Preaching Conformity While Acting Nonconformist

It is a fact of political life that many politicians display a psychopathically tainted behavior. With the distinction between true and false less defined, some politicians abuse their position of power and blatantly manipulate the public. Take the case of congressman James A. Traficante Jr., who in 2002 was convicted of racketeering, bribery, and fraud by a federal jury or of Rudy Cunningham, congressman from California recently convicted for taking bribes from contractors of over $2.5 million. The latest casualty is Congressman Rangel, who at the time of starting the investigation was chairman of the powerful Way and Means Committee, and who didn't report income from his properties to IRS for years, among other tax evasions. Finally, he was censored by the Congress but not prosecuted for his illegal tax dealings. But how many politicians with a psychopathic bent pass for normal until their devious behavior give them away?

A blatant case of a congressman's corruption fought politically and racially was that of William J. Jefferson of Louisiana who was indicted on fourteen charges of bribery, racketeering, and money laundering on June 2007 by a federal grand jury.[21]

The case started in 2005 when one investor representing a technological company, iGate Inc., paid $400,000 in bribes to a company under the name of the wife of Congressman Jefferson. Money was given to persuade the army to test a technical product of iGate company and to arrange its sale to the Nigeria, Ghana, and Cameroon.

A couple of months later, the FBI videotaped Jefferson receiving $100,000 cash in a hotel in Virginia. It was followed by a raid to Jefferson's home where they found $90,000 wrapped in aluminum foil hidden in the freezer. Serial numbers of the currency corresponded with the money given by FBI to the informant. FBI was also able to videotape Jefferson receiving the stock certificate from iGate of a company set up in Nigeria which was supposed to grow in five years to a revenue of $200 million.

After the raiding of Jefferson's congressional office, the battle turned to court for illegal search of a congressman's office, to change into a political scandal with racial overtone when the House Minority leader asked for his resignation from the Ways and Means Committee and he refused, supported by the majority of the Congressional Black Caucus.

Finally, he was tried and convicted in 2009 on eleven counts of corruption to thirteen years of jail.[22]

What is dramatic about this case is the fact that Jefferson was the son of a farmer and heavy equipment operator who grew up in a modest environment with neither of the parents graduating from the high school. However, he ambitiously pursued and received a bachelor's degree from the Southern University in Baton Rouge and a law degree from Harvard in 1972 and LLM in Taxation from Georgetown University Center in 1996. In 1976, he moved to New Orleans and in 1979 he became a state senator. A rising star in Louisiana politics in 1990, he was elected to the Congress where he served in the Ways and Means Committee. He was the first African American Representative since Reconstruction and was reelected seven times. In 1999, he ran for Governor of Louisiana and lost.

By possessing the right social and political credentials he could have gone far in politics, if he hadn't been involved in the massive corruption scandal that brought him down. What made him change from a powerful respected congressman to a sleazy operator of crooked schemes for fast enrichment? The combination between the ability to use the power of the office at his will and his overriding want to get rich proved to be disastrous when confronted with the tempting opportunity to achieve his dream. Blinded by his all-consuming greed, he ignored the obvious risk involved in his illegal actions. Magically, he truly believed that they wouldn't be able either to catch him or to convict him. He was too smart for them.

However, most politicians are not so blatantly cheating the public; they are more subtle in their ways of manipulating or deceiving the constituents. They just make false campaign promises about changing bad social policies, they pushed pieces of legislation favoring selective groups, or they lie to the public about their illegal campaign funds.

The politicians who psychopathically bent are initially hard to detect since they start their political careers with tolerable civil record until their dedication to the public services is gradually changed to a self-serving operation. If they succeed to convince the public of their integrity, leadership skills, and of their dedication to better the life of their fellow men and society, they feel free to promote their interest under the protection of their position beyond immediate scrutiny. While an honest politician uses his skills to master the variables of social-economic problems in order to reach valid solutions, the psychopathically disposed politician relies most often on deceptive practices. Gradually, during his tenure, he dispenses with any real commitment to any set of political beliefs and depends on opportunistic solutions. Truth becomes either expendable for the sake of political expediency or for personal gains. His demagoguery and moral corruption become an issue only when he brazenly violates the law as recently happened to a few members of the Congress or governors and state senators, particularly in the New York State.

As expected, sometimes successful opportunistic politicians with the help of talented but unscrupulous campaign operatives may ultimately reach the pinnacle of political power, used by them for aggrandizement and double dealings. After convincing the voters of their irrefutable qualities for leadership and mesmerizing them with their deft manipulations of facts and persuasive oratory that offered a glorious vision of a better future, when in the office their behavior betrays their conniving orientation. This was the case of governors Don Siegelman (D) from Alabama, John Symington III (R-AZ) from Arizona, and recently John Rowland (R) from Connecticut and Rod Blagojevich (D) from Illinois.

But what about the controversial behavior of Bill Clinton when president? Clinton is an unusual case, as governor and president he displayed traits of lack of empathy, exploitations of others, egocentrism, disregard for the society rules and dissocial pattern of behavior starting with a disposition to misrepresent facts typical of a habitual liar and proclivity to sexual scandals, all inappropriate behavior for a president. His mixed unethical behavior had been assumed by psychologists to be related to his turbulent childhood, which has led to lifetime problems in dealing with truth. As a matter of fact, he almost drowned under the flood of shenanigans ranging from outrageous political "gates" to scandalous sex affairs. Under him, political spinning reached a high degree of perfection as used by the White House and him in support of his controversial activities. The spinning game went so far as to justify Clinton's sex affairs and political shenanigans as part of his attempts to demystify the White House. His spin doctors, twisters of truth gained social respectability and became part of the political process as experts in damage control and public image repairs.

Interestingly, most of the media or citizens were less irate by his outrageous behavior during his presidency, as they were about his unjustifiable last minutes pardons of certain convicts or fugitives. Topping it all, it was his surprise at the public's negative reaction that indicated his blurred distinction between permissible and not permissible actions. Even his presidential library in Little Rock bears the imprint of his inability to fully accept the responsibility for his actions. The section of the library exhibiting the documentation of his impeachment starts with this introduction: "The impeachment battle was not about the Constitution or rule of law, but was instead quest for power that the president's opponents could not win at the ballot box."[23] As Reuters' news remarked at the opening of the library, "he still is unable to level with America on Lewinsky."

Forget about false statements made on TV about his affair with Monica Lewinsky, about her stained dress which crushed his defense, just keep in mind his perjury before the court that later resulted in his disbarment as a lawyer.

A closer look at all the "smart" equivocators, some of them bordering on a benign psychopathy while others being just habitual liars or spinners of truth, holding positions of social leadership and ranging from that of policy makers to media experts or financial operators show certain general pattern of manipulation of truth. They use specific methods for recasting the truth in order to deceive others and meet their goals. One is to dissect, fragment, and eviscerate truth of its substance in order to recombine it with pseudotruth and the other is unverifiable projections in a new formulation that blurs the distinction between facts and assumptions. This manipulation of facts tends to create confusion in the mind of the public and it is beneficial to the manipulator of facts. This semblance of truth sold to other people as unadulterated truth which tends to create the impression of legitimacy is an art in itself. An example of recasting the truth had been the debate about targeting the alleged agencies responsible for failing to prevent the 9/11 attack. The arguments were based on hindsight knowledge while defensively ignoring those ill-thought decisions in the nineties, taken by Central Intelligence Agency that impeded any cover-up operation or an infiltration of Iraq's regime. The same manipulation of facts goes on now in debating the proper course of action toward illegal immigrants. It starts with their classification as undocumented immigrant which is more than a misnomer, it is a calculated misrepresentation of facts since undocumented is not synonym with illegal, and they are not interchangeable by any stretch of imagination. The political intention is obvious to remove the stigma of illegality and to soften the blow of their illegal presence here with the goal of giving them all the federal and state benefits equal to the legal immigrants, instead of finding a fair legal solution to clear up their status here.

Another method used by these "respectable" manipulators is to twist the truth based on a classical principle that the redefinition of a situation within a new conceptual framework will give a new meaning to that situation. This slants its initial context and changes the focus of attention to a secondary aspect of it. This method was successfully used by the defendants during the congressional investigation of illegal campaign funds raised by Al Gore from Buddhist temple's donors. The issue got buried in misleading testimonies and rhetoric for reforms. The same approach was also used by Robert Torricelli, who as a New Jersey senator denied any wrongdoing in raising illegal funds for his political campaign against credible evidence pointing in the opposite direction. Later, faced with irrefutable proofs, he was forced to withdraw his name from the reelection campaign.

Disingenuous but elegant presentations of facts, interspersed with well-designed lies, are alarmingly used by these devious power brokers to manipulate people financially or politically.

Can a psychopathically tinted personality be called "normal-nonconformists?" Isn't it a misnomer? After all, the notion of psychopathy implicitly implies abnormal social behavior which is in conflict with the social norms of morality. However, well-known researchers of human behavior observed that certain people while presenting traits of psychopaths are able to gain social respectability as long as they avoid any serious confrontations with the law.[24]

Today, in our murky moral climate, more regular people, respectable citizens with a psychopathic bent feel free to take chances of promoting their dishonest schemes of fast enrichment.

The "Big" Social Lies of the Demagogic Leaders

A special category of politicians and social activists who present subtle psychopathic traits but appear behaving normally are in reality opportunistic, nonconformist, and demagogic leaders. People are faced with a most serious problem in dealing with the big lies of the alleged political and social reformers who have periodically reached for power in the name of social justice and equality for masses. The more appealing and generous their social or political platforms had been, the more opportunistic the leaders were. The same demagogic process filtered down to all levels of societal organization negatively affected the daily existence of common people. Unfortunately, naive people who had hoped for a better life have always been betrayed by their trusted "saviors."

The need of the masses to have their illusions reinforced by a rescuer who will miraculously solve their problems and take care of their needs is as old as mankind. They have been exploited by political demagogues, activists-magicians of social changes, phony spiritual leaders, or lately financial investment crooks. As the claims of these opportunist-demagogues for the purported schemes of changes that will bring the desperately sought betterment of life become more grandiose, the more inspiring the created vision of the future will be, the more enthusiastic the masses will become, and unreservedly they will support and follow these "saviors." Common people, because of their limited social horizon and endless frustrations, always have had difficulty to distinguish between what is real and possible and what is desirable but only remotely believable.

The charismatic political opportunist-leaders who promised a new era of prosperity and happiness happened to be subtle demagogues and accomplished liars with strong narcissistic-psychopathic bend, enamored with power and adulation of masses. During their campaigns for power, they sell to the masses an illusion of glorious, flourishing times to come, combined with a skillful attack on the present living social conditions which indeed were woeful either due to corruption or the ineptitude of the government. Under these circumstances, these clever alleged political reformers and masters of deceit are able to convince people and mobilize them to their cause and sometimes win the elections.

The rank and file ready for a change believe that they have only to gain by embracing the new leaders without any understanding of the true consequences of the newly advocated policies like the one of granting unchecked legality to the illegal immigrants while the country suffers high unemployment or increasing the entitlements with disregard for the effects on the astronomical national debt. Take, for instance, the position of then Governor Bill Richardson of New Mexico, who in 2003, welcomed in Santa Fe a bus caravan of illegal immigrants who were on their way to Washington, DC, by stating "Thank you for coming to Santa Fe. Know that New Mexico is your home." Furthermore, he signed a bill to give them free tuition to state colleges and right to driving license with total disregard for the law and at the expense of the taxpayers, while attempting to create the illusion of acting compassionately. In reality, it was a ploy for political gains to run for Presidency of America. These deceptive games reinforcing the moral relativism play a destabilizing role for society and in human interaction. In a different context, the same gains relying on the new duplicity of social conformity are played by the new Wild West recreated by the corporate and the Wall Street crowd in a more sophisticated and subtle form, but as lawless as the original one.

Part II
The Compulsive-Habitual Liars

However, there are other types of ordinary cheaters with less grandiose goals and whose dissocial actions are part of an alleged style of life based on an uncontrollable emotional need to distort facts and judgments by heavy lying. Regardless of other traits of their personality, one that is part of its core is the need for indiscriminate lying. The issue is to what extent they are different from the so-called "normal" psychopaths who in reality are "pseudonormal," and whose social functioning also relies on heavy lying. Certain liars are pathological liars in their daily interaction because of their compulsive need to lie and apparent self-destructive patterns of behavior, though their fibs have a minor social impact when compared to the "normal" psychopaths whose lying and elaborated schemes are significant and outright frauds. Habitual liars could be, for example, some lawyers who not only twist facts in court in order to win the case but also cheat their clients by overcharging or make promises which they know are false, but still functioning within a relative normal social range. The difference between them and the alleged "normal" psychopaths is mainly a matter of degree of interpretation of their acts labeled or not criminal.

The true habitual liars are people for whom lying is intertwined in their daily activities because of their difficulty to tell the truth even when the truth does not hurt them. These compulsive, pathological liars do not represent a special type of personality. They are found among other personalities who have developed a pattern of social interactions with a high reliance on lying. For these liars, lying takes place within a framework of thinking that attempts to make the actual circumstances more favorable to themselves. The habitual liars customarily relate to others by twisting, distorting, falsifying, or misconstruing facts and events in the belief that this will place them in a more favorable social light. They either imaginarily perceive being disadvantaged or want to create a desired effect. They confabulate every day to the point of blurring for themselves the distinction between truth and falsehood. Their lies become intertwined in their own head with true facts to the point of becoming sometimes almost indistinguishable.

A good example is that of Jayson Blair, a twenty-seven-year-old, ex-national reporter at the New York Times whose false reporting shook the credibility of the newspaper and led to a shake-up of its editorial leadership. Blair made a farce out of reporting news by sending dispatches from places where he was not present, fabricating statements as if made by people allegedly interviewed, created nonexisting scenes related to investigated events, constructing imaginary interviews with people from photographs and personal assumptions and plagiarizing content of facts about events from other newspapers. Gradually, his deceptions surpassed all limits of responsible reporting by becoming a total fraud and on many occasions, facts couldn't be separated from fictional stories.[25]

The explanations of the newspaper, caught red-handed for not supervising him in order to detect the obvious inconsistencies of his reporting, were weak and self-serving. In reality, the young reporter showed for years a pattern of deception with total disregard for honest journalism, albeit tolerated for apparent political reasons.

From the detailed investigation of the New York Times leading to his termination, it resulted that his behavior exhibited during his tenure at the New York Times had belonged more likely to the domain of pathological lying, underlying obvious other personality problems. Intelligent, talented, he could have done the reporting without resorting to fraudulent devices, but the desire for quick success without doing the work combined with a belief in his ability to pull it off led to his defiance of superiors and contempt for truth. This attitude led him into a pattern of deception which, ultimately was self-destructive.[26]

This style of relating to others gives these people the illusion of coping more smartly with everyday life, while quite often failing to meet their social standards of reliability or responsibility. By remaking reality according to their immediate needs, they reduce the pain of possible failure while receiving instant gratification. Their number is legion. One finds them in all walks of life. However, they do excel in some professions such as lawyers, politicians, advertisers, public relations, diplomats, and so forth.

While some habitual liars seem to try to uplift an underlying low self-esteem by conveying a positive image against evidence to the contrary, others are just manipulating people for enhancing their social status. In the first case, the fear of projecting an image of inadequacy due to their unreliable behavior is compensated by lying, a fast and apparently an immediate salutary solution. Yet, they like to think of acting cleverly in responding to immediate social demands and hence inviting the much sought acceptance or friendship of others. It is an expeditious but inefficient way of social adaptation. Other compulsive liars lie without scruples for financial gains or to get a feeling of importance.

Consider the case reported by newspapers of a police stooge who within one week was an eye witness at two murders. In both cases, based on his testimony, two people were convicted for murder. In his testimony, in the first murder he claimed to have witnessed the murder with his girlfriend. Later it was proven that neither one was in New York on that date. His girlfriend denied any knowledge about the shooting. But it took seven years for the convicted man to prove his innocence. In the second murder case, he claimed to have witnessed the shooting while waiting for his mother near a subway station. The trouble was that a later investigation showed that the mother contradicted his story by denying being in that area at the time of the shooting. There was other evidence questioning his testimony. Furthermore, members of his family and relatives described him as having difficulty in telling the truth.[27]

Various forms of pathological lying are at the core of distortion of truth perpetrated by other malignant types of liars such as career con artists or certain imposters who breathe and live a life of deception. But the crown jewel of pathological lying is the "creative" sociopath, who adjusts relatively well socially. The main trait of his personality is represented by his antisocial behavior fighting to overcome the obstacles of the law while using various schemes for deceiving others. These sociopaths are looking for any available loophole in the law or negligence or naiveté of persons to cheat without being caught.

Most of the skillful crooks or con artists display various degrees of antisocial behavior. In the past they were known as psychopaths.

However, it was noticed that not all psychopaths commit antisocial acts. There are relatively distinct differences between the ones called "normal" psychopaths and the true antisocial sociopaths, particularly related to various degrees of severity of antisocial behavior. The terms of sociopath have been equated with antisocial personality because his social interaction with others is based on continuous attempts to defraud, cheat, and lie to them. His general psychological profile is that of an intelligent, articulate, charming, superficially considerate person, who is emotionally suspicious and detached cold, and unscrupulous. He cultivates the skill of talking smoothly and lying convincingly while looking straight into the other's person eyes. Confident and alert during conversation, he has a knack for picking upon some of his potential victim's possible weakness of personality by skillfully asking the right questions before entrapping that person. In the process of expounding on his elaborate and persuasive schemes, he does not display any verbal or nonverbal signs of emotional or physical discomfort. It is assumed that sociopaths have a less developed capacity than the general population to show visible responses of the autonomous nervous system when subjected to powerful emotional stimuli. Free of unpleasant physical reactions and guilt, the sociopath does not experience anxiety or fear of being exposed for cheating others. Calm and self-assured, he is ready to sell anything, even the "Brooklyn Bridge," to anyone naive or foolish enough to get involved in any of his scams. He likes to deceive people either for fun or, most often, for gains, as his late needs may dictate. When he succeeds in putting something over on someone for fun, he is delighted to be able to prove his cleverness and superiority. But most often, he lies and cheats people for financial gain. For most sociopaths, it means a way of making a living in an environment viewed by them as full of suckers.

Take Sam, a junior college student of above-average intelligence, articulate, and of pleasant demeanor, academically in good standing, who gradually started to display serious antisocial behavioral problems. One of his bizarre acts was to write racially obscene slurs against his own ethnic group on classroom desks. Later, while surrounded by classmates, he would read the insults aloud and would then indignantly complain to the administration. At other times, he would send obscene letters to female students signed with the names of various top students or young faculty members. The resulting uproar, screaming, and complaints of these women were a source of great enjoyment for him and his friends. When the administration caught up with him, he was temporarily suspended from attending classes and was referred for psychiatric treatment as a condition to remain at college. Anyway, these prankish activities were regarded by the college psychologist as an attention-seeking device and were dismissed by the officials with a reprimand only after the school received a hefty monetary gift from his rather well-to-do family. However, over time his personal behavior got worse as he started stealing food from supermarkets and clothes from department stores for fun. In fact, a few times he devised very sophisticated schemes to steal from department stores. On one occasion, he went to a department store, bought a pair of jeans, paid for them and left. He came back one hour later, put the same jeans on the display table and started trying on other jeans. After he tried on numerous pairs of jeans, he put all of them back on the display table, took his original jeans from the same table, stuffed them furtively into his briefcase and nonchalantly moved toward the store exit. He knew that his behavior would be noticed by the store detectives who were monitoring the aisles. Indeed, one detective ran after him and stopped him in an attempt to check his briefcase. An argument broke out as to whether he had bought the jeans as he had claimed or he had stolen them. Unaware of his game, the store detective thought that he had stolen them and attempted to detain him for interrogation. Sam resisted, and a scuffle followed, at which point he shouted for police's help while customers started to gather around. He suddenly freed himself from the store detective's hold and triumphantly showed the receipt, proving that he had bought the jeans. In front of witnesses, he threatened to sue the store for false arrest and asked to see the management, but not before taking the names of a few witnesses. Later, the store settled the claim and compensated him handsomely. This game worked out very well and thrilled him to no end. It also gained him a high mark with his friends.

Sam continued his petty criminal behavior until he graduated to more sophisticated and crooked deals. After graduating from college, he got a job in another state at an investment firm which sold, among other financial products, offshore tax shelters. Sam masterminded a business scam related to these offshore transactions which were used by high net-worth people for sheltering income. The investment product was considered to be legitimate, but was required to be reported to IRS. As a salesman for the company, he became friendly with some buyers and tried to extract personal and business information from them whenever it was possible. If he suspected that an investment might represent the hiding of unreported money offshore, he would, according to a prearranged plan, inform his partner in crime, who, posing as government insider, would attempt to extort money from the investors by claiming to have knowledge of alleged tax irregularities or to accuse them of possible tax evasion. When his confederate was arrested for extortion, Sam denied any cognizance of his alleged acquaintance with the criminal activity, but admitted to being careless by leaving records of the business transactions on his desk at home, accessible to the other person when he occasionally visited him. Sam left town when he was physically threatened by his former partner because of some dispute about money. He moved to the south where he started another series of outright swindles, cashing unauthorized pension checks left at the building mail boxes, which temporarily landed him in jail. In order to receive a more lenient sentence, he invoked a plea of emotional distress allegedly related to a longstanding psychological problem: that of having been sexually abused as a child by a nanny. Based on this defense, he received a six-month jail sentence and three years on probation with a requirement for psychiatric treatment. Afterward, his antisocial activities continued because of his low tolerance for frustration, lack of sustained perseverance in any task, and need for immediate gratification combined with a need to prove his cleverness. These negative traits were counterproductive for holding a regular job and adapting socially. Furthermore, he lacked respect for the rights of others because he viewed people either as careless in handling their business or using poor judgment. "If they are cheated, they do not deserve compassion or concessions because they do not protect their interest," argued Sam. No guilt, no problems of conscience for Sam, he just wanted to stay a step ahead of the arm of the law. What makes sociopaths behave as they do?

The psychological explanation for their antisocial behavior is presumably related to two unfavorable interacting factors of their personality make-up, a genetic component which interfaces with an ego-damaged trait of personality assumed to have been the result of frustrating developmental experiences. Most people exhibiting antisocial behavior have a history of lying, cheating, stealing, and other deviant behaviors since childhood. This represents a way of coping for some children who have a low tolerance for frustration, a need for immediate gratification, and a denial of satisfaction by acceptable means. They gradually learn this deviant behavior that pays off for them, at least for the short term.

Interestingly, not too many intelligent crooks with sociopathic traits are arrested and fewer if convicted get long jail terms for their crimes. Incidentally, some sociopaths are imposters, but not all imposters are sociopaths. In most cases the sociopathic behavior is an outcome of a narcissistic core personality which displays antisocial traits oriented toward sensation seeking, risk taking, and deception.[28]

Antisocial behavior is exhibited in our society by a variety of people ranging from those cunning to others but able to maintain a facade of "normal-behavior" by covering their illegal activities very skillfully to those more daring fraudsters, who commit various types of swindles, fraud, etc., and try to battle the law quite often successfully. Most of them are familiar with all loopholes of the law which they intend to break. As previously mentioned, the difference between "normal" psychopaths and sociopaths is considered as depending on the persistence of a pattern of antisocial behavior as related to their different levels of acceptance the risk involved in the projected crime. In general, it is assumed that the "normal" psychopath is more selective and cautious in calculating the acceptable risk to be taken and more careful in selecting a target for his projected crime under the radar, in his desperate attempt to protect his social status in the community. On the other hand, the common antisocial, the sociopath—most often a con man—has a personality less integrated socially that drives him to take much higher risks to the point of recklessness. This difference is also induced by a sociopath's trait of a high feeling of skillfulness that makes him able to beat the odds. In addition, sociopath's long pattern of life style is focused on duping others in order to make a good living beyond his realistic social possibilities.

As previously mentioned, the criminal behavior of the sociopath seems to have a genetic underlying, mostly not yet deciphered. Some genes have been associated with criminal behavior. For instance, the low monoamine oxidase inhibitor A has been associated with either antisocial impulses or with impairment of internal resistance to control the impulses.[29]

What is interesting about these people who exhibit at various degrees antisocial behaviors is the fact that they behave otherwise within the range of socially adjusted behavior passing for normal. In fact, outside of their cheating deals they function socially as conformists. Some of them, if caught and convicted get light sentences like placed on probation or only reprimanded. They maintain, as such, their ambiguous status of relative social pseudo-conformity.

Notes

1. R. C. Boddy, "The Corporate Psychopaths Theory of the Global Financial Crisis," *Journal of Business Ethics* 102 (2011), 255–59.
2. A. Eichler, "One Out of Every Ten Wall Street Employees is a Psychopath, Say Researchers," *Huffington Post*, February 29, 2012.
3. R. D. Hare and C. S. Neuman, "Psychopathy Assessment and Forensic Implications," *Canadian Journal of Psychiatry* 54 (December 2009), 791–802.
4. P. McGeehan, "SEC Begins Investigation into Analysts," *New York Times*, April 26, 2002, C1.
5. Ambereen Choudhury and Christine Harper, "Goldman Sachs Employee Criticizes Firm for Ripping Off Clients," *Bloomberg News*, March 14, 2012.
6. C. Gasparino and S. Craig, "Lehman Broker Vanishes," *Wall Street Journal*, February 2, 2002, A1.
7. D. Henrique, "Hedge Fund Manager to Pay $405 Million in Madoff Settlement," *New York Times*, June 24, 2012.
8. IB Times Staff Reporter, "Allen Stanford Trial: Billionaire Ponzi Schemer Found Guilty of Fraud," IBTimes.com, March 7, 2012.
9. A. Hoffman, "Waksal: 'May Arrogance Did Me In,'" *New York Post*, October 6, 2003, 17.
10. K. Crawford, "Ex-World.com CEO Ebbers Guilty," *CNN Money*, March 15, 2005.
11. F. I. Norris, "Pension Folly-How Losses Become Profit," *New York Times*, April 28, 2002, C1.
12. B. Berkowitz, "Earthlink Financier Pleas Guilty to Fraud," *Yahoo News*, April 20, 2002.
13. "Waksal Gets More Than 7 Years, to Pay $4.3M," *CNN Money*, June 10, 2003.
14. D. Barrett, "Shamed DeDe Home 'Bound,'" *New York Post*, April 30, 2002, 3.
15. R. Blumenthal and C. Vogel, "Ex-Sotheby's CEO Sentenced," *San Francisco Chronicle*, April 30, 2002.
16. M. Brick, "Former Judge is Convicted of Bribery in Divorce Court," *New York Times*, April 30, 2007.
17. B. Golding, "$42M Holocaust-Fund 'Rip-Off,'" *New York Post*, November 10, 2010, 5.
18. AP Service, "Crooked Eye Doc Gets Jail," *New York Post*, September 4, 2003, 15.
19. D. Seifman, "City Lawyer Accused of Giving Himself a Raise," *New York Post*, December 19, 2001, 32.
20. F. Dicker, "Michael Boxley Rape Record," *Free Republic Forum*, August 1, 2003.
21. D. Stout, "Ex-Rep. Jefferson Convicted in Bribery Scheme," NY Times.com, June 8, 2009.
22. Ibid.
23. J. Zelny, "His Library, His Way ... Chicago Tribune," *News*, November 18, 2004.
24. H. Cleckley, *The Mask of Sanity* (St. Louis, MO: C. V. Mosby, 1982).

25. "Correcting the Record: Times Reporter Who Resigned Leaves Long Trail of Deception," *New York Times*, May 11, 2003, Front Page.
26. Ibid.
27. B. Herbert, "Justice Confounded," *New York Times*, December 31, 1998, A19.
28. Ibid.
29. A. Levine, "As Genetic Data Increase," *Psychiatric News*, December 7, 2012, 18.

6

Social Conformity in a Polarized Society

Social Functioning in a Conflicting Social System

So far, the concept of well-adjusted behavior translated in conformity might capture one's ability to master various relatively stressing events within the framework of societal rules and regulations. The degree of experiencing distress or not is an open question. As previously discussed, adjustment can neither be fully equated with social conformity nor with normalcy. A debatable issue is the fact that the individual's social functioning when confronted with unexpected adverse situations could test his ability to respond properly and his ability of whether to act in a conformist manner or not. Some people, as we have seen, might feel compelled to change their degree of conformity to the point of becoming nonconformists when faced with controversial social policies that might be viewed as harmful to their well-being. Furthermore, the same narrow concept of conformity has excluded the most socially creative people or the real "movers and shakers" who are most often the agents of societal changes. As such, they are more likely to be less-compliant citizens to the social rules and more free in their behavioral responses that make them act in various degrees as nonconformists. As known, the nonconformists tend to ignore to various extents authority's regulations which promote a consensus of socially acceptable responses that enhance conformity. In our present stage of social transition governed by significant values' change and supported by controversial if not inconsistent conduct's rules, society seems plagued by conflicting and polarizing policies that have destabilized the concept of proper social adjustment. The acerbic and uncontrollable conflict between individual needs and social contradictory policies has inherently led to a gamut of individual responses ranging from customary compliance or negotiated agreements to explosive reactions or weird acting out, often accompanied by a wild array of negative emotional reactions. The implicit assumption of this psychosocial concept of conformity, that it should capture the high resilience of the individual to make it possible for him to pursue his ultimate drive for self-fulfillment, has proven to be overoptimistic. The fact is that man doesn't always have the ability to cope and adjust to the whole range of positive and negative crisis and stressful events confronting his life, particularly when induced by twisted laws and norms of conduct. This is exacerbated by the gap between many people's present social constraints by dealing with the arbitrary restrictions imposed by society and their nagging aspirations of what they want to achieve and be.

Despite these noticeable inconsistencies of the concept of proper social adjustment or its equation with "normal behavior and good health," it has still been the ultimate goal in mental health treatment for the humanistic psychotherapist. After the assumed control or resolution of the client-patient's intrapsychic conflict, the humanistic psychotherapist tends to urge the client-patient to attempt to work for the growth of his personality and to do his utmost to increase his capacity for self-realization as part of developing his innate potentials. The problem starts when client-doctor goals are confronted with the new conflicting social state of affairs. After attempting to improve patient's emotional condition, if the psychotherapist tries to eventually emphasize those assumed attributes of alleged acting "normally," implicitly favoring our societal standards of acceptable behavior, he opens up a Pandora's box for the client. Wittingly or unwittingly this would amount to a subtle indoctrination of the patient in the new norms of conformity that embodies our present social values viewed by many as unsettling or equivocal. However, by doing so he might antagonize the very set of values espoused by the patient while promoting the ones which could have caused or contributed to the patient's emotional problems. As such, this discreet reinforcement of social conformity might have in reality, the opposite effect on patient's well-being. It stifles his creative expression or desire to make his contribution to the reformulation, modification, or restructuring of some dissonant, incongruent governmental rules. On the other hand, if his drive for self-expression, particularly the desire to reform aspects of the social organization, met with the authority opposition, he either might be forced to protest or to strongly confront the official position. The consequences for him might be dramatic and detrimental. Then, the exhorted self-realization as promoted by the humanists could inadvertently lead to a situation of maladjustment.

The individual's pursuit of self-fulfillment is a controversial issue even within the framework of humanistic thinking considering the implicit assumption of a delicate, unstable balance between the existent social norms and someone's attempts to express his different social concept. This different social concept might be viewed as dissonant or dissident, thereby antagonizing the very core of his social acceptance with its unforeseen consequences for his future.

Under these circumstances what an alleged well-adjusted-normal individual pursuing self-fulfillment could do? Should he have an attitude of submission toward the socially controversial norms, which as adaptive as they may sound at first presuppose a willingness to forgo any affirmation of his cherished ideals or of his integrity when they contradict the official policies, even if they might suggest immediate safety? Does this intellectual and emotional conflict when translated in behavioral dissenting responses to the existing policies that stifle his aspirations or sense of justice make him maladapted? This is a basic controversy of defining what would constitute "normal" behavior within the larger concept of proper social functioning, particularly in a multicultural society in transition reigned by contentious, shifty, and contradictory norms of conduct.

In this context a puzzling example might help to show the paradoxical dilemma created by the concept of well-adjusted behavior "normalcy" as elaborated by armchair theorists. Socrates, the Greek philosopher who was sentenced to death for his philosophical theories and considered harmful and seditious for the state had the opportunity to leave the city with the help of his disciples and not to take the poison, whereas Galileo, the Italian astrologist who was brought before the Roman Inquisition as heretic was faced with the alternative of renouncing to his scientific cosmological knowledge or die. Socrates, faithful to his beliefs, stoically took the poison and died, whereas Galileo renounced and reneged on his scientific knowledge in order to live. By the criteria of conformity equated with normalcy, both of them had the capacity to evaluate the consequences of their acts, but only Socrates took responsibility for his teachings while rejecting the authorities' allegations of corrupting the youth and of antistate subversive activity. Was Socrates acting "normally" by submitting to the unfair punishment of the system of his society that arbitrarily convicted him to death without valid charges or was Galileo acting "normally" who reluctantly disavowed responsibility for his scientific theories to avoid death? From the social point of view, their creeds and actions that opposed the official social system made them more than nonconformists, in fact, rebels, and as such "maladjusted." In the end Galileo survived by conforming to the demands of society. He became again proforma well adjusted, while Socrates the alleged rebel died acting as a conformist.

As we may see the idea of self-realization and self-assertion as ultimate goals of accomplishing the ideal of normalcy has always contained the seed of an insurmountable contradiction with the idea of conformity, the backbone of community adjustment. On the other hand, the emphasis on the acceptance of the individual's inalienable right for self-expression and free rejection of any social action which is not in accord with his beliefs or sense of right and wrong is totally unrealistic and impractical. To pursue it, it would be detrimental to the society and ultimately to the individual by satisfying anyone's fancy concept of right and wrong that would lead to anarchy. The conclusion is obvious that the present formulation of normalcy and social adjustment are complementing each other on a very limited basis. Carrying the argument further, even considering a society where the norms of conduct imposed by the government are supposed to be strictly obeyed by the fear of heavy punishment, still some alleged "obedient" normals would have problems to follow them because of the inherent conflicts with one's specific traits of temperament (risk takers, reward dependent, etc.) and personal drives. In our unbalanced societal system, the conflict is open and any individual's social functioning that follows the duplicitous and irreconcilable norms of conduct would not be protected from being abused by others and frustrated in the quest of his social aims.

In this context, the changed social-moral values have not only fallen short of meeting the human diversified and changeable needs but also have tended to interfere and hinder the individual's pursuit of his social undertakings. To complicate further the issue, the composite list of normal social behavior extolled by humanists and accepted by society contains attributes of personality that do not correlate positively with each other. For example, uncritical trust of others is questionable to be pursued in our morally relativistic society. Worse, it doesn't correlate with social success which as a rule is based on the manipulation of others and is not necessarily decided by honesty and merit. In the same vein, the pursuit of independence for reaching personal goals doesn't associate with altruism or with successful handling of a marital partnership.

All in all, if a person would follow the prescriptions of humanist view of their "healthy psychology" in the pursuit of self-realization, he or she could end in bitterness, aggravations, and frustrations. Ironically, as a whole, personality qualities which tend to cover all-encompassing, general goals as advocated by the culturalists, are loosely defined in terms of their relationship to the complex needs exhibited by the human nature making the pursuit of most of them unrewarding. However, in some cases, they could be helpful for achieving social adjustment as used in specific situations. For instance, attributes of social adjustment like self-control, self-reliance, and social responsibility are highly beneficial traits when used properly to safeguard one's interests within the daily human transactions. However, the same qualities of self-control and cautiousness highly protective in social transactions are less useful in intimate relationships where the expression of love and more openness are desirable. The same applies to self-reliance, a personality trait highly valued in the organization of one's life but disadvantageous in situations where the individual's high confidence precludes asking for advice to solve properly a difficult situation, making him proceed without the necessary knowledge to deal with the task at hand.

The question asking for clarification but unanswered by these theoreticians of personality is whether one can assume the existence of a cluster of personality traits that increases individual's capacity to solve adverse situations. As we have seen from the previous chapters, there is not a specific cluster of traits to guarantee a constancy of responses and reactions within the range of what is called normal behavior that would secure one's continuous adjustment to his environment. More likely, it depends on the dynamics of one's holistic interaction with his environment. The interaction is multifactorial starting with one's intellectual capacity and ability to apply a dispassionate judgment in the evaluation of the stressful event to one's facility to use judiciously his appropriate past experiences and emotional resources to deal with that situation. Ideally, a well-adjusted personality assumed to act normally presupposes to have acquired a judgmental ability to manipulate his environment successfully. Theoretically, this would create the most favorable conditions to make the best available choices in coping with a diversity of favorable and unfavorable circumstances. But, if one's ability to cope successfully with crises is hindered by insurmountable realistic difficulties that reduce his possibilities to find a proper solution to the problem, should we assume that he is not "well-adjusted or normal?" Certainly not.

Successful coping is only one facet of the assumed concept of social adjustment, the other one should be the ability to accept one's limitations and thereby to attempt to maintain a degree of mental control over the confronting stress or overwhelming crisis. Furthermore, should one assume that the normal individual as defined by humanists confronts the adversities of life less affected by negative emotional responses? Should he be able to deal stoically with crises and unfavorable events without experiencing too much worry, distress, or bouts of anxiety? Far from true; in reality, he would experience the whole gamut of the above human emotions, not to mention anger, rage, or hate, depending on his view of the nature of the event and the impact on his life. What is important to note is that in most cases, all these emotions should subside at the resolution of the stressful event. It is also expected that they should have a relatively minimal impact on his regular functioning and not unreasonably affect his judgment. Any acute emotional discomfort when confronted with overwhelming problems is more often rather short lived either because either he has been able to find at least a temporary tolerable solution or to avoid its deleterious impact by compensating for the sustained losses in redirecting his energy and skills toward other more controllable activities. Not to mention, that people who might appear at a particular time socially uncomfortable and stressed, hence not quite "normal," would become well integrated at another time when they are able to deal with the sustained emotional or material losses by finding valid explanations for social events that are uncontrollable by him, like natural disasters, impairment of health, and so forth, for the change of his social fortune.

While there is a remarkable element of resilience in individual's adaptability with a flexible integrative approach, operating socially has its own limitations. People's personalities have areas of strength and weakness and if a weak trait is under assault, the negative emotional response will be relatively compensated by the areas of personality strength. It is well known that successful professional people, businessmen, or regular citizens who might have serious problems in their personal life from unhappy marriages, relationships with partners, or problems with their children or relatives compensate for them by relying on their areas of social success, translated in personality strength. In general, in interpersonal relationships, the conflicts or changes are made more acceptable by the well-known fact that a good adjustment in these areas is difficult to attain in these days of affirmation of independence of each partner. This might create situations when both parties are not necessarily emotionally evenhanded to be able to make the desirable concessions for mutual benefit. In case when only a partner is well adjusted, then the burden is on him or her to cope with the other who tends to feel prejudiced, to be egocentric if not disinterested to cooperate.

The social adjustment is complicated when traits of personality considered as part of a personality disorder are allegedly disruptive in interpersonal relationships, but could represent an asset for specific jobs or for succeeding in the public life. Let's take the example of a successful Hollywood movie executive whose private life was a long series of abortive or contentious relationships with women. He had many short-lived unsatisfactory affairs that were either mutually terminated or more often by women who found him, though generous and socially entertaining, too self-centered, demanding, and behaviorally unpredictable. After years of looking for the right woman to accommodate him, compelled by age he decided to make all the necessary social moves to get married. Finally, he convinced an attractive business woman who was pursued at that time by another man to have an exclusive relationship with him in order to marry her. Though in the period of dating she had some reservations about his intimate erratic and odd behavior, she decided to marry him. What she didn't realize was the extent to which he was consumed by his movie business which was taking most of his time from morning till late at night. The difference in time and working hours between New York and California made the running of the business more difficult and because of it he was rarely able to spend time with her in the evening or go to bed together at night. He was compensating his neglect for her by buying her expensive gifts and supporting her child from a previous marriage. However, gradually the relationship deteriorated anyway because of his controlling and autocratic manner of organizing their private life. After divorce, the best they could do was maintaining a superficial friendship since he was partly supporting her and the child. Afterwards his pattern of relationships with women continued in the same erratic and superficial manner as controlled by his total dedication to his work. Indeed, he became even more successful career wise which was translated in getting richer and inviting more business respect from his peers.

Ironically, his success was favored by his psychological traits of personality that classically belong to the domain of abnormal psychology.

He suffered from an intractable obsessive-compulsive disorder that was combined with a personality profile exuding ambitiousness, egocentricity, and arrogance affecting his relationships with subordinates and other people. He was looking down on most of his subordinates as unproductive and undisciplined and whose work couldn't be trusted. The volume of his office work was enormously self-increased because of his conviction that it was his duty to strictly direct and control his subordinates as to assure the best execution of tasks according to his specifications. He was an ultraconformist. After years of undergoing various kinds of psychotherapy, he was aware that his working habits and compulsive behavior were viewed as unwarranted if not odd by others. But he justified his conduct by the quality of his work and his social achievements. Though his private life was more or less in shambles, he coped relatively well with the disappointments generated by his poor relationships with women and acquaintances by deriving his gratification from his business career that made him appear socially well adjusted. As long as he was able to cope with this emotional limitation in his private life compensated by his successful career, and as long as he was able to accept and insulate the emotional conflicts of his intimate relationships he passed the test of social adjustment but not necessarily that of what has been called "normal conduct."

He is not by any means alone. There are many people who successfully dedicated their life to their career as writers, explorers, scientists, and so forth, to the detriment of a satisfactory organization of their private life. Their conduct of life though appearing to be to some extent objectionable by the general norms of social functioning, it is compensated by their achievements in their careers that make them to seem well-adjusted "normal," while functioning within the framework of an ambiguous conformity.

It should be evident by now that the concept of social adjustment doesn't entirely stand the scrutiny of either fulfilling the criteria for a balanced social and private functioning routinely or, at least, to meet the criteria of a continuous smooth social interaction. There are discrepancies, holes, and disparities at various levels of an individual functioning which makes his social conduct uneven and sometimes unpredictable. These problems of behavior are often associated with deviant conduct and/or negative emotional reactions which might convey a degree of maladjustment poking holes further in the hypothetical concept of what should constitute a "normal" conduct.

This poses the issue of separating the alleged "normal" behavior with its wide variations of conduct from the also ill-defined, marginal personality disorders considered weakly adjusted by displaying what is popularly called a neurotic comportment representing a gray area of overlap with so-called well-adjusted behavior. It comprises the alleged well-adjusted-normal behaviors, but accompanied by social areas where there are degrees of conduct deviance and emotional discomfort often provoked by stressful conditions or by strong inner irrepressible drives. These neurotic behaviors labeled as "abnormal" could be displayed routinely as inappropriate, negative reactions in specific social interactions representing nonconformist behavior. It is psychologically assumed that the so-called emotionally charged responses of the so-called neurotic-maladjusted person to environmental situations are part of his habitual skewed coping with perceived unfavorable events or with unacceptable pursuit of his inner drives. To some extent, this is an arbitrary division of human way of coping with crisis and events viewed as overwhelming by him, mainly because of societal arbitrary restrictions.

The problem starts with the fact that most people according to their skewed perception of events viewed as possibly detrimental to them, might overreact out of proportion with the situation, which by this definition would make them automatically maladjusted, at least temporarily. However, this does not represent a fixed, indisputable law of behavior to a perceived stressor. This situation is more evident for many people who are faced with new situations, new type of activity where they unexpectedly encounter problems of adjustment. Under these circumstances, one's major traits of personality could make or break his ability to adjust. Take the case of someone displaying temperamental traits of risk adversity or harm sensitivity but otherwise relatively well adjusted, considered as normal, who under new untested conditions might display some transient negative emotional reactions that could be erroneously identified as maladjustment by someone adhering to the stereotypical definition of neurotic behavior as maladjusted. This also could happen to people who are adjusted to perform their routine tasks viewed as unrewarding and frustrating until they have the opportunity to change their job to a more demanding one. If they failed to evaluate properly their ability and willingness to meet the potential demands of the job, they might have serious difficulty to readjust and respond to the new responsibilities. Their responses could be sometimes out of line with the demands of the situation inducing negative emotional responses.

For example, Trudy, a housewife who was bored performing her routine household duties and taking care of her six-year-old child felt that the only compensatory pleasant diversion had been meeting her friends for lunch, shopping for clothes, or going out to movies with her husband. This organization of life was viewed as ungratifying emotionally and frustrating intellectually. After mulling over her options she reckoned that she would be able to satisfy her needs for self-realization by opting to get rid of the home drudgery when the child entered elementary school and be able to go to work like her husband. An additional impetus was her conviction that she has been emotionally used by her husband and relegated to a secondary, housekeeping role. Liberated in her thinking from the old sex stereotypes, she decided to get a job that to her surprise opened a Pandora's box.

In her new role, Trudy was unable to take proper care of the house and had no choice than to delegate the care of the child after school to a regular babysitter. In addition, she was frustrated by her arguments with the husband about sharing of household obligations and paying among other expenses for a housemaid. Her dissatisfaction with the hired housemaids was endless because she found them quite sloppy and argumentative. Tired of changing maids and fighting a losing battle with her husband about responding to each other's needs, she progressively started to think that she didn't have another alternative than to get a divorce, to be free from all marital obligations. The divorce moved smoothly by invoking "irreconcilable differences," and after solving financial matters with the help of the lawyer she was a free, independent woman.

Finally, she was ready to readjust her life to the new status of working as a divorcee-single parent. However, her sense of liberation was spoiled by the realization that her standard of living fell more than she had expected. Trudy also realized to her chagrin that the societal institutions have not done too much to facilitate her social life as a single parent by offering good child-care places for single parents, properly supervised. The solution to develop new patterns of social interaction by relying on an undependable social network of women with similar problems or on transient unreliable nannies proved to be rather unsatisfactory. She also found out that the exchange of her set of marital problems for the new one of single mother didn't increase her sense of comfort and peace of mind. Something was amiss about her liberation. Worries and insecurities plagued her and she didn't have anyone to blame or ask for advice or to share her endless concerns about her child, dating, and her job or to protect her.

Now Trudy is reconsidering her attitude toward marriage, particularly since her ex-husband remarried and seems quite content. She wonders whether her divorce was a too impulsive action triggered by her misperception about her own aspirations. Now she is toying with the idea of getting remarried, but she is afraid that the same pitfalls will confront her unless she has a clear arrangement with a prospective husband about the limitation of her marital obligations that would not antagonize the pursuit of her career. She has also become aware that her independent style of social interaction could put strains on the contemplated marital relationships unless she would be able to bring home a relatively fair income to permit her to spend extra money on herself, lunches with her girlfriends, and so forth, after her equitable contribution to the household expenses. Otherwise, it might lead to a disastrous spousal interaction because of a competitive assertion of their independence at the other's expense.

From her perspective she seems to be faced with a temporary intractable dilemma. That of staying as a single parent and dealing with all issues related to it while still chasing after occasional lovers, or at best, temporarily accepting a cohabitant partner who might be more accommodating to her needs and hoping for the best. However, any of these provisional choices wouldn't solve the long-term issue of finding a permanent partner to share the joys and sorrows of life. The disquieting awareness of getting older doesn't help either.

But the main issue for the concept of well-adjusted person in a humanist framework is whether her fragile social adjustment has met her pursuit of self-realization. By our present social standards, Trudy functions within the parameter of acceptable social behavior striving to be become self-fulfilled; hence, she appears to act as a "conformist-normal person." However, can one say that she is well adjusted while coping with her new carved life, considering her constant worries, insecurities, sleeping difficulties and bouts of sadness? At best, her social adjustment is tenuous, it could get destabilized any time if her prized love relationship suddenly goes sour or the career becomes stagnant. The gamble for social self-realization is still uncertain in her case. Why should it be so?

Basically, it might have to do with fancy attempts of society to tinker with unalterable instinctual programming of human nature. While incremental changes of the interaction between sexes have continuously taken place, spurted by technological advances of society that it truly liberated women from house chores, it didn't change the reproductive needs of women. It provided jobs where they could function well but society didn't find the right formula to deal with the aspect of the simultaneous satisfaction of her maternal instinct by practical social-agencies support of the mother-child bond, paramount for the healthy development of the child. Inadvertently, society has tampered with the mother-child bond and has affected its strength by manipulating the child's rearing practices that has created a serious dilemma for the mother's use of surrogate child's care. When conditions of child rearing deteriorate, it has had dramatic consequences on the emotional development of the child as demonstrated long ago by John Bowlby[1] and others. One way or another, the child, or more likely children's rearing interferes with the fast track of social climbing of many women. It has provoked a sober debate of what is the best way to pursue a woman's self-realization. It pitted social trends against maternal needs. In a way, it has attempted to work as a natural selection for their social competition in business favoring those women with no children or the ones who have their extended family's help in the upbringing of the children. Furthermore, the present condition with 46 percent of the children out-of-wedlock is an unworkable emotional and social solution.

An interesting case of misguided expression of emotional self-fulfillment is reported by the New York Times which presented the convoluted story of the parenting of Lisa Miller and her daughter Isabella. Miller was one of the partners in a same-sex marriage with Jenkins in Vermont.[2] They decided to have a family and Miller became pregnant by in vitro insemination. However, the relationship between the two women progressively deteriorated to the point of Miller moving out, followed by divorce. Miller became guilt stricken for practicing lesbian love and was drawn back to religion. She started to restrict Jenkins' visiting rights for Isabella on the grounds of undue sexual influence by calling herself "Mummy" and narrating stories with lesbian flavor. Miller moved to Virginia, a state which doesn't offer same-sex marriage. The issue of custody battle reached the Supreme Court of Virginia pitting the religious position of Miller, supported by lawyers from Liberty Counsel, affiliate with Liberty Law School, Virginia, against the high battery of American Civil Liberties Union, Lesbian Alliance, and so forth, legal rights lawyers defending Jenkins lesbian's marital rights. Her case became a political and civil rights battle regarding the rights of the same-sex union. Jenkins won the reinstatement of visiting rights.

Distressed, Miller decided to leave the country and take her daughter Isabella to Nicaragua with the help of Mennonites in order to protect her from the influence of lesbianism. The Federal Bureau of Investigation eventually found her and meanwhile the judge in Vermont threatened her that if she continues to interfere with Jenkins' visiting rights, he will give Isabella's custody to Jenkins. The drama of humanist self-actualization which became a nightmare for Miller and her daughter goes on. So much about humanists' concept of reaching one's potential, self-realization, and fulfillment!

By the same token, the marital interaction also affects the male who is subject to the same new conflicting marital values and whose sense of balanced approach to marriage is heavily tested by the emotional demands of the wife or by his inability to satisfy her reasonable social needs because of his egocentrism and personal priorities resulting in similar problems of poor adjustment. As important as it is, this is just one controversial aspect created to be the ambiguous social policies and incongruous set of values affecting the presupposed congenial relationships of sexes.

The Redefinition of the Assumed "Well-Adjusted" Behavior by Authorities

The problem of acting "properly" in our society becomes confusing if not frustrating when the individual has to deal with a variety of new controversial and contradicting social beliefs-values, most of them created by ambiguous official policies that quite often lack a reasonable justification as general norms of conduct and seem to be of questionable moral validity. As it is known, the most notorious twisted policies are those related to political correctness which are by definition arbitrary, imprecise, and open to wide interpretation and political abuse. Consider this silly incident which took ridiculously official proportions.

On April 2007, a student placed a ham stake in a bag on a lunch table where Muslim Somali students were eating. Since Muslims consider pork unclean, they felt offended and complained to the school administration.[3,4] The incident was investigated by the local police that categorized it as a "hate crime," a very serious political and social offense. The immediate result was the suspension of the student for his intolerable crime. The interpretation of his act went beyond treating it, as an act of insensitivity. It metamorphosed in an outright premeditated act of hate against another religious and ethnic group. They reached these dubious conclusions without any due process of law. One might think that this is an isolated case of an opportunistic or misguided police interpretation supported by an overzealous school authority, which is far from true.

Another case is of a seven-year-old boy charged with misdemeanor for shooting a toy gun at school. The boy allegedly shot a $5 Nerf-style toy gun in Hammonton, New Jersey school in January 2011. No one was hurt, but the boy faced misdemeanor criminal charges. The school alerted the police which investigated the "suspicious activity" at the Early Childhood Education Center. They found out that nobody was threatened and the mother of the child stated that she didn't know that the boy took the gun at the school.[5] Where is the criminal case if not in the biased mind of politically correct police officers? The incident took a wild proportion because people in position of authority are either biased or narrow-minded employees, who only care about being in the good graces of the higher-ups who decide their jobs and promotions.

Think about the case of a family with a four-year-old boy who used leg braces for walking and was forced by the Transportation Safety Administration (TSA) at the airport to remove the braces while attempting to cross the safety detector. The father explained that the boy born prematurely has weak muscle tone at the legs and can't walk without the braces which were custom fitted. The TSA agent insisted on taking off the braces if they expected to reach their destination Orlando, Florida at Disney World. After the removal of the braces the mother offered to walk the boy through the security checkpoint. Her request was denied by the allegedly "clever" law implementing agent. Finally, the boy was patiently coaxed to walk holding the frame of the checkpoint and to slowly make it to the other side of the detector. Was the agent afraid of breaking the security rules by letting a four-year-old "suspected terrorist," slip through or did he assume that the leg braces might have contained explosives put in by the father? There were other better methods to verify this assumption if ever they crossed his mind. That said, it wouldn't explain why he rejected the request of the mother to let her hold the boy's hand while helping him cross the security point.[6] The security agent abused his position by his autocratic and perverse use of the rules. What is important is the fact that he didn't care about the unnecessary anxiety and emotional discomfort inflicted on the family. Were his actions morally correct?

The issue of abuse of political correctness gets quite weird if one considers the absurd case of the Maine Human Rights Commission that proposed banning any gender bathroom divisions in public schools.[7] It all started when the school was accused of discriminating against a twelve-year-old transgender boy by denying him access to the girl's bathroom. The Maine Human Right Commission has spent tax payers' money, debating very seriously whether to eliminate any gender differences about their access to male-female bathrooms by a simple political decree. The real problem is not only the aberrant orientation of a politically ill-advised Commission which was put on the spot by a social activist family but also by the confusion and worries which have been created in the minds of citizens who have difficulty in understanding the purpose of the debate or to relate to it.

How should an assumed well-adjusted person deal with it? Should he accept and follow their decrees regardless of how unsettling they might be to his family or should he obey under protest or disobey and pay for the consequences? Either way his desirable psychological state of well-being will be affected by these out of place demands imposed by misguided activists. But what could happen if an individual who in the past always behaved within the framework of acceptable social conduct reached the point of saturation and decided to protest?

Let us follow the convoluted experience of an Oklahoma police captain, Paul Fields, who filed a federal lawsuit claiming that his civil rights had been violated after being reassigned and placed under investigation for refusing to order his subordinate officers to voluntarily attend a social event at a mosque.[8] They were supposed to attend a law enforcement appreciation day at the Islamic Society of Tulsa. Fields refused to execute the "voluntary" request since it violated his religious beliefs. His lawyer called the lawsuit a case of political correctness that went too far. The lawsuit named the deputy chief as the lone defendant accusing him of retaliating against Fields for exercising his First Amendment rights and not "voluntarily" attending the mosque event. However, Tulsa police chief told Fox23-TV that the mosque event was about community relationship, not about religion. He continued, "We are not going there because they are Islamic. We are going there because they are Tulsa citizens."

However, the event was advertised as a social gathering offering food, watching a Muslim prayer service, and an invitation to join lectures on beliefs, human rights, and women. According to the lawyer, no officer responded to the invitation and no one volunteered. The following day Fields received a directive ordering him to find officers to "volunteer" for it. Interestingly, he received an order to find a voluntary participant to the event but not specifically asking him to order someone to go. If Fields had ordered someone to go, he would have broken the police regulations. The impression was that the program was organized by the mosque for the familiarization of officers with the official position of the Muslims. Nevertheless, according to the same lawyer, "never in the past the police department was obligated to attend social events at synagogues or Christian houses of worship." The Council on America-Islamic Relations capitalized on this controversy to attack police attitude as an example of "anti-Muslim bigotry."

The interpretation of the invitation by the deputy chief seemed to be based less on a sound judgment and sense of fairness and more on his political ambitions to advance his career, even disregarding the rights of others. Interestingly, his "voluntary" order was ambiguous enough suggesting an unwillingness to take full responsibility for his decision. By our new social criteria at first sight, the chief had appeared to have acted normally, although one might have suspected him of overreach. However, on a closer look, his eagerness to arbitrarily reinforce an issue of political correctness to the point of demoting the captain is suspect of crass abuse. He imposed the execution of a nonconformist act in a total conformist manner, a typical behavior falling within the range of ambiguity of social conformity. In this context, the attitude of the captain basically didn't help him to advance his career.

By the same token, how should we judge the crisis of conformity of Fields? He had been in the police force for sixteen years and had about six commendations with no disciplinary action, but now because he asserted his rights by refusing to arbitrarily force the officers to go "voluntarily" to the Mosque lectures and religious service, he was demoted and under investigation apparently, at least for insubordination for not executing a voluntary order. This is another example of someone well-adjusted socially who under the pressure of the newly arbitrary and imposed social policies developed problems of proper social functioning. It is all part of the ambiguity of social conformity, which would be solved by the court. By these criteria his supposed sense of normalcy has been seriously damaged, all because of his resistance to the twisted act of conformity to his boss.

Incongruous Social Adaptation

As previously discussed, the new social and political climate has directly and indirectly encouraged a moral ambiguity that has basically ignored or defied adherence to truth or to the moral values. The misrepresentation and distortion of truth have been extensively practiced not only by crooked corporate executives and dishonest Wall Street investment bankers but also by biased government agencies, hypocritical politicians, prejudiced media, or manipulative lawyers and also by many regular citizens. The truth has become expendable and replaced by fiat with fabricated relative truths. The new reworked social ethics view truth as subjective, tainted by the social background of the individual's societal condition and class. In this context, multiple truths which have been initially debated as an intellectual exercise in philosophical sophistry, later become a smart argument to justify the new social policies by some disingenuous politically biased academicians. Multiple truths based on relative truth became apparently a valid explanation for the same factual event attempting to give it credibility. The direct consequence of this new pseudologic was the twisted reinterpretation of the ethical notions of right and wrong by social activists and lawyers. By and large, the distinction between their meanings has become blurred depending on the subjective version of relative truth used as a basic premise for evaluating the facts under deliberation. The power game of the social activists is amazing, who by using the relative truth, perversely try not always successfully to persuade people to accept wrong facts as right.

Take the case of a federal district judge who accused the federal appeals court of St. Louis of racial bias because of daring to reverse his "irrefutable" decision. The federal judge felt "offended, insulted, troubled and confused" because the federal appeals court rejected his ruling against a policeman on ground of improper judicial conduct. Part of the brilliant argument of this judge was to question their judgment by not so subtly accusing them of racism. "Had I been white and the plaintiff had been black, the appeal court decision would have been significantly different." Did the appeal court act racially, and misinterpret the law or did it disagree with the judge's personal interpretation of the code of justice?

In reality, the federal judge abusing his judicial power took the liberty to ignore judicial procedures and instead of recusing himself from this case as he should have done, he proceeded to try the case. The reason for recusal should have been his personal close relationship with a defendant woman who was part of the suit of the plaintiff-policeman. In his eminent opinion, his integrity couldn't be questioned by the law, supported by his use of veiled intimidation. To convince the appeals court of his rightfulness, he inappropriately played the race card. He was indeed "confused," as he admittedly stated, by the action of the appeal court that apparently from his perspective didn't distinguish right from wrong in the spirit of political correctness.[9]

As we may see, the relative truth fits well in the grand design of the moral relativism which has gone beyond the intended objective of the political ideologists and social activists of changing the thinking of society. The new fanciful social model of man conceived by progressive and activists politicians with the ideological support of some biased members of academia hardly has met the nature and the inalienable social rights of man. They have reinterpreted and redefined the basic man's social aspirations for equality, equal work opportunities, justice, and freedom for which he fought throughout history reducing it to a narrow political context of reinterpretation of social equality within the framework of gender and race. The free social competition with its concept of open hiring and entrepreneurial enterprise regulated by the economic market forces has been skewed by employment quota which in many cases led to inefficiency. It has fueled, among other things, a social conflict created by what has been called reverse discrimination with the replacement of a relative meritocracy by legislation of hiring people with less proper qualifications for the corresponding job.

In this context, equality, while a highly appreciated social principle has been by and large reinterpreted by the official in a biased manner by making some people "more equal than others" with reference to getting employed and other social privileges. While this has been justified as compensatory for the lip service paid by society before the civil rights revolution, it unreasonably destabilized society. It is also true that in the past, society didn't enforce the civil rights of the minority groups, though our Constitution guarantees their rights, but instead of finding fair solutions to redress the balance of inequity, it relied on expedient solutions that have succeeded to exacerbate the racial strife bringing again the issue before the Supreme Court. If the politicians would have found a more equitable solution by offering to all Afro-Americans, scholarships, well-planned preparatory programs and tutorial courses in high school to get them ready for college entrance in order to compete with whites from a position of equal competence, we

Social Conformity in a Polarized Society

would not face this unnecessary social conflict. The reparative approach succeeded to punish people who have not been responsible for past historical injustice promoting an ambiguity toward social conformity. Ultimately, did politicians' "smart solutions" favor a more successful and harmonious functioning of the society? There is no evidence of it.

As far as justice goes, it continues to be extolled as treating all people equally under law, except for the minor twists of offering special legislation for sentencing the crimes of sexual harassment or rape which circumvents the due process of trial discovery in support of accusation of the alleged victim. Otherwise, the justice continues to be manipulated by people able to hire the best lawyers that money can buy or by the ones too powerful socially or politically to be indicted. The moral relativism has surreptitiously permeated the integrity of justice and destabilized its desirable fairness.

Freedom, the buzz word of the politicians and social activists alike has undergone some not so subtle changes in its meaning. It still theoretically protects the free expression of people but provided that one adheres to preferential job treatment and obviously to the officially written and unwritten rules of political correctness, which seems to be at odds with some articles of our Constitution. All in all, it has added to the obfuscation and misinterpretation of what is right and wrong, or how to act "normally." The result is obvious: people have to cope with an ambiguity social conformity.

All these twists and turns of our equivocal social values most often subjectively interpreted have created resentment and frustration in the minds of many people requiring significant attempts for social readjustment if affected by them. The ability to adjust or not brings into question the emotional price to be paid by many individuals who try to function socially under these equivocal conditions that have loosely redefined the notion of what could be considered as well adjusted, normal behavior.

People try to survive and adapt as much as they can to the redefined social principles of equality, justice, freedom, and so forth within the boundary of moral relativism, skillfully manipulated by social ideologues and political opportunists.

However, could someone seemingly of independent and reasonable judgment be able to fully accept and justify to himself some of the lopsided values full of contradictions and interpreted through the subjectivism of the relative truth that defies logic and common sense? What mental gymnastics should he execute to feel comfortable in this new ambiguous moral order that ultimately relies on the support of moral relativism?

How Well Can a Society Function Twisted by Moral Relativism?

Under the umbrella of the moral relativism it would be easy for anyone pretending to act within the realm of conformity to attempt to benefit from the breakdown of societal ethical standards of conduct. It doesn't work, when swindles, frauds, scams, identity theft, false commercial promotions, and so forth, are engulfing society. It becomes even harder for a regular guy to try to "adjust" to the new equivocal business standards. He might not be able to succeed and might more likely become a victim of them. Just to contend with the gamut of poorly unmonitored business regulations and to be able to protect oneself from phony transactions schemed by respectable crooks of the financial or commercial markets is almost an unattainable task. Worse, after being cheated, if the victim expects any fair compensation or at least a judicial retribution, he might be out of luck. Isn't it strange that all the big executives, the fraudsters of Wall Street who engineered the most ingenious and dishonest deal of derivatives that ultimately led to the collapse of the economy weren't indicted and tried for their slimy operations? At best, only some dishonest investment firms were fined but not the responsible chief executive officer and chief financial officer or governmental supervising counterparts, the true culprits. At worst, they were forced to resign or at best remained in their positions free to continue their activities as alleged experts. As a matter of fact, some people responsible for the financial debacle were put in charge by their former partners in the government to solve the crisis created by them.

To fully understand the social significance of this explosion of corruption, systematic cheating, and victimization of the public we have to view it in the light of the new ethics and assault on the social truth whose validity has become questionable and has been conveniently replaced by the self-serving relative truth. It was done by political or judicial decisions that worked toward the advancement and reinforcement of the new confusing social order.

Take, for example, the case of falsifying the school records at the CUNY's Zicklin School of Business. Eight students, including Wall Street people and other full time financiers enrolled in this graduate program obtained failing grades at the school and were supposed to be expelled. To solve the problem, they appealed to CUNY administrators who forged their records changing their failing grades of "F" or "incomplete" to "A" minus. The administrator claimed that four faculty members helped him by letting the students in the class as if they passed the courses. The members denied the allegations. The administrator who stated that he didn't receive any financial benefit from this fraudulent operation received six months jail sentence. What is significant in this case is that eight mature people working in financial markets that would presuppose a high degree of integrity didn't mind cheating without any compunction in order to get passing marks and eventually get the post graduate degree of masters of business administration.[10]

The distortions of social conformity are even more dramatic if one considers the obfuscation of its norms of social conduct induced by some arbitrary decisions of the court. There are judges who from the bench have officially reinterpreted the social conformity by twisting its rules and making them confusing or paradoxical to support their fancy concept of right and wrong with disregard for the conventional norms. To appreciate the extent to which social conformity can be made ambiguous by the court, consider the arbitrary and controversial decision of a Florida judge in a dispute about paternity rights in an adoption case. A lesbian couple wanted to have a child. One of the partners, forty-three-year-old Maria Italiano, had tried unsuccessfully to get pregnant until she decided to ask her gay hairdresser, Massimiliano Gerina, to donate his sperm. According to the court depositions, all three persons met and agreed verbally for him to give the sperm for artificial insemination. However, before the baby girl was born, Gerina wanted the birth certificate to register him as the father of the child. The women refused and he sued. After two years of court wrangling, the inventive judge disregarding the existing rules of birth registration decided to approve a birth certificate listing three parents. It is unclear whether it was written that the baby has two women (mothers) and a man (father) or more likely, all three were listed as parents without specific sex role in procreation. Somehow the women will have sole parental rights and Gerina will have visiting rights (maybe as an observer). He wouldn't provide child support or act as a parent. According to Italiano, his role would be explained to the girl as "that of mommy's good friend who helped your moms have you because they wanted you so badly."

Now, imagine the grownup girl having to present this certificate of birth with three parents to schools, college administrations, or various institutions where the ambiguity of the certificate might require embarrassing explanations. The controversial judge, allegedly a defender of social conformity, acted in a nonconformist manner by deviating from the customary norm of two parents' birth certificate. By legislating from the bench, he would let the future young woman deal with the consequences of his puzzling decision emotionally and socially. The unconventional judge got notoriety and has created a legal precedent for further contentious disputes and psychological turmoil in similar cases.[11]

What is obvious is that the new relative truth and moral fudging tend to justify any outlandish action as acceptable as long as it's serving its political purpose under the cloak of the moral relativism. The irony is that the new relativistic attitude toward truth and falsehood, and right and wrong has offered a sham adjustment to many devious people giving the illusion of their relatively normal functioning by wearing this "mask of normalcy." On the other hand, moral duplicity has become, to some extent, part of the government conduct and of our multicultural society and has become part of all forms of human interaction affecting the way people do business and relate to each other either in intimate or social relationships with the result of increasing the reciprocal mistrust.

Worse than this is that all this social turmoil didn't improve race relations. According to a Rasmussen poll, quoted by Thomas Sowell, professor of economics, only 29 percent of the surveyed Americans believe that race relations got better, while 32 percent think that are getting worse. Incredibly, the same poll indicated that 31 percent of the Afro-Americans think that blacks are racist and only 24 percent of them view whites as racist. From the surveyed whites, 38 percent think that Afro-Americans are racist and only 10 percent believe that whites are racist.[12] There are many factors contributing to this racial polarization, but it seems that among them the implementation of some compensatory or retributive social-political policies have an undesirable effect.

Then, can one truly define a set of valid standards of proper social adjustment for someone functioning in this morally equivocal climate which requires unexpected readjustments to the changing social policies? Under these circumstances, for one to be considered well adjusted he or she has to successfully adapt to incongruous rules and precepts of the moral subjectivism. He has to act coolly and accept unemotionally the arbitrary and inconsistent laws, and while acknowledging the social dissonances to unflinchingly pursue his own interests.

Meanwhile, the ethical people, who might become nonconformists by rejecting or protesting the biased laws could end up being prosecuted by the ones in power in order to legitimize their self-serving policies. Who would be the "well-adjusted normal," the new conformists who had committed the social abuses or their victims?

This means that to be well-adjusted allegedly functioning normal, one has either to conform uncritically to the social system or to act opportunistically and unscrupulously by blocking any sense of fairness and exhibiting a transparent moral insensitivity. Some of these opportunists are self-appointed activists for self-serving cause. They are basically callous climbers and are ambiguously adjusted to the system while satisfying their egotistic wants. They belong to the new genre of duplicitous conformists, pseudoadjusted people, who manipulate well the disquieting social environment. Should this new category of opportunists, socially privileged, the new pillars of social equivocal respectability, play the role models for the new generations? Should it follow that their social power and prerogatives to the new societal scene make them automatically well-adjusted "normal," while the ones who have difficulty dealing with moral ambiguity or are in conflict with the new social-political policies are the ones maladjusted, the "abnormal?"

All considered, one can safely say that the assumptive notion of normal adjustment as elaborated by past theoreticians contradicts and fails to address to the reality of the present social functioning of an average individual in an unsettled and polarized society. As previously said, it had been based on the premise of an ideal, stable society, spared of constant crises, dramatic changes, and turmoil that affect the adjustment of the individuals. The attribute of stereotypical concept of well-adjusted behavior previously equated with conformity has to go beyond this limited aspect of conformity, itself changeable in the new social environment. Under the pressure of a personal or social crisis a more ingenious, unconventional coping to overcome stressful events is required. As we discussed, the conformist adjustment will temporarily fluctuate to various degrees of nonconformist behaviors according to the nature of confronting situation. It is quite possible that a nonconformist approach and an unconventional solution would help the person to deal better with the amount of anxiety or depression or other negative emotions triggered by the threatening event. While his social adjustment might appear to be marginal, he is not an "abnormal" person as psychologists might tend to classify him.

In this context, abnormality represents extreme personality disorders showing significant persistent deviancy in conduct and problems of impaired relationships with others resulting in serious interpersonal dysfunction. From this perspective it removes the stigma of abnormality from most mild personality disorders who attempt to cope with adverse social events and present problems of conduct and whose emotional reactions do not meet the arbitrary standards of alleged normal behavior. The acceptance of the fact that there is nothing abnormal about reacting behaviorally and emotionally outside the range of routine conformity's responses when confronted with serious unfavorable situations, helps the individual to maintain his self-esteem and a cool reasoning in the search for at least a temporary solution. It is erroneous to assume that because one is overwhelmed with emotions and unable to find a salutary solution quickly to a critical situation, he is less "smart" and socially less "skillful," which in turn adds to his emotional discomfort and might delay any solution.

All these psychological considerations take an even more significant meaning considering that the individual is conflicted everyday with new problems created by the ambiguities and vagaries of a culturally dissonant and polarized society.

Notes

1. J. Bowlby, "Human Personality Development in an Ethological Light," in *Animal Models in Human Psychobiology*, ed. G. Serban and A. King (New York: Plenum Publishing Corp., 1974).
2. E. Eckholm, "Which Mother for Isabella? Civil Union Ends in an Abduction," NYTimes.com, July 29, 2012.
3. "Student Suspended for Ham Sandwich 'Hate Crime,'" *Bluffton Today*, April 24, 2007.
4. M. Thomas, "Federal Judge Rules Fox News 'Gullible and Unprofessional,'" *Open Education*, June 10, 2008.
5. "7-Year-Old with Misdemeanor for a Nerf Gun," dumbASS government .com/taxonomy.
6. Political Correctness, "TSA Force Disabled Boy to Remove His Leg Braces to Pass through Security," dumbASS government.com.
7. Ridiculous Cases of Political Correctness, "The Maine Human Rights Commission and the Gender Bathroom Access."
8. T. Stames, "Oklahoma Police Captain Sues Supervisor for Mandatory Attendance at Islamic Group Event," FoxNews.com, February 24, 2011.
9. A. Liptak, "Federal Judge is Scolded for Attack," *New York Times*, November 5, 2002, A18.
10. M. C. Giove and S. Edelman, "CUNY BIG: I F'D UP Admits Grade Fix," *New York Post*, December 20, 2012, 17.
11. K. Gray Florida, "Judge Approves Birth Certificate Listing Three Parents," www.Reuters.com/article (accessed February 7, 2013).
12. Thomas Sowell, "Strange New Face of American Racism," *New York Post*, July 8, 2013, 19.

Index

aberrant behavior 58, 75, 78, 87
ability 1, 4, 11, 37, 40, 49, 76–7, 79–80, 84–5, 99, 132–3, 165–6, 169–70, 173
abnormal behavior 13–4, 55, 61, 83
abnormal personality 17, 24, 27, 44, 55, 73, 128
abnormal social behavior 153
abnormality 13–4, 27, 32–3, 35, 44, 63, 73, 187–8
abortion 5, 26, 66
acceptable behavior 13, 20, 24, 26, 34, 58, 70, 99, 166
accusations 65–6, 68–9, 102, 106, 183
actions, nonconformist 50, 133
activists 92, 95
  social 91, 115, 153, 181–3
activity 8, 25, 31, 48, 50, 53–4, 56, 80, 116, 129, 131–2, 173
acts 4–5, 11–2, 18–9, 22, 25, 32, 56–60, 64, 99–100, 123–6, 128, 131–2, 183–7
  nonconformist 64, 180
  self-concept 49
  terrorist 116, 120
  violent 116, 125
adjustment 5, 13, 25–6, 37, 44, 49, 55, 85, 99, 108, 165, 170, 173, 177, 187
administration 64, 68, 71, 80, 82, 92–3, 106, 158, 185
admission 71, 81, 90, 123
adultery 10, 72
affirmative action 72, 89, 91
Afro-Americans 61, 90, 182, 186
aggression 18, 22–3, 95
Alexander 137–8
allegations 68, 102, 105, 167, 185
ambiguity 87, 183, 185, 188
Ambiguity of Normalcy 37

American Psychiatric Association (APA) 51, 131
analysts 88, 135, 140, 162
anger 22, 47, 75, 78, 83, 91, 170
antisocial 56–7, 77, 118, 127, 158
antisocial behavior 24, 32, 62, 116, 121, 127, 157–8, 160–1
anxiety 5, 13, 29, 41, 46–7, 53–4, 56, 75, 89, 101, 108, 170, 179, 187
argument 2, 19, 67, 70, 78, 96, 100, 103, 125, 152, 159, 168, 174
army 93–4, 130, 149
artists 129, 146, 157
aspirations 75, 108, 126, 166–7, 175
assassination 116–7, 127–8
assault 66, 68–9, 97, 102–3, 170, 184
assumptions 14, 19, 23, 29, 40, 42, 46, 49, 52, 55, 59, 61–2, 64–5, 106
attention 16, 27–8, 74, 98, 103, 113–4, 149, 153
attributes 14, 140, 168–9, 187
authorities 28, 33–4, 59, 81, 87, 91, 112, 119, 122–4, 127, 129, 146, 177–8

baby 18, 26–7, 46, 67, 185
Baird, W's case 107
Barr, S., (Homeland Security, male's sex harassment) 102
beat 64, 81, 141, 147, 161
behavior 15, 17–8, 20–2, 31–3, 35–6, 38–9, 43–5, 50–1, 56–9, 61–3, 82–5, 113–5, 131–2, 151, 171–3
  conformity-normal 14, 25, 71, 77, 173
  controversial 46, 151
  nonconformist 32, 38, 85, 109, 137, 187
  patterns of RESPONSES 15–6, 23–4, 44–5, 55, 57, 82, 161, 165, 167

189

Berger, S. 80–1, 87
biology 39, 95
birth 17, 20–1, 46, 51, 148, 185
birth certificate three parents 185–6
Blagojevich, R. (convicted governor) 82
body 19, 28, 40–1, 43, 63, 76, 100, 114
bosses 1, 3, 28–9, 49, 80, 100, 108, 114, 180
boyfriend 26–7, 68–9
boys 6, 10, 20–1, 94, 178
brain 41, 50
bribery 57–8, 134, 147, 149
Brodsky, M. 73
business 8, 57, 88, 95, 139, 143, 145, 160, 171, 176, 184, 186
businessmen 31, 120, 141–2, 144, 170

campaign 79, 133, 154
capacity 11, 13, 79, 108, 158, 166–7
care 9, 27, 96, 104–5, 146, 154, 174, 178–9
career 1, 3–4, 27, 30, 80, 84, 92–3, 96, 99, 105, 115, 129–30, 171–2, 175, 180
Cecil 'case of hostile work milieu 100
census bureau 97–8
CEO 62, 134–5, 141, 146, 184
character 7, 19, 47–9, 55–6, 62, 73, 81, 128
charming 2, 29, 144, 158
cheat 99, 104, 107, 141, 146, 155, 157–8
cheating 64, 72, 88, 139–41, 144, 146, 150, 158, 160–1
chest 69, 85
child 2–3, 10, 16–8, 20–3, 42, 46, 51, 56, 82, 133, 160, 171, 174–6, 178, 185
children 9–10, 16–24, 30, 35, 42, 46, 76, 96, 98–9, 104–6, 137, 160, 170, 176
chromosome 20 (SNAP) neuroticism 47
civil rights 89–90, 179, 182
clients 3, 8, 52, 80, 140–3, 155, 162, 166
Clinton Administration 79–80
Cloninger, R.C. 73
CNN Money 138, 162
Coetzee, S.' case 67
college 1–2, 6, 71, 90, 92, 104, 130, 159
community 9, 11, 13, 24, 26, 30, 33–5, 38, 113–4, 128–30, 142–4
company 2–3, 6, 36, 59, 100, 102, 114, 134–6, 141, 145, 149, 159
compassion 49, 84, 129, 160

compromise 25, 96–7, 100–3, 123–4, 158
compulsive behavior 53, 172
concept 5–6, 9, 11–3, 15, 19, 21, 25–6, 33, 35, 40, 55, 69–71, 89–90, 165–7
conditioning, social 41–2
confident 48, 141, 143, 158
conflicts 5, 14, 25, 29, 35, 38, 82–3, 89, 95–7, 99, 104, 108, 168
 inner 5, 7, 40, 71–2
conformists 6, 111–3, 115, 117, 119, 121, 123, 125, 127, 129, 131, 133, 135, 137, 161
conformity 9, 25–6, 32–3, 37–8, 55, 61–2, 84–5, 112, 125, 136–7, 165–8, 180, 187
conformity-normalcy, social 29, 54–5, 61, 66, 69, 71, 89
Congress 82, 136, 149–51
conscience 23, 144, 160
conscientiousness 47, 70
consequences 22, 56, 59, 64, 79–80, 83, 128, 146–7, 154, 166–7, 176, 179, 186
constituents 133–4, 150
Constitution 11, 152, 182–3
contacts 30, 67, 146
context 5, 9–10, 13–4, 17, 21, 25, 33, 38, 42, 45, 124–6, 167–8, 180–2
continuum, behavioral 14, 24, 44–5, 50
contributions 2, 121, 134, 166
control 4, 11, 17, 28, 37, 40, 57, 75, 77, 79, 81, 83, 88, 101, 131–2
conviction 5, 65, 68, 103, 105–6, 113, 135, 137, 146, 150, 152, 172, 174
corporations 87–8, 134
country 10, 12, 70, 87, 116–9, 122, 124, 130, 154, 177
couple 76, 83, 96–7, 127–8, 149
court 29, 31, 59–62, 65, 73, 87, 91, 99–107, 112, 139, 141, 147, 149–50, 185
Crayton, J. (narcissism-aggression theory) 120
credibility 129–30, 156, 181
crime 31–3, 59–62, 65–6, 68, 76–7, 128, 147, 160–1, 183
criminal behavior 60–2, 65, 81, 119, 125, 129, 140, 161
criminal lawyer 76–7, 81
crises 14–5, 75, 79, 131–2, 169–70, 173, 180, 184

Index

culture 10–1, 41–2, 69–70, 72, 139
customs, social 5, 10–2, 70

DA (District Attorney) 34, 58, 66, 93
Danny's case 56–7
date rape, 65
daughter Isabella 176–7
David's case 5–6
death 7–8, 10, 35, 56, 76, 113, 122, 124, 126, 131, 167–8
deception 23, 31, 71, 87, 101, 139, 147–8, 156–7, 161, 163
defendant 31–2, 36, 59–61, 80, 93, 103, 106, 153
defense 32–3, 59–61, 64, 152, 160
defense lawyer 59, 61, 80
defining social conformity 32, 62
degrees 14–6, 35, 41, 45–6, 49–50, 53, 79, 83, 94, 99, 105, 128–9, 172–3
depression 5–6, 13, 29, 46–7, 54, 89, 108, 187
destruction 81, 107, 116, 118, 120–1, 125
detectives 76, 159
development 17, 23, 42
deviant behavior 20, 23, 34, 82, 85–6, 131, 160
Didi's case 1–4, 6
differences 16, 23–4, 44, 48, 69, 96, 104, 130, 146, 155, 161, 171
discipline 18, 98, 130
discriminations 89, 91
disorders, dependent personality 52
disorder of will 60
display 20, 22, 55, 75, 114, 132, 137, 140, 158, 173
dissonant 166–7, 188
distress 4, 13, 44–5, 142, 165, 170
divorce 2, 10, 30, 56, 70, 97–8, 147, 171, 174–6
DNA Study 47, 65, 73, 93
doctors 101, 114, 120, 144
Dollard, J. (learning theory) 42
drugs 33, 37, 60, 97
Durkheim, E., Boas, F., Kroeber, H. 39
DSM-4, DSM-5 51

eccentrics 112–5
emotional responses 14, 16, 27, 51, 166, 170, 172–3
empathy 94, 140, 142, 151
employees 59–60, 80–1, 94, 102, 148
enemies 121–3

environment 11–2, 15–7, 23–4, 35, 39, 44, 46, 50, 56, 108, 112, 150, 158, 169, 187
hostile work 17, 61, 69–70, 100, 102–3, 107
equality 154, 182–3
equivocation 37, 39, 41, 43, 45, 47, 49, 51, 53, 55, 57, 59, 61, 63, 65
ethnic group 12, 70, 121–2, 158, 178
events 14–6, 18, 24, 26, 35, 45, 56–7, 75, 79, 82–3, 86, 108, 156, 173, 179–80
evidence 65–6, 68, 78, 80, 82, 85, 93, 100, 105, 126–8, 137, 157, 183
executives 144–6, 184
expenses 8, 15, 133, 155, 174–5
experience 9, 14, 17, 37, 47, 78, 132, 169–70
expert witnesses 105–7, 152
extraversion 46–7
extremists, political 116, 118
Eysenck, H. 46

factors 15, 18, 20, 24, 39, 42, 46–9, 70, 79, 90, 186
  genetic 24, 42–3, 55, 62, 131
  mitigating 12, 41, 51, 60–1
failure 4, 13, 57, 120, 132, 135, 137, 147, 157
False Rape Society 74
family 5–6, 16, 23–4, 30, 34–5, 62, 94, 104–5, 118, 122, 128, 178–9
father 20, 27, 57, 64, 104, 125, 142, 178, 185
FBI 80, 94, 126, 131, 147, 149–50, 177
fighting 28, 81, 117–8, 122, 125–6, 174
Fisher, Abigail (affirmative action) 91
Federal Judge case 61
Flushing Hospital's case 101
formation 11, 16–9, 21, 23–4, 39–40, 42–4, 46, 49, 51
framework 4, 12, 25, 29, 57, 65, 69, 97, 99, 116, 132, 156, 165, 167
fraud 69, 88, 129, 136, 144–5, 148–9, 155, 161–2, 184
Fred's case 7–8
freedom 13, 25, 122, 182–3
function 4–5, 7, 9, 20, 24, 29, 31, 40, 44, 54–5, 108–9, 111, 131

Gail's case 29–31
Galileo 167–8
gambling 29, 54, 102, 130, 139, 159

191

gender 20–1, 71, 90, 182
genetics 24, 39, 42, 46–7, 51, 62, 161
girlfriends 6, 34, 67, 133, 157, 175
girls 6, 9–10, 20–1, 67, 185
God 5, 33, 86, 116, 133
Goldstein, K. (organismic/holistic theory) 43
government 71, 87, 89, 99, 112, 117, 121, 123, 127, 143, 154, 168, 184
gratification 20, 40, 50, 160, 172
group 23, 43, 45–7, 49, 67, 89, 94, 114, 120–2, 124–5
guilt 6, 22–3, 47, 59, 69, 136, 138, 147, 158, 160
Gupta, Rajat (insider trading) 62

HA (harm avoidance) 48, 56
habitual liars 151–2, 155–7
Hamas 117
harassment 100–1, 107
Hasan, Nidal Malik psychiatrist terrorist 93–4
Hinckley, J., Jr. 128
Hippies 114–5
histrionics 52, 79
hobos 114–5
Hofstra's false rape case 68
home 3–4, 9, 21, 24, 27, 53–4, 63–4, 104, 143, 155, 160, 175
homosexuality 5–6, 10, 52
human predictability 12, 37, 39, 41–4, 153
humanists 22, 38, 167–9, 177
husband 30, 96–7, 103, 174

illegal immigrants 153–5
illusion 29, 31, 44, 82, 122, 154–6, 186
impairment 32, 44, 51, 131, 161, 170
imposters 129–30, 157, 161
inability 4–6, 11, 25–6, 30, 32, 53, 59, 86, 97–8, 122–3, 132, 152, 177
independence 3, 12, 25, 92, 95, 97, 116–7, 168, 171, 175
individuals 16, 43, 48, 57, 62, 70, 98, 111–2, 126, 183, 187
innocence 76, 103, 106, 157
insanity plea 32–3, 59–60, 128
insider trading 136, 138, 144, 146
interaction 4, 16, 18, 24, 45, 49, 51, 58, 72, 97, 108, 115
Internal Revenue Service (IRS) 144, 149, 159
interpersonal relationships 40–1, 170–1

investment bankers 31, 88, 136, 139–40, 143, 146, 159
Islamic Society of Tulsa 179

J. Arehart-Treicher 73
Jefferson, Th. 11, 150
job 1, 3, 6, 27–9, 53–5, 84, 88, 91, 107, 112, 115, 127–8, 130–1, 159, 173–6
Jones, H.'s case 84, 87
judge 57–8, 61, 64, 92, 99, 103–4, 106, 134, 147, 177, 180–1, 185
   federal 61, 148, 181, 188
judgment 4, 26, 32, 38, 56–7, 62, 78–9, 81–2, 84–6, 107, 132, 155, 160, 170
judicial system 103, 106
jury 99–102, 105–6
justice 65, 68, 93, 102, 106–7, 110–1, 144, 167, 181–3

Kagan, J. (genetic factors) 46
kleptomania 63
knowledge 12, 16–7, 24, 39, 42, 62, 79, 129, 152, 157, 160, 169
Knutson, J. (damaged self-concept theory) 120
Korean War 129

lawsuit 31, 33–4, 58, 60–2, 65–6, 70–1, 99–100, 106–7, 111–3, 144–5, 147, 151–3, 160–1, 178–9, 181–3
lawyers 2, 28, 31, 57–8, 75, 77, 80–1, 102, 106–7, 113, 129, 144, 147–8, 179–81
leaders 111, 117, 124–5, 133, 153–4
liars, pathological 155
liberation 122, 174
life 2–4, 7–9, 15–6, 18–9, 26–8, 35, 37–8, 56–7, 112–6, 118–20, 123–4, 126–7, 154–5, 157, 169–70
   style of 1, 3, 7–8, 38, 40, 50, 108, 113–4, 161, 170–2, 174
limitations 42, 170, 175
livelihood 88–90, 112
logic 61, 83, 125, 183
Los Angeles 85, 146
Louisiana 149–50
love, passionate 2, 4, 9, 22, 59, 95–6, 98, 124, 169
lovers 1, 3–4, 27, 86, 98, 123, 133, 175

Madoff, B. 88, 109, 142–4
magical thinking 64, 73, 82, 109, 146

Index

marital obligations 96, 174–5, 177
marital rape 103
marriage 2, 9–10, 20, 30, 95, 97–8, 103, 171, 175–7
Mary's case 1 26–7
Mary's case 2 64
mask of normalcy 2, 4, 6, 8, 10, 28–30, 78, 88, 186
Maslow, A. 41, 72
maternal deprivation 21
McCaffrey, W. (false rape conviction) 67
McCrae, R. R. 73
members 33, 68, 70–1, 100, 104, 124, 134, 136, 142–4, 151, 157, 185
mental health 33, 58, 60
mental illness 13, 125, 127
meritocracy 90–1
Miller, N. (learning theory) 42
Miller, Lisa (lesbian divorce) 72, 176–7
minority 119–20
money 1, 5, 29–31, 64, 67, 76, 80, 88, 101–3, 118–9, 133, 139, 141–4, 146, 149–50
moral relativism 31, 34, 65, 69, 72, 87, 99, 103, 134, 155, 182–4, 186
mother 10, 17–8, 21–3, 30, 51, 64, 76, 94, 98, 157, 178, 185, 188
motivation 65, 72, 120, 124
motives 16, 58, 76, 122, 128, 136, 139
Muslims 10, 93–4, 123, 177, 180

nation 12, 92, 94, 133
National Archives 80–1
nature, human 11, 38–9, 73, 169, 175
neuroticism 46–7, 57, 73, 83–4, 132
New Jersey 73, 153, 178
New York Post 36, 73–4, 109–10, 137, 162,
Nifong, M. (prosecutor) 69, 106
nonconformism 112, 115, 129, 149
nonconformists 55, 63, 111–5, 117, 119, 121, 123, 125, 127, 129, 131, 133, 135–7, 165
normal behavior, identifying 33, 62
normal conduct, social-adjustment 13, 70, 72, 108, 172
normal person, well-adjusted 4, 14, 27, 40, 58, 63, 109, 131
normal personality, assumed 14, 21, 40–1, 47, 53, 58, 62–3, 131
normal Psychopath 139, 141, 143, 145, 147, 149, 151, 153, 155, 157–9, 161, 163

normal social range 41, 54, 84, 89, 128, 131, 155, 168
normalcy 8–10, 14, 20, 26, 30–2, 36–74, 76–8, 88, 90–2, 106–8, 114, 130–2, 165–8, 180
alleged psychological 6
flexible 62, 72, 78, 108–9
normalcy 13, 27, 38, 62, 85
normals 11–3, 24–6, 34, 38, 44–7, 54–5, 59, 86, 111, 130, 134, 144, 170, 172, 187
norms 7, 10–1, 13, 33–4, 42, 58, 72, 89, 92, 166, 168, 185
NS (novelty seeking) 48, 50, 55–6, 126
nurse 59, 68, 101

O'Conner, Sandra (Supreme Court) 65
O'Connor Danny (affirmative action) 90–1
obsessive-compulsive condition 54
offenses 23, 32–3, 60, 92
officers 90, 97, 135, 144–5, 147, 180, 184
organization 12, 14, 25, 45, 52, 87, 91, 117, 120–1, 124–5, 169, 172
social 24, 34, 114, 154, 166
outsiders 7, 105, 121–2, 136

persistence 48, 56
parents 5, 9, 17–8, 20–4, 34, 64, 98–9, 185–6, 188
partners 37, 78, 95–8, 160, 170–1, 176, 185
patient 49, 166
patterns 15–6, 18, 20, 22, 29–30, 48, 87, 131, 136, 147, 155, 161, 171
peers 24, 98–9, 171
perception 16–7, 26–7, 51, 69–70, 78, 89
Perez-Olivo 's case 76–7
person 5, 14–6, 19, 26, 32, 35, 37, 55–6, 58–9, 76–7, 79, 83, 129, 157–8
maladjusted 23, 25–6, 187
personal gains 85, 105, 151
personality 13, 15–7, 19, 24–5, 39–52, 54–6, 72–3, 98, 121–2, 131–2, 155, 157–8, 160–1
antisocial behavior 50
development of 18, 23–4, 40–1, 45, 51
theories of 37–9, 41, 43, 45, 47, 49, 51, 53, 55, 57, 59, 61, 63, 65, 67
traits of 2–3, 11, 15, 18, 38, 44–5, 52, 55, 126–7, 131–2, 140, 169, 171, 173

193

personality disorders 13–4, 31–2, 45, 47, 49–52, 54–5, 63, 75, 97, 123, 127–8, 131, 137, 171
polarized society 165, 167, 169, 173, 175, 177, 179, 181, 183, 185, 187–8
police 59, 61, 66–8, 76–7, 80, 84–6, 102, 107, 114, 118, 149
policeman 84–5, 105, 181
political assassins 80, 123–4, 127, 151
political correctness 69, 92–4, 109–10, 177, 179–80, 182–3, 188
politicians 31, 92, 134, 141, 144, 149, 151, 153, 157, 182–3
Post-Freudians (Adler, K., Karen, H., Fromm, E., Sullivan Stack) 40
Post, J. (terrorists abnormalities theory) 138
power 8, 21, 29, 42, 80, 82, 88, 99, 118, 122, 134, 139, 149–50, 152, 154
president 31, 62, 81, 117, 127–8, 133, 151
prevarication 69, 71–2, 82–3
prison 58, 67–8, 106, 135–6
professions 76, 91, 129–30, 137, 157
prohibitions 21, 23, 108
promotions 53, 71, 90–1, 99, 107, 178
prosecution 33, 36, 59, 65, 68–9, 92–3, 99, 102, 105
protest 2, 112, 119, 166, 179
Psychiatric News 73–4, 163
psychologists 7, 19, 38, 105, 115, 117, 125, 129, 140, 151, 187
psychology 35, 58, 72, 122, 138
psychopaths 140, 143–4, 153, 157–8, 162
psychotics 13–4, 46, 52, 55, 61
pursuit 8, 96, 116, 122, 124, 127, 167–9, 175

Al-Qaeda 80, 94, 117–8
qualities 5, 14, 16, 23, 25, 32, 52, 71, 120, 132, 169, 172

rabbis 31, 148
race 71–2, 90–2, 94, 99, 109, 182, 186
rage 78, 120–1, 170
rape 20, 65–8, 84, 101–2, 149, 183
  alleged 67–8, 84
RD (reward dependence) 48, 56
rebels 125, 129, 168
regulations 5, 21, 25, 55, 70, 89, 108, 111, 131, 165

relationships 1, 3–4, 26, 48, 53, 55, 64–5, 71, 78, 95–7, 169–72, 176
relative truth 12, 70–1, 86–7, 181–3
religious beliefs 33, 116, 124, 179
Reno, Janet 105–6
resentment 25, 90–1, 99, 112, 183
respectability, social 30, 81, 135, 137, 152–3
responsibility 60, 64, 86, 125–6, 135, 152, 156, 167, 180
revenge 33, 66, 76, 102, 105, 120, 122
revolutionaries 12, 118–9
Richardson, W. (governor) 155
rights 28, 78, 83, 92–3, 9 9, 104, 108, 112, 122, 160, 176–7, 180, 182, 185
risk 47, 50, 54, 57, 62, 85–6, 126–7, 135–7, 147, 150, 161
role 9, 12, 14–5, 17–8, 21–4, 31, 33, 38–9, 41–3, 45, 47
rules 5, 8, 12–3, 32–3, 40, 46, 55, 89–92, 108, 111, 125, 147
Ryan, G. (convicted governor) 82

Sam' sociopath case 158–60
schizophrenia 47, 62
school 6, 23–4, 41–2, 46, 68, 72, 94, 130, 159, 174, 178–9, 184–5
SD (self-directedness) 48–9
self 8, 45, 77, 107, 132, 138, 144
self-concept 20, 48–9, 120, 132
self-directedness (SD) 48–9
self-realization 4, 43–4, 166–9, 174, 177
Serban, G. 73, 109, 188
sexes 4, 6, 18, 20, 23, 67, 86, 92, 94–8, 103, 149, 176–7
  consensual 66–7
sexual harassment 65, 94, 100–2, 110, 183
Sheldon, W. constitutional typology
shot 75–8, 85, 93–4, 109, 127–8, 137, 157, 178
snip rs6441.48-extraversion 47, 73
Skinner, B.F. (social conditioning) 40
Snowden, G. (case of abuse of justice) 105–6
social adjustment 5, 12, 16, 24–6, 29, 31, 38, 43, 53, 104–5, 128–9, 165–6, 168–72, 186–7
social behavior 12, 33, 83, 87, 175
social conditions 8, 11, 19, 24, 41, 44, 50, 58, 119, 123, 131, 167
social conflict 88, 90, 103, 182–3

Index

social conformity 18, 37, 50, 60–2, 75, 77, 91–3, 95–7, 99, 165–7, 183, 185
  ambiguity of 72, 136, 180
social environment 16–7, 55, 86, 95, 108
social interaction 29, 33, 41, 57, 63, 89, 96, 98, 104, 113, 125, 155, 158, 173–5
social rules 5, 24–5, 38, 42–3, 50, 111, 134, 136, 165
social standards 4, 7–8, 26, 31–2, 53, 131, 134, 156
social status 8, 29, 88, 144, 157, 161
social system 12, 25–6, 115, 119–20, 168, 187
social values 9, 71–2, 87–9, 95, 97, 183
socialization 4, 17–8, 21, 174
societal concept 5, 63, 71, 78, 115, 181
societal rules 26, 70, 86, 108, 111, 114, 121, 151, 165
society norms of 5, 75, 83, 109
  pluralistic 12, 34, 70, 89, 167, 186
  relativistic 33, 62, 116, 168, 182
sociopaths 127, 158, 160–1
Socrates 167–8
son 2, 56–7, 125, 145, 150
Sowell, Th. 186
spouses 10, 70, 96–7, 104
ST, transcend himself 49
Stalin, J. 118–9
Stanford Allen, international fraud 143
standards 4, 26, 28, 33–4, 38, 58–9, 84, 87, 90, 113, 123, 128, 188
  societal 13, 38, 166, 184
stealing 63–4, 72, 80–1, 88, 130, 159–60
Stenroos, J.'s case 81
story 23, 37, 66–8, 75–6, 84–6, 93, 104, 107, 127, 148, 157
stress 14, 26, 29, 45, 47, 50, 56–7, 75, 77–9, 81, 83–5, 87, 89, 91, 101
stressful events 88, 131, 166, 169–70, 187
stripper's case 68–9, 93
success 3, 8, 48, 63, 80, 126, 128–9, 137, 146–7, 156, 171
Sudik's case 27–8
suicide bombers 93–4, 120, 122–4
Sullivan Scot (fraudster WCOM) 41
superiors 59–60, 93–4, 100, 107, 156
Supreme Court 72, 91–2, 176, 182
Supreme Court judge (bribery) 57–8
swindles 139, 142, 146, 160–1, 184
symptoms 13, 27, 50–1, 137

Taylor, M. (terrorist-normal theory) 138
temperament 16, 43–4, 46–8, 50, 55–6, 73, 79–80, 168
temperament traits 16–7, 43, 47–9, 168
Temple University Hospital's case 68
terrorism 93, 117, 119–21, 125–7, 137–8
terrorist groups: (IRA, LEHI, FARC, HAMAS, HIZBOLLAH LTTE, AL-QUEDA) 117–25
terrorists honored (I. Shamir, Stalin) 115–27, 138
testimonies 65, 103, 105–6, 153, 157
traits 15, 17, 35, 38, 43, 45–51, 55–6, 71, 80, 113, 121, 128, 140, 147, 169
trial 22, 32, 69, 105, 107, 117, 134, 144–5
truth 65, 68–71, 83, 87, 102, 106, 141, 147, 151–3, 155–7, 181, 186
  multiple 69–70, 87, 181
TSA (Transportation Safety Administration) 178
types 17, 24–5, 32, 38, 41, 43, 45, 61, 64, 82, 87, 141

UN 27–8, 117
unstable social conformity 1, 3, 5, 7, 9, 11, 13, 15, 17, 19, 21, 23, 25, 27, 29
USA 118, 130

validity 46–7, 52, 69–70, 91–2, 184
values 6, 11–2, 25, 33, 40, 44, 49, 61, 63, 114, 140–1, 145, 165–6, 177
Weiner, A. (ex-congressman) 82
victims 34, 74, 88, 94, 100, 109, 125, 148, 184, 187
Virginia 149, 176

Wall Street 2, 5, 62, 88, 139–40, 143, 155, 184
Wall Street Journal 110, 162
weapon 93, 117–8, 123
well-adjusted normalcy 12, 14, 34–5, 38, 52, 63, 81, 97, 115, 165, 167, 173, 177, 187
well-adjusted-normals, alleged 82, 167
well-being 14, 22, 25, 27, 56, 88–9, 91, 95, 99, 112, 165–6, 179
White House 151–2
whites 90, 182, 186

195

wife 2, 75–6, 88, 96, 104–5, 109, 133, 149, 177
Wikipedia 73, 109, 137–8
witnesses 65–6, 76, 100, 106, 159
Wolfe, K's case 77–8
woman 4, 6, 64–7, 77, 82, 96–7, 100–1, 104, 137
women 6, 10, 35, 56, 65, 95–6, 102–3, 114, 158, 171–2, 174, 176, 180, 185
work 1, 7, 28–30, 53–4, 58–9, 71, 79, 90, 98, 100, 102–3, 107, 116, 171–2
WorldCom 145

Yung, C. (introvert-extrovert) 45